cusses Dante's early and middle period, when, in addition to the *Vita Nuova*, he wrote the *Canzoni*, the *Convivio*, and other works. The second half is devoted to a searching and inspired analysis of the *Commedia*, Dante's journey of three stages: the *Inferno*, the *Purgatorio*, and the *Paradiso*. Professor Fergusson makes clear that this is not only a poem but also the poetic expression of the spiritual structure of the Middle Ages. Included in the book is a diagram showing the plan of the *Paradiso*, as well as full bibliographical notes.

FRANCIS FERGUSSON is University Professor of Comparative Literature at Rutgers University. He is the author of *Dante's Drama of the Mind*, *The Human Image*, and *The Idea of a Theater*.

MASTERS OF WORLD LITERATURE

PUBLISHED:

GEORGE ELIOT *by Walter Allen*
JOHN KEATS *by Douglas Bush*
JOHN MILTON *by Douglas Bush*
JONATHAN SWIFT *by Nigel Dennis*
DANTE *by Francis Fergusson*
HONORE DE BALZAC *by E. J. Oliver*

IN PREPARATION:

PROUST *by William Barrett*
FLAUBERT *by Jacques Barzun*
COLERIDGE *by W. J. Bate*
SAMUEL JOHNSON *by James L. Clifford*
YEATS *by F. W. Dupee*
JOYCE *by Leon Edel*
D. H. LAWRENCE *by Monroe Engel*
CONRAD *by Elizabeth Hardwick*
THOREAU *by Granville Hicks*
HARDY *by Irving Howe*
EMERSON *by Alfred Kazin*
SHAKESPEARE *by Frank Kermode*
JANE AUSTEN *by Louis Kronenberger*
POE *by Dwight Macdonald*
FIELDING *by Midge Podhoretz*
HENRY JAMES *by Richard Poirier*
GOLDSMITH *by Ricardo Quintana*
TOLSTOY *by Philip Rahv*
MELVILLE *by Harold Rosenberg*
BEN JONSON *by Raymond Rosenthal*
WORDSWORTH *by Lionel Trilling*

MASTERS OF WORLD LITERATURE SERIES

LOUIS KRONENBERGER, GENERAL EDITOR

Dante

"And like a pilgrim who is travelling on a road where he hath never been before . . . even so our soul, so soon as it enters upon the new and never-yet-made journey of life . . ."
—*Convivio* IV, xii

by Francis Fergusson

THE MACMILLAN COMPANY, NEW YORK

COLLIER-MACMILLAN LIMITED, LONDON

First Printing

The Macmillan Company, New York
Collier-Macmillan Canada Ltd., Toronto, Canada

Library of Congress catalog card number: 66–14202

Printed in the United States of America

Contents

Preface

This book was written for the Masters of World Literature Series, on the invitation of Mr. Louis Kronenberger. It is intended as a "short critical biography" for readers interested in Dante, whether or not they are, as yet, acquainted with his works.

Little is known with certainty about the objective facts of Dante's life, but a great deal is known about his Florence, and about the wider European scene where he played his passionate part in the political-religious conflicts of the time. I have tried to say enough about the historical background to make what we know of his doings—his involvement in Florentine politics, his banishment and exile, his espousal of the Emperor Henry VII's lost cause—intelligible to a reader with no special knowledge of the period. But in endeavoring to trace the course of Dante's career I have relied mainly on his own works. They all emerge quite explicitly from his experience as lover, or politician, or studious explorer of his long tradition. In all of them he tries to fathom the meaning of his experience, and to take full responsibility for what he is—or thinks he is at the moment; for what he does, and for what he is writing. For that reason I have made this book chiefly an introductory reading of Dante's works in chronological order; and the second part is devoted entirely to the *Commedia.*

I have to thank my wife, Peggy Fergusson, for making the diagram of the *Paradiso*.

In quoting Dante's poems in Italian I have followed the text of the Temple Classics edition (*The Vita Nuova and Canzoniere of Dante*). In quoting from the Divine Comedy in Italian I have also followed the text of the Temple Classics edition of the *Inferno, Purgatorio,* and *Paradiso,* except for Paradiso XII, 21, where I have followed the text of the *Società Dantesca* edition. For the poems of Guinizelli I have used *I Rimatori del dolce stil novo.* The translations of all the verses are mine. They are intended to give the literal meaning, even though it may sound strange or clumsy in English.

The passages from Dante's prose works are all quoted from the English translations in the Temple Classics edition, translated by Philip Wicksteed (*The Vita Nuova,* the *Convivio,* and *Latin Works of Dante Alighieri*). I have to thank J. M. Dent & Sons, Ltd., London, and the Oxford Press, New York, for permission to quote from the Temple Classics edition; the Princeton University Press for permission to use a diagram from my *Dante's Drama of the Mind;* and Professor Enrico De' Negri, of the University of California, for permission to use a diagram from his essay Tema e iconografia del *Purgatorio* (*The Romanic Review,* Vol. XLIX, No. 2).

I wish to record my gratitude to the Research Council of Rutgers University for enabling me to devote a term to work on this book; to the John Simon Guggenheim Memorial Foundation for a fellowship in the autumn of 1963; to Professor Kenneth Murdoch, formerly Director of I Tatti, Florence, for a visiting fellowship there; and to Professor Gianfranco Contini, of the University of Florence, for his kindness in making the facilities of the library of the Società Dantesca, in Florence, available to me.

F. F.

PART ONE

The Road to the *Commedia*

I

Youth in Florence, 1265–1293

Dante in Florence

Tempo era dal principio del mattino;
e il sol montava in su con quelle stelle
ch'eran con lui, quando l'amor divino
mosse da prima quelle cose belle;
sì che a bene sperar m'eran cagione
de quella fera alla gaietta pelle
l'ora del tempo, e la dolce stagione.

(The time was the beginning of the morning,
and the sun was rising upward with those stars
that were with him when Divine Love
moved for the first time those beauteous things;
so that, for me, causes to have good hope
of the wild beast with the gay hide,
were the hour of day and the sweet season.)
—*Inferno* I, 37–43

THE BEAUTIFUL LEOPARD that Dante meets in the dark wood, at the beginning of the *Divine Comedy*, its often supposed to stand for Florence, as that city seemed to him when he was young, passionate, and hopeful. Florence certainly was both beautiful and perilous: it provided Dante with what he needed to nourish his genius from earliest childhood to maturity, and then turned on him so savagely that he had to flee for his life, never to return. The only way to form some conception of Dante's beginnings, and of the human scene that preoccupied him all his life, is to consider

Florence at the end of the thirteenth century, for we know very little about his own doings there.

The few undisputed facts that we have about Dante's birth and family are soon told. He was born in Florence in May or June, 1265. His father was a notary, Messer Alighirro di Bellincione di Alighiero. Nothing is known about him; but the family was old and respectable, and Dante (in the *Paradiso*) makes much of an ancestor, Cacciaguida, a cavalier and a crusader. His mother was named Donna Bella, and died soon after his birth. His father married again, had one son and two daughters by the second marriage, and died during Dante's boyhood.

Florence, at Dante's birth, was entering a time of greatness, and its citizens were well aware of that. A contemporary chronicler, Dino Compagni, introduces his city as follows:

> And in order that strangers may better understand the things that happened, I shall tell the form of the noble city: the which is in the Province of Tuscany, built under the sign of Mars on an ample imperial river of sweet water that divides the city almost in half; with temperate air, protected from harmful winds; with little land, but abounding in the good fruits of the earth; with citizens of prowess in arms, proud and quarrelsome; a city rich in illegal gains; feared for its greatness in neighboring lands rather than loved.

One feels in Dino's description that mixture of pride and despair that Florence inspired in all her gifted children. It is Dante himself, of course, who expresses it most poignantly (*Inferno* XXVI, 1–3):

> Godi, Fiorenza, poi che sei sì grande,
> che per mare e per terra batti l'ali,
> e per l'inferno il tuo nome si spande.

> (Rejoice, Florence, since you are so great
> that over sea and land you beat your wings,
> and through all hell your name is spread.)

The visible, envied greatness of Florence was founded upon the manufacturing of woolens, silks, fur and leather goods, and arms; and upon banking; it was perhaps the richest city of its time. It had about ninety thousand inhabitants, and Florentine merchants and bankers (with their famous golden florins) were in every important city of Europe. It was a strictly bourgeois, or capitalistic, society, with respectable families whose wealth was old, and newly rich families who exhibited the nimble enterprise and the ruthless greed that we associate with modern capitalist societies in their nascent stages. But capitalism itself, then and for several hundred years thereafter, was illegal, for the Church taught that usury (lending money at interest) was a sin against nature. The borrowing of money that everyone had to resort to—princes, merchants, the Papacy itself—was permitted by all sorts of hypocritical casuistries, but there was no way to regulate it by law, and the lender was free to extract as much "usury" as he could get. Dino Compagni had such abuses (as well as others) in mind when he spoke of the "illegal gains" that were making Florence rich.

The wealthy Florentines could afford the pleasures of the mind and of the senses. They had the reputation of celebrating festivals, with gorgeously costumed processions, music, and dance, more frequently than any other city. Architecture, painting, and sculpture were flourishing. According to Dino Compagni, Florence was already attracting tourists:

> The said city of Florence is very well populated and prolific because of the good air; the citizens well-mannered, and the women very handsome and well-dressed; the houses most beautiful, filled with many useful artifacts, more than the other cities of Italy. For such things, many come from distant countries to see the city; not through necessity, but because of the excellence of its arts and trades, and because of the beauty and adornments of the city.

The modern tourist will not find the *palazzi,* with their fortified towers, in which the rich families lived in Dante's time, for they were all destroyed in savage civil broils. But there is enough left to give one some idea of how the city looked to him.

Florence and the other cities of Tuscany and northern Italy are often likened to the ancient Greek city-states. There was the same deep attachment to the native town: the "commune" was the focus of life for every citizen, and exile was regarded as a fate next to death. Florence and the other Italian cities dealt with each other, in their incessant wars and intrigues, as sovereign powers; but (unlike the Greek city-states) they remembered a "universal" authority, that of Rome. Both the Emperor and the Pope laid claim to the political authority of Rome, and Italy was divided between the partisans of the Emperor, the Ghibellines, and the partisans of the Pope, the Guelfs. In Dante's time the northern cities were the Ghibelline strongholds, while Florence was controlled by the Guelfs; but all the cities, and indeed many families, were divided into Guelfs and Ghibellines. As though that were not enough, the new national powers of France and Spain were continually intervening in Italian politics. Florence, because of its own ambitions, and because of its wealth, which everyone coveted, was involved in all of the treacherous struggles between these rival powers.

It is very difficult for the modern inquirer to discover what the Guelf and Ghibelline parties actually stood for. They were, of course, derived from the struggle between the Empire and the Papacy that darkens the whole history of medieval Europe. When Dante, in his maturity, endeavored to make sense out of the political chaos, he carefully defined the relations between the secular authority of the ideal Emperor and the spiritual authority of the ideal Pope, and his *De Monarchia* is, among other things, a classic discussion of the necessity of separating church and state. But theory had little to do with the power-battles of the two parties in Dante's youth; and it is even hard to see what class or economic interests they represented. The Ghibellines were originally the feudal lords who lived in their castles on the hills around the city; as descendants of Germanic invaders, they naturally looked to the Emperor, in Germany, as ally and protector. The Guelf party was originally bourgeois, and looked to the Pope, not as a spiritual leader, but as a political power, always eager to help them in their struggles with the feudal lords. But the feudal order, never as important in Italy as it was in northern Europe, was already fading away in Dante's time. The uncouth country lords tended to move into the city, acquire the glamorous Florentine urbanity, and become city families. The rich bourgeois liked to acquire aristocratic titles, along with aristocratic pride and cruel insolence. The struggle between burgher and feudal lord was giving place to that between the rich and the poor, and in this time of rapid change it was common for powerful leaders to shift their party labels with bewildering frequency.

The Guelfs gained firm control of Florence in 1266, the year after Dante's birth. That was the beginning of thirty years of prosperity, of artistic and intellectual life, and of comparative peace, for the most serious fighting during those years was outside the city. Dante's family, though of noble origin, had been settled in Florence for generations, and had long been Guelf. The young Dante might, therefore, have felt secure in his native town, and in fact there is nothing to indicate that he was especially concerned with party strife for the first twenty-five or thirty years of his life. He was, as we shall see, deep in his youthful loves, in the writing of poetry, and in thought and study. For the rest, we may suppose that he was leading the usual life of a citizen of his age and social position.

One of the things expected of a citizen of Florence was military service. In 1289 Florence and its Guelf allies were at war with neighboring Arezzo, then controlled by the Ghibellines, including some Florentine exiles of that party. As a young man "accustomed to bearing arms," Dante was in the cavalry, the more aristocratic part of the army, and he took part in the campaigns of the summer of 1289. In June he was in the big battle of Campaldino, which Florence and its allies decisively won, and in August he took part in the siege of the Pisan fortress of Caprona, and witnessed its surrender. That is all we know about his military experiences, but he remembered them many years later when he wrote the *Commedia*, and recorded there a few fragmentary impressions which show how he felt, then, about war. In *Purgatorio* V, Campaldino is glimpsed through the sad, bewildered story of Buonconte da Montefeltro, who was mortally wounded in that battle, fled, died from the loss of blood, and was washed down into the Arno by a sudden mountain freshet. In *Inferno* XXI, frightened by his treacherous escort of demons, Dante remembers the surrender of Caprona (line 94):

E così vid'io già temer li fanti
ch'uscivan patteggiati di Caprona,
veggendo sè tra nimici cotanti.

(And I once saw the foot-soldiers frightened so,
coming out, under truce, from Caprona,
when they found themselves among so many enemies.)

He pays his respects to military pageantry (Canto XXII, line 1) in another memory of that campaign, just after the commander of the demon-escort *avea del cul fatto trombetta,* "had made of his arse a trumpet":

Io vidi già cavalier muover campo,
 e cominciare stormo, e far lor mostra,
 e talvolta partir per loro scampo;
corridor vidi per la terra vostra,
 o Aretini, e vidi gir gualdane,
 ferir torneamenti, e correr giostra,
quando con trombe, e quando con campane,
 con tamburi e con cenni di castella,
 e con cose nostrali e con istrane:
nè già con sì diversa cennamella
 cavalier vidi muover, nè pedoni,
 nè nave a segno di terra o di stella.

(I have seen, before this, horsemen moving camp,
 and starting the assault, and holding muster,
 and sometimes leaving to escape;
harriers have I seen in your land,
 O Aretines, and seen foragers marching;
 the crash of tournaments and the course of jousts,
sometimes with trumpets, sometimes with bells,
 with drums and with castle-signals,
 and with things native, and with foreign;
but never yet with so odd a flageolet
 have I seen horsemen move, nor infantry,
 nor ship by landmark or by star.)

I have seen this passage cited to prove that Dante enjoyed the military life, but its very gusto strikes me as ironic: the demons and the nimble troops appear as similar. The spirit is like that of a modern bawdy GI in a disillusioned mood.

Some time between 1284 and 1292 Dante married Gemma di Manetto Donati. The date is uncertain, and all we know about Gemma is that she belonged to the important and powerful Donati family, bore Dante four children, and survived him by about eleven years. It has been conjectured that the marriage was arranged by the two fathers while Dante and Gemma were children; in any case, one must remember that marriage at that time was a matter of family convenience rather than of the wishes of the bride and groom. Gemma did not follow Dante into exile when he left Florence in 1302, and he never mentions her in his writings, though he has so much to say of Beatrice, and of other, unidentified, women. His biographers, beginning with Boccaccio, are often tempted to paint us a dreary picture of Gemma.

Boccaccio suggests that she was an impossible shrew, and gratuitously adds that intellectuals should never marry. But Boccaccio is not to be trusted in this matter, and we must recognize that we simply do not know enough to understand Gemma, or the marriage.

One would like to know much more than we do about Dante's doings as a youth; but on the other hand his writings make it evident that his intense energies were focused inward, upon the awakening life of his mind and spirit. He was already acquiring the culture of his time, and the end of the thirteenth century, the culmination of the Middle Ages and the beginning of the Renaissance, was a time of great intellectual activity. Paris was the chief international center of thought and learning. It was there that the German, Albert the Great, and his greater disciple, the Italian Thomas Aquinas, were rebuilding Christian thought on the basis of Aristotelian philosophy. Nearer home, the University of Bologna was exploring law, philosophy and the arts of language. Dante may possibly have spent some time in Bologna as a young man, but in any case he could have acquired the standard Latin education, the Trivium* and the Quadrivium,† as well as more advanced theology, in the Franciscan and Dominican schools in Florence. He knew the painters, musicians, and poets of Florence, and he worked with the greatest Florentine teacher of the time, Brunetto Latini. Latini was a jurist, politician, and savant, the author of an encyclopedia in French, the *Trésor,* which was read and admired all over Europe. He had the reputation, among his contemporaries, of being the man who first "polished" the vigorous Florentines; Dante must have owed him a great deal, for he wrote a touching and famous tribute to him many years later (*Inferno* XV, line 82 ff.):

chè in la mente m'è fitta, ed or mi accora,
  la cara e buona imagine paterna
  di voi, quando nel mondo ad ora ad ora
m'insegnavate come l'uom s'eterna.

(For in my memory is fixed, and strikes my heart now,
  the dear, good, fatherly image
  of you, when in the world, time and again,
you would teach me how man makes himself eternal.)

* The Trivium includes Grammar, Logic, and Rhetoric.
† The Quadrivium includes Arithmetic, Music, Geometry, and Astronomy.

We are not in the habit of thinking that patient study could make a man eternal. But Dante and other men of his time, who were bringing about the Renaissance through the study of classical authors, could more easily think so. When Dante wrote the *Commedia* he felt the timeless and ghostly communion with the great spirits of the past as hardly less "real" than intercourse with his own contemporaries. As a young man he was already "searching" the works of ancient saints, philosophers, and poets with "long study and great love," as he puts it in *Inferno* I, to form and guide his own spirit. In some sense, this communion did lift him above time.

In the chapel of the Bargello, in Florence, among the faces in the frescoes attributed to Giotto, one can see the profile of Dante as a very young man. It is both strong and visionary; it seems to convey a convincing impression of Dante, as he was in youth. But of course the best way to get to know him is to read his earliest masterpiece, the *Vita Nuova,* in which he carefully presented what he thought significant in his own life during these years in Florence.

The New Life

The *Vita Nuova,* as the title suggests, is Dante's own account of the central inspiration of his passionate youth. In spite of the music of its lyrics and the delicate charm of the prose narrative, it is a mysterious little masterpiece, for it speaks in a reticent, enigmatic style derived from Troubadour songs and medieval allegory. It is easier for us to understand it (as Eliot points out) after reading Dante's later, more explicit works, especially the *Commedia.* Nevertheless I have thought it necessary to say something about it here, for it is the best, indeed practically the only, account we have of Dante's marvelous beginnings as a man and a poet.

The prose narrative of the *Vita* is based on thirty-one lyrics which Dante selected from his early works to illustrate the theme of his love for Beatrice. He himself never collected his other poems, and the dates of their composition, and even the canon itself, are uncertain. They show that Dante, like other beginners of genius, was experimenting widely and freely. He could write a carefree love song, or he could make the famous sonnet, *Guido, vorrei . . .*

(VI in the Temple Classics edition of the *Vita* and *Canzoniere*), which may remind one of Baudelaire's *Voyage à Cythère.* He could also engage in the notorious *tenzone* (or "contest") with Forese Donati, which resembles some calypso songs or some of Aristophanes' mud-slinging sequences. Connoisseurs of the vernacular poetry of the period can recognize many diverse influences in Dante's early verse.

It was through his association with Guido Cavalcanti and his fellow poets that the young Dante found his own poetic style and the theme of the *Vita.* These poets, adepts in the *dolce stil nuovo,* the "sweet new style" as it is often called, were self-consciously building Italian poetry, against the disapproval of those who thought that Latin was the only proper language for serious writing of any kind. They recognized their predecessors in this effort: the Provençal Troubadours, who had already produced a vernacular literature; and the Sicilians, who had imitated the Troubadours in Italian in the time of the famous Frederick II (1194–1250). But the *stil novisti* regarded Guido Guinizelli of Bologna (who died in 1276) as the founder of their school, the father, and the best, of "those who used sweet and gallant rhymes of love," as Dante put it many years later.

Guinizelli and his Tuscan followers took a great deal directly from the Provençal masters. They admired and imitated the intricate Troubadour prosody based on musical forms, as Dante explains in his *De Vulgari Eloquentia.* They also took over many of the rules and conventions of the cult known as "Courtly Love." The singers of Provence were attached to the small courts of their region, and their love cult probably reflects the situation of the poet who woos his master's wife, and must therefore keep her identity secret, idealize her image from a distance, and be content with very little erotic satisfaction or "consolation." The Tuscans lived in the freer and intellectually more lively cities of central Italy, and the conventions of Courtly Love must have had a different value for them. But for them too the cult of love and the cult of poetry were inseparable. When they called themselves "love's lieges" (*fedeli d'amore*), they meant that they were faithful both as men, to their mistresses, and as writers of verse, to the feelings and visions that love inspired. In spite of their interest in intricate musical forms, the *stil novisti* endeavored to serve, first of all, the inspiration of *amor*; and in so doing, they achieved more vitality and freshness than the Sicilians, who had imitated the Troubadour forms more mechanically.

But one must try to see what they meant by *amor*. We tend to think of love inspired by a woman as aiming directly (if not exclusively) toward sexual gratification; but this earliest European love poetry dwells, rather, upon the iridescent colors of the passion itself before the biological mechanisms take over. Hence the young women of this tradition, who, by merely floating into the poet's line of vision, produce the delights of Eden itself. And hence the despairing death wishes, as well as the new insights and the ambitious dreams, which the *fedeli d'amore* may receive when they are *really* faithful to that disturbing passion itself. It is, of course, a "romantic" conception of love; the word itself is derived from the Romance languages of these early poets, and many modern romantic poets have found this school to their taste. But when Ezra Pound studied them (in his *Spirit of Romance*, in 1910) it was their unromantic clarity and objectivity that chiefly attracted him. "Than Guido Cavalcanti no psychologist of the emotions is more keen in his understanding, more precise in his expression," he wrote; "we have in him no rhetoric, but always a true description." They took *amor* seriously enough to try to discover its precise properties, and what it might mean, in their varied experiences of it.

The *fedeli d'amore* often addressed their poems to each other, inviting their fellow connoisseurs to help them interpret some amorous vision or dream. This procedure has been compared to the dialectic of the schools, whereby the theologians in the universities, in formal debate and by the strict use of Aristotelian logic, were defining *their* faith. Perhaps the theologians did influence the Tuscan poets: the poets, too, used Aristotelian psychology (if not logic) in their definitions, and they were often aware of analogies between the love they served and the orthodox love of God. But the *stil novisti* did not construct a consistent doctrine of love comparable to the theology of Saint Thomas Aquinas. Their "discussions" must have helped them to objectify and clarify their visions, and so attain the hard, elegant consistency that modern writers like Pound, Eliot, and Joyce have admired. But for them *amor* remained a mystery (deathly or heavenly, as the case might be), reflected in a particular temperament at a moment of time. That, of course, is the way of lyric poets; and the *stil novisti* (except Dante) never proceeded from their lyric inspiration to the larger forms of epic or drama.

Guinizelli's *canzone, Al cor gentil ripara sempre Amore,* is often cited as the basis of the *stil nuovo.* The first stanza clearly presents the theme:

Al cor gentil ripara sempre Amore
com'a la selva augello in la verdura;
né fe' Amore anti che gentil core,
né gentil core anti ch'Amor natura,
ch'adesso com fu il sole,
sì tosto lo splendore fu lucente
nè fu davanti il sole;
e prende Amore in gentilezza loco
così propriamente
come calore in clarità di foco.

(To the gentle heart Love always makes repair
Like bird to the verdure of the woods;
Nor was Love before the gentle heart,
Nor gentle heart before Love, made by nature;
So, as soon as there was sun
There was shining light,
Nor was it there before the sun;
And Love takes place in gentleness
As properly
As heat in the brightness of the fire.)

The *stil novisti* always assumed (and often explained again) that the *amor* they were talking about could be experienced only by the "gentle" or "noble." Their cult was therefore esoteric; but the nobility they required had nothing to do with birth or social status: it was a matter of moral and aesthetic sensibility. Guido Cavalcanti, a generation later than Guinizelli, in his famous *Donna mi prega, perch'io voglio dire,* "A Lady begs me to speak," still proudly, if somewhat ironically, insists that only the "gentle" connoisseur can understand him, as he defines *amor* for his lady. This is not the place for a discussion of this poem, a fine example of Guido's "dark humor," as Joyce calls it. The reader who wishes to study it for himself, however, will see what deep and delicate sophistication these servants of *amor* could reach in their lyric art.

What should be pointed out is that Dante, too, first found himself by accepting and exploring Guinizelli's theme, which might be called the basic article in the creed of the *stil novisti.* It helps one to understand the *Vita Nuova,* to see it, first of all, as Dante's contribution to the discussion of *amor.* He writes, introducing the first of his sonnets, "Forasmuch as I had myself already learned the art of saying words in rhyme, I proposed to make a sonnet in which I should salute all love's lieges (*fedeli d'amore*), and praying them that they would interpret my vision, I wrote to them what I had seen in my dream, and began this sonnet." He dedicates the book to Guido Cavalcanti, his "first friend," and he certainly could not have written it without the example and the encouragement of Guido and his school. But, as we shall see, the more Dante finds himself and his "New Life," the more he goes beyond his school, both in his understanding of love and in his art.

A Short Reading of the *Vita Nuova*

Dante wrote both the poems and the prose of the *Vita Nuova* to explore the nature and meaning of the love that his lady, Beatrice, had revealed to him. The poems were written, presumably, over a period of about nine years; but the prose narrative was composed after Beatrice's death, which occurred in 1290. He found the story, he tells us, in "the book of his memory." Thinking over in retrospect his love for Beatrice, he sees the dramatic sequence of that love: the changing motives and situations which had given rise to the thirty-one lyrics. Thus he himself appears in the little book in two complementary ways: as the very young man meeting each experience all unprepared, and trying to record and place it in a poem; and as the somewhat older man who can see it all more objectively, in the light of an experience remembered, accepted, and rationalized to the best of his ability.

When one first reads the *Vita Nuova* it may seem charming (especially if one encounters it in Rossetti's elegant but old-fashioned English) but hardly more than charming: a frail romance in a remote convention. Dante provides no documentation of the kind we expect in an autobiographical narrative, nor does he characterize any of the *dramatis personae.* The three women he uncandidly woos, the pretty young ladies that are always passing in and out of the scene like a *corps de ballet*—tittering among themselves, or regarding the doleful figure of the distressed lover with such melting pity that he has to pity himself—have no more individual "character" than Botticelli's nymphs. Beatrice herself appears in the story as the miraculous *donna* of the Troubadour tradition, rather than as the woman she is known to have been: the daughter of Portinari, a substantial citizen of Florence, and the wife of a banker named Simone de' Bardi. But the experience behind the decorative surfaces is at least as real as the young Werther's, with its more violent chiaroscuro, or as the passionate time that Baudelaire describes:

> Ma jeunesse ne fut qu'un ténébreux orage,
> Traversé çà et là par de brilliants soleils.
>
> (My youth was only a shadowy storm,
> Crossed, here and there, by brilliant suns.)

As one comes to know the *Vita Nuova,* one sees that in writing it Dante already had that psychological insight, and that realistic scruple, which would eventually enable him to present the countless brilliantly "real" personages of the *Commedia* itself.

The dramatic narrative of the *Vita* consists of a prologue, or *proemio,* and three large movements, or acts. In the prologue Dante tells us that Beatrice first revealed love to him when they were both nine years old; and he describes the symptoms of that incomprehensible disturbance in careful psychological and physiological terms. But he knows (he says) that the reader may doubt the possibility of love at so early an age, and so he picks up the story nine years later, when he has the prophetic dream described in the first sonnet (*Vita Nuova* III). He sends the sonnet to his fellow poets for their interpretations, and so begins the quest for love's meaning. The first movement (III–XIX) ends with the *canzone, Donne ch'avete,* which marks his first inspired triumph of understanding. The second movement (XIX–XXVIII) is centered around the *canzone, Donna pietosa* (XXIII), which presents his prophetic dream of Beatrice's death. It is the climax and peripety-plus-recognition of the whole narrative. The third movement (XXIX–XLIII) takes place after Beatrice's actual death and shows the wavering course of his love until he gets a final vision of Beatrice corresponding to that of the first sonnet of the book. It is Dante's intention, in this narrative, to stage himself as he was in early youth, objectively, even with a certain rueful humor.

The naïve and very young Dante (about eighteen) tries at first to obey the rules of Courtly Love, and to understand his infatuation in its terms. He tries to conceal the identity of his mistress, the miraculous Beatrice, and love inspires him to write poems to another lady, his "screen lady," as he calls her, to make people think that she is the cause of his amorous sighs. She moves to another city, and "love" obligingly inspires him to acquire a second screen lady; but all the time, Dante tells us, the real happiness of the young lover lay only in the heavenly feelings he received when Beatrice greeted him. But Beatrice then hears the gossip about her adorer and his second screen lady, and refuses to greet him at all (X), thereby throwing him into despair.

There follows a sequence (XI–XIX) of great psychological and moral interest, showing how the young lover almost lost his faith in Beatrice's revelation, and then found it again in a new way. Neither his visions nor his poem-making avail, at first, to cure his errors. He dreams of "love" as a young man in white, who tries to tell him that there is a distinction between love itself, which is "perfect as the circle," and the lover, who is not; but though this vision embodies the truth of his situation, the amorous youth cannot understand it. By this time he has lost the secrecy of his attachment to Beatrice, and he tries writing a pretty *ballata* directly to her. When that fails he writes a sonnet on love's paradoxes (XIII), but that also does little good, for circumstances are forcing him to face his plight as it objectively is. He meets Beatrice and a flock of young ladies, her friends, at a wedding feast; they all make fun of him, and now he is more lost than ever. The sonnets he writes then (XIV, XV, and XVI) are the bitterest in the book, foretelling the savage *canzoni* of amorous frustration (the *Pietra* group) of his maturity. He is almost ready to stop trying to be one of "love's faithful," since he gets only pain for his loyalty. But it apparently helps him to get the bitterness out of his system, for he reflects (XVII) that he has wailed enough about his own troubles, and needs "more noble material" to write about. It is at this point that his audience of pretty young ladies, some mocking, some sympathetic, but all extremely inquisitive, corners him, and they ask him some very searching questions about his love for Beatrice (XVIII). He tries to tell them that his happiness is no longer in Beatrice's salutation, but in what can't fail him, the poems he writes about her; but they point out that he has not, in fact, written such poems, and he creeps away deeply ashamed. It is after that, walking along a clear stream, that he is rescued by a new inspiration, the first line of the *canzone, Donne ch'avete intelletto d'Amore,* "Ladies who have intelligence of Love"; and so ends the first movement of the book.

The "reality" of this sequence is not to be found in the *dramatis personae*—conventional, decorative figures as they are—but in the carefully plotted movements of the poet's groping psyche, from frustrated longing and ambiguous dream, to the painful but finally accepted experience of love disdained and poetic inspiration gone, to the unexpected inspiration that at last shows him his lady in a new and wider light and releases his poetic imagination once more. Years later, in the *Purgatorio,* Dante will present the stages of the "creative" process more elaborately and more knowingly, but at this point he has already identified it in his own experience.

Dante's fellow poets must have recognized that this *canzone* marked a new achievement, for he tells us that they answered it and asked for more definitions of love. The young poet responds in two delicately beautiful sonnets (XX, XXI) which are, in fact, "more noble material": they rejoice in the love Beatrice reveals, with a new serenity, and with a clarity unshadowed by his personal selfish troubles. But then Beatrice's father dies, and that introduces the main theme of the second part of the book, that of death, the classic enemy of mortal love.

In the Romance tradition that Dante inherited the love-death theme is presented and interpreted in various ways. In the *Vita* it first appears (VIII) when one of Beatrice's friends dies, and the young poet writes two sonnets, which apparently suffice to dispel the shadow. This time the mourning sonnets he writes are not enough; he begins brooding upon the fact that he and Beatrice must both die; he falls ill, and on the ninth day of his illness he sees Beatrice's death in a dream. He yells in terror and is awakened by a girl (perhaps his sister) who, with her companions, tries to comfort him. He then writes the *canzone, Donna pietosa* (XXIII), to explain to them the dream that had so disturbed him. This, as pointed out earlier, is the center of the book, perhaps the best passage to study if one seeks to understand the basis of Dante's growing vision of love, which now decisively diverges from that of all the other poets of his tradition.

The *canzone* recounts the episode in a style appropriate to the naïveté of the passionate young poet; but here again Dante the author has given it a complex structure which one must consider in order to see the reality behind the figures of convention or dream. In the prologue (first two stanzas) we see the young poet, with the young ladies who waked him, turning back to rehearse his dream. Within the dream his appalled spirit approaches the hidden (or "repressed") reality: his own mortality, then Beatrice's; and with that a vision of the end of the world and a voice crying, "Do you not know the news? Your lady is dead, who was so fair." He sees angels ascending with a little cloud; then love shows him Beatrice's face in death, and that vision ends the terror: "She had such humility that she seemed to be saying, I am in peace." She thus enables him to accept mortality; he can even see death as "very sweet." The *canzone* ends as he returns from his "vain vision" or "empty dream," as he surprisingly calls it, to the girls in the world that we know as real when we are awake.

It is evident that this *canzone* is beautifully constructed as the peripety-via-recognition of the action of the whole book. Seeking to explore his faith in love as revealed by Beatrice, the young poet encounters the irresistible sense of mortality, which threatens to destroy the whole motive; his "recognition" of her death as it really is (or would be) then brings about the reversal of his whole view of his situation as a mortal lover, and quiets him down once more—this time almost permanently, for the story is nearly over. That much one can make out quite clearly; but the whole episode, precisely because of its reticent, figured style, is so suggestive that one might mull over its possible meanings for a long time.

It seems to show, for one thing, how the young Dante succeeded in rejecting one of the most seductive Romance interpretations of the love-death theme, that which identifies them both with the mystic sweetness of night and the void. It is this strand in the tradition that Denis De Rougemont studied in his famous *Love in the Western World*, finding its culmination in the Wagnerian *Liebestodt*. We find Dante longing for death at the beginning of this episode, but at the end the sweetness of death signifies his faith in Beatrice's immortality, thereby bringing about a reaffirmation of the human being, and restoring the poet to the waking world with a new sanity.

The most striking sign of the return to everyday reality is the criticism we get here of the poetic imagination, and of the figura-tive nature of the poet's language. As the young poet of the story, Dante insists that his dream is literally unreal or "vain"; and as the author of the book, Dante interpolates at this point (XXV) a very sophisticated account of the use of poetic "figures" and "rhetorical colors." He has personified love, he explains, but he knows very well that love has no separate being in that sense. Poets are by tradition allowed the use of figures, but he and his first friend (Guido Cavalcanti) would think it a great shame for a poet to use any figure he could not explain intelligibly.

The rest of the book partakes of this new realism, or sobriety: Dante the young poet has nearly reached the understanding of Dante the author, and all the threads are being drawn together. Part III, the last act, seems to have been planned as a "dying fall"—not to say a "falling away"—after the intense revelation of the death-dream. It is devoted to the period after Beatrice's actual death, but Dante explains that it is beyond his power, and outside his theme, to handle that terrible event directly. Part III is devoted chiefly to his infatuation with the "lady in the window," and that is indeed important to his theme, for it shows how he met a new and subtle threat to his faith that Beatrice was the unique and destined guide, for him at least, to love in the deepest sense.

The new lady appears while he is mourning the death of Beatrice. She looks at him, from her window, with such pity for his distress that he is forced to pity himself, and so he can enjoy the relief of tears. He thinks that love itself—the very "love" that Beatrice had first revealed to him—must be speaking to him again through this beautiful lady. They gaze at each other, "love" grows; but then he realizes with dismay that he is becoming happy. Is he then disloyal to Beatrice? He writes a dialogue (XXXIX) in the form of a sonnet between the *heart* (which, he explains, means "appetite") and the *soul* (which he glosses as "reason"). The appetite very gracefully explains that love itself has appeared again through the new lady, and reason makes no answer, seeming therefore to give tacit consent to the new attachment. This difficult moral-psychological discussion is, however, not so much concluded as it is broken off by the direct intervention of Beatrice's spirit. We read (XL), "Against this adversary of reason there arose one day a mighty vision within me, almost at the hour of noon; for methought I beheld this glorious Beatrice, in those crimson garments wherein she first appeared to mine eyes. . . ."

By identifying the heart with "appetite" Dante offers a consistent and very understandable interpretation of his affair with the window lady. His love for her, though so eloquently and musically rationalized by the "heart," is only "appetite" and thus, in essence, irrational. But it is not so easy for the modern reader to see what reason itself would say in this situation. The love of Beatrice is not to be identified with reason either—no form of love, even the highest, coincides with reason. We shall see that when Dante writes the *Convivio*, years later, he identifies reason, not with Beatrice but with the window lady, and declares his allegiance to "her." In the *Commedia* he returns, of course, to Beatrice, but by that time he can set forth the manifold relations between love and reason in the full light of his faith and of the elaborate wisdom of his tradition. In the *Vita*, as he carefully points out, he is not ready to deal with the ultimate questions raised by Beatrice's actual death.

In the *Vita* the sudden vision of Beatrice as she had first appeared, in childhood, sharply reaffirms the theme of the whole book. The first sonnet (III), a prologue, presents the prophetic dream of love, who brings Beatrice, feeds her the poet's heart, and departs weeping. The last sonnet (XLII), an epilogue, presents a love-inspired sigh rising to heaven and there meeting a lady of incomprehensible splendor, whom the poet feels sure is Beatrice.

Vita Nuova: The Symbolism of Number, Figure, and Form

I have been trying to bring out the realistic story in the *Vita Nuova*, for it is that which we can most readily read with sympathy. But the symbolism of number and color, the personifications, all that we think of as merely "medieval," are also important in Dante's scheme. It is by means of his symbolism, especially that of number in its connection with the form of the whole, that Dante seeks to "place" the story and suggest the wider meanings it may have.

Dante certainly intended to present the essential truth of a real experience of his own, which he found, he tells us, in the "book" of his memory. But the realism of that "book" is obviously not the modern realism of Joyce, for example, in *A Portrait of the Artist as a Young Man,* though that too represents a most impressive effort to get at the truth of a quest recorded in memory. In recent years the nature of Dante's realism has been elucidated by sympathetic students of his tradition, notably the late Erich Auerbach, and, more recently, Professor Charles Singleton, whose *Essay on the* Vita *Nuova* is indispensable.

In the second paragraph Dante writes, "Nine times already since my birth had the heaven of light returned almost to one and the same point in relation to its own proper revolution, when the glorious lady of my mind first appeared to mine eyes, who was called Beatrice by many who knew not what they were calling her." That does not sound realistic to us, but Dante was thinking of the real world as he understood it: the Greek-Christian cosmos, God's creation, filled in its every part and its every changing aspect with meaning for the perpetually-seeking human psyche. The cosmos was sometimes called the "book" that God wrote, and the book of Dante's memory would be significant only because it reflects a bit of what God himself had written. At the beginning, therefore, Dante places the little drama of the love of Beatrice in the cosmic setting from which it had emerged, the context which gives it meaning. Hence the astronomical references in this passage; and hence, throughout the book, the traditional symbolism of numbers, colors, and figures, all of which are regarded as signs that could show us the truth if we could only read them correctly.

The number nine, introduced at the very beginning, reappears throughout the first two parts of the book in connection with crucial events, like a carefully planted clue in a detective story. But Dante does not discuss it until after Beatrice's death (XXIX, XXX), when he pauses and interrupts the story to explain that he will not try to deal with the actual death of his lady directly. Instead he will try to guess what she signifies, and the number nine must be a clue since it has been associated with her all along. The date and hour of her death is connected with nine too, according to all three calendars then known, the Arabian, Syrian and Christian. What, then, might this association tell us about her?

His first guess is that the propitious conjunction of the nine heavens at her birth signifies her "perfection"—and he supports this hypothesis with reference to astronomy and astrology. But the number nine is itself significant, for its root is three, the number of the Holy Trinity. Beatrice would then be "a nine" and thus a kind of miracle coming from the Trinity itself. "Perchance a more subtle person might see in it a yet more subtle reason," he concludes, "but this is what I see therein and what pleaseth me most."

It would seem that Dante believed in astrology, like the "lonely hearts" who read the horoscopes in the newspapers. But he stages himself here, as he scans the heavens for signs of Beatrice's meaning, like the cautious weatherman who does not claim that he can read the signs with any certainty. It is always difficult to be sure of what Dante believes, for though his faith is that the visible cosmos and all the people in it *do* have meaning, he never forgets that his own view—that of one man in one place—is limited and fallible. Nevertheless, as author of the book, he built both the number nine and the three of the Trinity into the structure of the drama itself, in the belief that Beatrice did point to those exalted meanings.

The numerical arrangement of the poems on which the three acts of the drama are based depends upon nine in various ways:

Act I: the first sonnet (a prologue) followed by nine short poems, and then *Canzone* I, *Donne ch'avete,* which ends Act I and introduces Act II.

Act II: nine poems altogether—four short poems; *Canzone* II, *Donna pietosa,* the climax and peripety; and then four more short poems.

Act III: *Canzone* III, nine short poems, and then the final sonnet, an epilogue corresponding to the first sonnet of the prologue.

This scheme will reveal all sorts of abstract symmetries if one thinks it over; it is characteristic of Dante's elaborate form. Number had an almost mystic significance for him. He makes much of it (in the *De Vulgari Eloquentia*) in his analysis of the musical forms of the *Canzoni,* and the *Divine Comedy* has an elaborate numerical scheme to which he attached great importance.

But *nine* points to the *three* of the Trinity, as Beatrice points to God; it is that which makes her so unlike any other *donna* of the Courtly Love tradition. And Dante seems to have tacitly, but consciously, composed the three acts of his love for Beatrice on the analogy of the traditional three stages of the approach to God. It was pointed out earlier that in the first "act" the young poet looks inward and finds the dreams and the poetic images and figures of his own delighted or despairing passions. The second act begins as he turns outward, to rejoice in Beatrice herself, the miraculous bearer of love. When he encounters his own and her mortality he is obliged to turn again, away from Beatrice in the flesh to Beatrice as immortal and dwelling in the heaven of his creed. Professor Singleton has shown that these three directions of the young poet's quest, as he follows his lady, correspond to the stages of the soul's progress toward God, as described by various saints and theologians of the Christian tradition after Saint Augustine. Dante probably knew several of them; the best known and the easiest in our time is, I think, Bonaventura's *Itinerarium mentis in Deum,* where the three movements we must make in the search for God are *intra nos, extra nos,* and *super nos.*

There is a great deal of psychological insight and a great deal of the wisdom of experience in this picture of growth or enlightenment, whatever one may think of the faith of the ancient religious thinkers. It throws light, by analogy, on any of our efforts to find and accept the truth; and Dante makes full use of it again, in the *Purgatorio,* when he is ready to present the soul's progress in many aspects. Both the overall form of the *Vita Nuova,* and its symbolism, suggest that basic theme: the psyche trying to find its way through the mysteries of God's world, which preoccupies Dante all his life.

Dante as *Fedele d'Amore*

Io mi son un che, quando
Amor mi spira, noto, ed a quel modo
che ditta dentro, vo significando.

(I am one who, when
love breathes in me, take note, and in that mode
which he dictates within, go signifying.)
—*Purgatorio* XXIV, line 52

There can be little doubt that the youthful Dante first found himself as one of that circle of poets who called themselves "love's faithful" (*fedeli d'amore*). The "new life" of the title is not a misnomer; it refers to Dante's inner life: that of the loving, seeking, poem-making psyche itself. In writing his love poems, then making a selection and arrangement of them, and finally composing the prose narrative that places them within a complete dramatic action, Dante was finding both himself and his art. Or should we say, rather, that he was *inventing* himself and his art? Is that tearful and ecstatic youth really young Dante, or is he a mask, a Poundian "persona" imagined and projected as an expressive device, part of the process of poem-making?

It was obviously not Dante's intention to try to present himself "as he was," in the manner of our modern autobiographical novelists. I have pointed out that the poems in the *Vita* represent a selection from his youthful output, which reflects several quite different loves and attitudes to love. The few facts we have about Dante's life in Florence, his marriage, and his war service do not appear in the *Vita* at all. His intention was not to offer his readers either confessions or documentation, but to present, honestly and clearly, the *new* direction his spirit was taking: that was what seemed to him sufficiently noteworthy to be written about. Convention, poetic invention, and fresh insight probably all entered into the *Vita*. But one must remember that the human is always and inevitably making myths of himself, especially in the creatively changing time of youth. Modern writers do not escape that: when they recount their early adventures "as" lost and depraved, they too are following convention, oversimplifying, and myth-making.

The *persona* (or "working hypothesis," as one might call it) of the *fedele d'amore* enabled Dante to make certain discoveries about life and art which he would build on long after he had left his youth behind. It was his habit all the rest of his life to think over the lyrics that emerged from his experience and to try to understand their meanings intellectually. The realistic scheme of the *Vita*, in which Dante appears both as protagonist and as author, enables him to present the story critically, in the light of two simultaneous points of view, and he will use the same scheme, greatly and very consciously developed, for the *Commedia* itself. Most important of all was his discovery that the inspired subject, or true content, of his poetry was *amor*. The formula quoted at the beginning of this section was written near the end of his career. It applies to the *Vita Nuova* and the early lyrics of the *dolce stil nuovo,* but also to his later poems, including the *Commedia.* But by that time he understood *amor* far more deeply, widely, and objectively than he had in youth—as we shall see when we look at his later works.

The *Vita Nuova* is strictly confined to the *amor* that Beatrice inspired in earliest youth. He explores the dreamlike visions it produces as far as he can, and with all his candor and insight. He learns thereby a great deal; but by the end of the book it is clear that neither Courtly Love, nor *la gloriosa donna della mia mente,* "the glorious lady of my mind (or memory)," as he calls Beatrice, nor "amor" in just that form, have anything more to offer him. The *persona* of the *fedele d'amore* has served its purpose; to try to stay within it any longer would have been artificial, unnatural and imprisoning.

It is probable that by the time Dante was finishing the *Vita* he was already being drawn more deeply into the cruel turmoil of Florentine politics. That was the beginning of another life and a new phase of his development as poet and seer.

II

Dante's First Participation in Politics: 1293–1302

Politics in Florence

As mentioned earlier, Dante's party, the Guelfs, gained control of Florence in 1266, and for the rest of the century the city prospered greatly. But success, it seems, made the citizens more "proud and quarrelsome" than ever: as Dante put it years later (*Inferno* XVI, 73), "The new people and the sudden gains have generated pride and excess." Most of the Florentines may have been nominally Guelfs, but they had no trust whatever in each other. Their complicated tussles for power at last erupted (in 1300) in the ruthless civil war between the Blacks and the Whites. Dante's part in these troubles cannot be traced with any certainty, but it is known that he held various offices, after 1295 at least; that he was one of the six Priors governing the city when the fighting started, and that he was banished in 1302. One needs to have some conception of this period in Florence in order to understand what happened to Dante, for it is all reflected in his later writings.

It is very hard for modern inquirers to make out a consistent pattern in Florence's broils. The rich and powerful bullied and exploited the little people, but they were also bitterly, often violently, divided among themselves. The little people beat back the rich, both with votes and with clubs; but Florence was not, at this time, neatly lined up for a "class struggle." Perhaps it could best be described as a radical and rapidly changing democracy. Del Lungo puts it this way in his *Da Bonifazio ad Arrigo VII*:

> The twenty years from 1282 until a little beyond 1300 include perhaps the most eventful period of the Florentine Commune, the stabilizing and strengthening of the democracy, the definitive constituting of what our ancestors, like the Greeks, called "people" (*popolo*). "People" was for them the government, since that conformed entirely to the power and authority of the majority in the republic; and that same word, in the phrases "old people," "first people," "second people," "beginning of the people," applied to the revolutions of 1250, '67, '68, '93, signified the political changes in which, varying only in form, the democratic character remained unchanged. (Author's translation)

The city was small enough so that direct majority rule seemed possible, and almost everyone was "in politics."

The actual constitution was apparently intended to assure majority rule. The real power was vested in the four Councils (*Consigli*): that of the *Potestà* or Commune; that of the *Capitano del Popolo*; the Council of One Hundred, and the Council of the Wise. The latter was appointed to give advice; the other three were elected every six months by the Guilds (*Arti*) in the different wards of the city. The Councils elected six Priors to perform the judicial functions and to rule the city day by day; but they served only two months. In the Councils every member had a chance to express his views, if he dared, and to vote; but nobody was allowed to hold office long enough to consolidate his power—or to effectuate his policies. Del Lungo, who read a great many of the ancient records of the Councils, concludes that, under that form of government, "the citizen was lost in the citizenry." It was a system made for the demagogue, and in this period a number of fascinating popular leaders appeared, some sinister, like Pecora the Butcher, some noble, like Giano della Bella.

One must understand that the *Arti*, or Guilds (whose members were entitled to vote), were associations not only of craftsmen, like the workers in wood, and of professional men, such as the notaries and judges, but sometimes of all of those in one industry. The "Arts of Wool," for instance, included not only the skilled workers but also the great merchants and exporters. The original intention in providing that only the members of Guilds could vote was to make sure that all political power was firmly in the hands of the "people." But according to Davidsohn, in his *Storia di Firenze*, the rich soon found ways to use the Guilds themselves to acquire power.

The "revolutions" mentioned by Del Lungo were crises in the perpetual struggle for popular control of Florence. The most important in this period was that of 1293, which was led by Giano della Bella. He belonged to a very old and rich family, but he succeeded in making a set of severe laws, the "Orders of Justice," which effectively deprived the rich, and the cavaliers, of all their power, even the right to vote. It is probable that Dante did not support Giano, for the Orders of Justice excluded him too, and there is a tiny reference in the *Paradiso* (XVI, 132) which suggests that he thought Giano had gone too far and damaged his own people. But it seems certain that Dante did not like the man who upset Giano either: Pecora the Butcher, whom Compagni describes as a cruel and lying bully. As the result of Pecora's intrigues, Giano della Bella had to flee for his life (1295) only two years after his success, and the Orders of Justice, though they remained on the books, were slightly mollified—enough so that Dante could participate actively in politics. From 1295 his votes in Council are recorded.

One would like very much to know how Dante, with his learning, his strict intellect, and his scorn for the ignorant and dishonest, could rise to the top in that faithless free-for-all. He pays his respects to the Florentine government in *Purgatorio* VI, directly addressing the city,

. . . che fai tanto sottili
provvedimenti, che a mezzo novembre
non giunge quel che tu d'ottobre fili.
Quante volte del tempo che rimembre,
legge, moneta, offizio e costume
hai tu mutato, e rinnovato membre!
E se ben ti ricordi e vedi lume,
vedrai te simigliante a quella inferma,
che non può trovar posa in su le piume,
ma con dar volta suo dolore scherma.

(. . . who make such subtle
provision, that to mid-November
does not reach what you spin in October.
How often in the time that you remember,
law, coinage, office and custom
have you changed, and made new your members!

And if you remember well, and see clearly,
you will perceive yourself like that invalid
who cannot find rest on the pillows,
but by twisting veils her pain.)

That passage, however, was written many years later. In Florence, before 1300, he must have hoped, like Giano della Bella or Dino Compagni, or the few other men of good will, that he could accomplish something of value. Probably, also, he was thinking of the somewhat legendary civic virtue of ancient Romans like Cato, for such figures were already haunting the imaginations of the men of his time.

After the fall of Giano della Bella and the liberalizing reforms of 1295, Dante appears as a member of the Guild of Physicians and Specialists (*Arte dei Medici e degli Speciali*). Unfortunately that does not tell us what he was actually doing to make a living, for the experts are uncertain what businesses or professions that oddly named Guild included. Davidsohn says that the "Specialists" were dealers in things like drugs and herbs. Del Lungo points out that the Physicians were associated, at that time, with the Liberal Arts, and suggests that Dante may have been enrolled in that Guild in recognition of his humane learning. But we may be sure that, as a member of that Guild, his status was honorable and that he was free to vote and to hold office. He participated in the deliberations of the Councils. He was appointed Florentine Ambassador to the neighboring town of San Gimignano, to conduct the affairs of the *Taglia Guelfa,* an organization that Florence used to dominate her allies. He probably went to Rome in 1300 for the great Jubilee. And it was in that year that he became a Prior.

The summit of Dante's career as a practical politician coincides with the tragic crisis in the affairs of Florence: the outbreak of the ferocious struggle between the Whites and the Blacks. All of the political forces in Italy were involved, sooner or later, in this struggle: the other cities of Tuscany and the North; the Pope; the Emperor; the canny and ambitious royal house of France. It changed Dante's life suddenly and completely, and it was to haunt his poetry and his thinking for the rest of his career. It is, therefore, necessary to try to understand it, even though we know so little of Dante's own role as Prior in the very center of the crisis.

The Revolution of the Blacks and Dante's Banishment

The party to which Dante belonged, the Whites, was led by the rich and powerful family of the Cerchi. Their wealth was comparatively new, and they were identified with the prosperous merchants, who wanted peace with the neighbors so that trade might flourish. The Blacks were led by the Donati family, whose wealth was older. The Blacks had banking interests all over Europe and were less interested in peace than in Florentine imperialism; and that is supposed to have been one of the reasons why the Whites mistrusted them. Both Whites and Blacks insisted that they were zealous Guelfs, but the Pope, Bonifazio VIII, sided with the Blacks, because his finances depended upon the Florentine bankers who belonged to the Black party.

Bonifazio VIII is one of the Popes whom Dante, later in his life, would blame most bitterly for the chaos and the demoralization of Italy. Some students maintain that Dante's hatred for Bonifazio was a matter of personal enmity. But much of what we know about Bonifazio's doings supports Dante's view, and there were very many in his time who shared it. Bonifazio procured his election as Pope, in 1294, by persuading his unworldly predecessor, Celestine V, to abdicate, and then purchasing the support of Charles of Anjou with promises of the Imperial Crown. As Pope, Bonifazio enriched not only the Church, but his own family, the Caetani; and he used his power to ruin his hereditary enemies, the Colonna family. There is, I think, no reason to doubt that Bonifazio sincerely believed that the Pope ought to have absolute political authority, and as much secular wealth and power as possible, and he was ready to pursue those ends by any means. He was probably one of those strong, passionate figures (common everywhere, but especially in Italy then) who could not distinguish what he instinctively wanted from what it was his duty to want.

There were plenty of material interests at stake in the complicated struggle between the Whites and the Blacks. But the beginning of overt hostilities suggests that the high-spirited Florentines wanted to fight anyway. There had been a feud in the nearby city of Pistoia between two families that were nicknamed the "Whites" and the "Blacks." Florence, as a more powerful ally, tried to pacify Pistoia by arresting the leaders of both sides and imprisoning them in Florence. But the Florentines themselves then began taking sides, lining up either with the Donati, who supported the Blacks, or with the Cerchi, who preferred the Whites. In this rather haphazard way the Florentine parties got their names. The dispute soon produced street fights between partisans of the two families. It was on the fifteenth of May, 1300, that the brawling got out of control. There was a dance of young women that evening (as Villani reports) in the Piazza di Santa Trinità, and there some young gallants of both factions met (like the Montagues and the Capulets) and, of course, got into a fight. The disorder spread through the city; the Priors could not stop it; and the formidable Bonifazio VIII was then bound to intervene to support the faction closest to him, the Blacks.

The Popes, with their claim to universal political power, were interested in all the little wars of Italy, and a Papal legate was always on hand to patch up a peace. Guelf Florence, of course, recognized Papal authority in such matters, and the Guelfs had often benefited from the Pope's support. But in this case the Signoria (the six Priors) mistrusted Bonifazio and his legate in Florence, Matteo d'Acquasparta, and in April they had taken matters into their own hands and banished three Blacks whom they thought responsible for the trouble. When d'Acquasparta demanded that they be reinstated, the Priors refused. A new Signoria then took office; Dante was one of the six. The new Priors supported their predecessors, and when the fighting grew worse after May fifteenth, they issued an order (signed by Dante along with the rest) that some of the leaders of both parties be confined outside Florence. Bonifazio demanded that the Blacks be freed, but the Priors defied him again, and in September, 1300, d'Acquasparta, on the order of Bonifazio, excommunicated the rulers of Florence.

It appears that the Priors were endeavoring, with courage and integrity, to rule justly, to safeguard the welfare of the city as a whole without reference to party, and to maintain, even against Bonifazio, the legitimate authority of the city's government. But it was perilous to resist the Pope, and it must have been very hard for them to banish their own colleagues and political allies. Florence was a small city (by our modern standards) and political strife there had the intimate bitterness of feuding within a single family. Certainly it must have been a dark time for Dante; one of the Whites whom he banished was Guido Cavalcanti, and one of the Blacks was Corso di Donati, his wife's cousin, and the brother of his close friend Forese.

Guido Cavalcanti was one of the conspicuously quarrelsome Whites, a patrician like Corso Donati, and as proud and scornful as he. It was probably inevitable that the Signoria should make an example of him. In that situation the fact that he had been the first of Dante's friends, the man to whom he had dedicated the *Vita Nuova*, was irrelevant. Guido was confined at Sarzana, and there he wrote the wonderful *canzone, Perch'io no spero di tornar giammai,* "Because I do not hope to turn again," in which his exile is almost identified with his approaching death. Exile was feared like death in those days; and Guido, in fact, sickened in Sarzana, and died on August 28, 1300.

Corso Donati, unfortunately for Florence and for Dante, did not die, but lived to lead the Blacks to their decisive triumph. Dino Compagni described him as follows, in his clumsy but vivid prose:

> A cavalier of the type of the Roman Catiline, but crueler than he; of gentle birth, handsome in body, a pleasing speaker; embellished with good manners; subtle in mind; his spirit ever intent on evil-doing. . . . Many arsons and robberies he caused to be done, and great injury to the Cerchi and their friends; much wealth did he gain, and rose to a great height. That was Messer Corso Donati, who through pride was called *il Barone*; for when he passed through town many shouted, "Viva il Barone!" and it seemed the town was his. (Author's translation)

In Dante's mature view Corso shares the blame for the ruin of Florence with Bonifazio, and the traces of his destructive career are to be found in several parts of the *Commedia.*

Bonifazio's excommunication demoralized Florence, and especially, of course, its White rulers. The Signoria was still determined to maintain their independence and authority at all costs, but they rather weakly hoped that Bonifazio might be persuaded to relent, if they gave him everything he wanted except civil authority. They organized a solemn mission to Rome, in November, with delegates not only from Florence but from the other Guelf cities, including Lucca, Bologna and Siena, to try to influence the Pope. Dante was one of the three ambassadors from Florence. But Bonifazio was listening to the Black bankers; and, moreover, he was already bringing Charles of Valois into Italy, to enforce his will with the aid of the French.

Charles of Valois was the brother of the French King, Philip the Fair. As a result of the ancient struggle with the Empire, the Popes had, for many years, been trying to use French power to support their claims to absolute authority in Italy. At this time Bonifazio wanted to use Charles both to assist the rather shaky French regime in the Kingdom of Naples, and to reduce Florence to obedience.

When Bonifazio received Dante and the other Tuscan ambassadors, he relented to the extent of allowing Florence to resume religious services, but with the warning that he might restore the interdict at any time. Perhaps he succeeded in deceiving the Tuscan mission; at any rate the Florentine Signoria continued to try to mollify him, acceding to his requests for money and military assistance. But Charles of Valois even then was making his cautious descent into Italy. He had only five hundred horsemen, and he avoided the cities he thought might be dangerous, including Florence. When he reached the Papal summer residence at Anagni, Bonifazio received him with great magnificence; "granted" him absolute powers in Romagna and Tuscany, and an impressive list of titles, including that of *Paciere di Toscana*, "Peacemaker of Tuscany." And so equipped, Charles proceeded, at last, to Florence.

Guelf Florence had enjoyed most cordial relations with the House of France. Dante himself had become a devoted friend of Charles Martel, when that prince passed through Florence with great pomp and circumstance on his way to Naples, in 1294. One can see why the Signoria, isolated as they were, did not want to break with an old ally, even though they knew that Charles of Valois was very dangerous. Moreover, Charles gave them all sorts of assurances of good will and promised that their independence and authority would be respected. They did not dare to oppose him by force, though they had the strength to do so; and Charles entered Florence in November, 1301.

Once inside the city, Charles used his authority to betray the legitimate government, the White Signoria, to their enemies. The Blacks inside Florence were emboldened to rebel, and Corso Donati sneaked back into the city. He opened the prisons to gain more followers, and five days of arson, murder, and pillage followed. While the Signoria tried, without much success, to call the demoralized citizens to arms, Charles did nothing. But when Corso had successfully completed his ruthless revolution, and the White leaders had either fled or been killed or imprisoned, Charles stepped forward in his role of Papal "Peacemaker." He and Corso set up the government again, with the Blacks, of course, in complete control.

Corso and his party feared that the Whites who had fled would rouse their friends in the rest of Tuscany and return. They moved swiftly to complete their enemies' ruin. They summoned the important Whites to stand trial for crimes against the state, and when they refused to appear, their absence was officially taken as a confession of guilt. The accusations were barratry and disturbance of the peace by defying the Pope and his legates. The penalties usually started with very heavy fines and banishment or imprisonment for two years; went on to confiscation or destruction of all property owned by the accused, registering of their names as traitors, sometimes banishment of the whole family, on pain of death. Dante was "tried" *in absentia* for barratry and defiance of the Pope, found guilty, and banished with the loss of all his property, on January 27, 1302.

Very little undisputed information is available about Dante's doings between his term as Prior, in May and June 1300, and his banishment in 1302. He continued to play a responsible part in the government, for it is recorded that he spoke in Council several times, the last being in September, 1301. In November of that year he was (as has been said before) one of the three Florentine ambassadors in the fruitless mission to Bonifazio. It seems probable that he was detained for a time after the other ambassadors had been dismissed and was therefore not in Florence when Corso Donati seized the city. Bruni, a contemporary chronicler with a good reputation for accuracy, says that Dante learned of the revolution and his own banishment when he reached Siena on his way home. Certain it is that he never saw Florence again.

One would like very much to know just what part Dante played while the Whites were making their last desperate efforts to retain control. The Whites seem to have been weak, indecisive and deluded, compared to their enemies; and Davidsohn tells us that they were capable of savagery, notably in their relations with the little city of Pistoia. I don't suppose that Dante could have been in the confidence of the White leaders during this painful crisis without sharing to some extent in their crimes and follies: that is one of the penalties of participating in party politics. But we do not have to assume that he agreed with all their policies. And there is no reason to believe that he was guilty of the barratry that he was officially charged with: his resolute refusal to recognize the Pope's authority in civic affairs amply accounts for his trial and banishment.

One can see what the brutally abrupt end of Dante's political career in Florence meant to him by reading what he wrote during the next few years. He could neither accept it emotionally, nor understand it to his own satisfaction, before he started writing the *Commedia* six or eight years later. In the years of wandering, writing, and study, he was burdened both with the exile's nostalgia and the bitterness of the defeated politician. Out of that stubborn suffering came the thought and poetry of his middle phase.

Of Dante's life in exile, apart from his writing, very little is known definitely.

The struggle between the Whites and Blacks continued for years, but the Whites had almost no success, and their party slowly and painfully dissolved. Dante participated in their councils, and possibly some of their battles, for a year or two after his banishment. There is a letter (Epistle I in the Temple Classics edition) which he may have written in their behalf to another Papal Peacemaker, the Bishop of Ostia. But by 1304, at the latest, he had ceased to work for the Whites, or pin his hopes to that party.

His personal situation is largely unknown. His brother Francesco was with him for a time; his wife Gemma never joined him; some of his children, at least, appear with him toward the end of his life. It is not known whether he had any means of support except the hospitality of his patrons, the della Scala family in Verona, the Malaspina in Sarzana, and a few other lords in northern and central Italy who are mentioned in the *Commedia*. He was in Verona with the della Scala very early in his wanderings, and with the Malaspina in 1306 and for a time thereafter. But there is no other definite information about his movements until Henry VII's arrival in Italy, when Dante went to Milan to meet him.

One might get some insight into Dante's life in exile by carefully considering the anecdotes reported by chroniclers and the early biographers, dubious and inconsistent as they usually are, and by digging into the extremely intricate histories of the cities of Lombardy, Romagna, and Tuscany. But one gets closer to Dante himself by studying the poetry and great prose works he was writing then, with their characteristic mixture of passion, aspiration, and candor.

III

The Middle of the Journey: Dante's Cult of Reason, 1293–1308

The Works of Dante's Middle Phase: *Canzoni, Convivio, De Vulgari Eloquentia*

Quanto ragion qui vede
dirti poss'io; da indi in là t'aspetta
pure a Beatrice, ch' opera è di fede.

(As far as reason sees here
I can tell you; beyond that you must wait
for Beatrice only, for it is a matter of faith.)
—*Purgatorio* XVIII, 46

THERE ARE MANY unanswered questions about the works of Dante's middle phase. He himself never collected his poems, and he left both the *Convivio* and the *De Vulgari Eloquentia* unfinished. The dates of composition cannot be determined accurately, and therefore we cannot tell in what order the poems and the prose works were written. It is, however, generally agreed that they were written after the *Vita Nuova* and before the *Divine Comedy*. Moreover, all of them clearly emerge from Dante's experience of the "world" after he turned away from the love of Beatrice; and the two prose works (both of which are based on his *canzoni*) show very clearly that in early maturity he was using classical reason to find his way through the problems of art, passion, and political conflict.

The *canzoni* must be regarded as the basis of Dante's whole intellectual effort during this period. Until the overwhelming inspiration of the *Commedia* struck him, the *canzone* was for him the supreme form of poetry in Italian, and he used it to explore every aspect of his experience, every possible path: metaphysical speculation, the assaults of erotic passion, the intricacies of his angry controversies about political or moral questions. Some of his *canzoni* impress a modern reader at once as great poetry; some are too frankly didactic for our taste; some are very difficult in spite of their beautiful music, as Dante says himself:

> Canzone, i' credo che saranno radi
> Color che tua ragione intendan bene,
> Tanto la parti faticosa e forte.
>
> (Ode, I think there will be few
> Who understand your meaning well,
> So hard and arduous is your utterance.)
> (Ode XV, Temple
> Classics *Canzoniere*)

The *canzoni* offer all sorts of insights into Dante's restless spirit, and the reader is urged to become acquainted with them, preferably with the aid of Professor Contini's fine edition of the *Rime*. But it is in the *Convivio* and the *De Vulgari Eloquentia* that one may see what Dante himself, at this time, was trying to make out of his own rich and varied work as lyric poet.

In the *Vita Nuova* Dante selected some of his poems in order to bring out the theme of new life, and in a similar way he chooses to discuss some of his *canzoni* in the two prose works, in order to bring out the path he was then taking as a man and as a poet. We find him, as usual, facing his experience in the faith that it has a true meaning for him, and endeavoring to embody it in a poem. He then collects a number of his poems, remembering the experiences they came out of, and seeks the meaning of the whole sequence. His method, if one can call it that, is the same in his middle phase as it was when he wrote the *Vita Nuova*: he thinks over his adventures as man and as poet, and so he redefines himself and his aims, continually moving from his individual, momentary perceptions toward a wider vision of human conduct and more general principles of art. In so doing he was unconsciously laying the foundations for the *Commedia*, when he would return to Beatrice, and to the supernatural faith with which she was always associated. But he did not foresee that freshly religious inspiration while writing the *Convivio* and the *De Vulgari Eloquentia.* He thought that what human reason could see was enough—until (for reasons we can never be quite sure of) both works were broken off unfinished.

In what follows the two works will be considered together, in order to bring out Dante's conception of himself and his art in this period, and also to indicate the outlines of the philosophic structure he built then and used later as the framework of the *Commedia.*

Convivio: Dante's Apology for Turning from Beatrice to Philosophy

The *Convivio* consists of four Treatises, the last not quite finished. Treatise I is an extended prologue in which Dante (as was his custom) introduces himself and the book to follow. He explains his purpose in the first sentence, with a quotation from Aristotle's *Metaphysics*: "All men by nature desire to know." He is inviting men of good will to a "banquet" (*convivio*) of true knowledge, in order to satisfy the basic need of all rational beings. His method will be to comment at length upon fourteen of his *canzoni,* those "treating as well of love as of virtue." The *canzoni* contain or imply the knowledge already, but he knows from experience that his readers cannot understand their true meaning without help: hence the full explanations which he will offer. He never completed this scheme, for he gets around to considering only three *canzoni,* in Treatises II, III, and IV, and then the book is abruptly broken off. But the commentaries on these three suffice to set forth his reasoned view of man, in society, in history, and in the cosmos. The *Convivio* is thus the best place to study that basically Aristotelian philosophy which he used, all his life, to form and guide his spirit.

The *Convivio* is also Dante's apologia for his own life and work up to that time, as he tells us himself (Treatise I, ii, 112): "I am moved by the fear of infamy, and I am moved by the desire to give instruction which in very truth no other can give." It is impossible to read the *Convivio* without realizing that Dante was finding it very hard to rise from the passions of his troubled life to the disinterested contemplation of the truth, and that he did not always succeed in that great effort. He presents himself (especially in Treatise I) as a man beset by enemies. There are his political enemies, to whom he owes the poverty and the humiliations of his unjust exile. There are enemies of a quite different kind, academic and ecclesiastical one may suppose, who will attack him because he writes philosophy in Italian instead of Latin. There are those who, reading his love poems, will conclude that a "great passion" had "dominion over him"; and "infamy," he believes, will completely discredit him as a philosopher. In the *Vita Nuova* he presents his credentials as poet and *fedele d'amore*; but in the *Convivio* he must be received as a man of knowledge and reasoned virtue; he must silence those who would accuse him of violent erotic passions. The "proper interpretation" of his love poems is thus a crucial part of his effort to write this book and to bring reason into his life and work. The attempt to understand himself as faithful to reason runs through all the *Convivio*, and the book is therefore the best place to study his change of heart from youth, when he was in love with love, to maturity, when he was in love with reason.

It is the apologetic theme of the *Convivio* that I wish to consider first. It gives the *Dantisti* as much trouble as the biographical problems of the *Vita Nuova*, and for similar reasons: we have no direct information about Dante's love affairs, and his own account is very reticent, inconsistent, and unconvincing. There is a learned and ingenious literature on the problems of Dante's veracity, and some of what I have read strikes me as valuable. But in the long run one must return to the *Convivio* itself, and the *canzoni*, in order to understand—if not to judge—the struggles of his spirit here in the middle of his life.

In Treatise I, chapter i, line 111, he writes: "And if in the present work . . . the handling be more virile than in the *New Life*, I do not intend thereby to throw a slight in any respect upon the latter, but rather to strengthen that by this; seeing that it conforms to reason that that should be fervid and impassioned, this temperate and virile. For a different thing is comely to say and do at one age than at another. . . . And in *that*, I spoke before entrance on the prime of manhood, and in *this*, when I had already passed the same." So he takes up the story of his inner life where the *Vita Nuova* had left it; and what he says at this point is clear, and obviously true.

The difficulties begin in Treatise II when he interprets the beautiful *canzone*, *Voi che intendendo il terzo ciel movete*, "You who by understanding move the third heaven." He tells us (chapter ii) that the *bella donna* of this poem is "that gentle lady of whom I made mention in the end of the *Vita Nuova*," i.e., the "window lady" who for a time replaces Beatrice as his love object. We have seen that in the *Vita Nuova* he thinks it is "appetite" that is arguing for the window lady, while reason is on Beatrice's side. That interpretation is, as pointed out before, essential to the whole dramatic movement of the *Vita Nuova*, which ends when the supreme value and meaning of Beatrice's love is reaffirmed. But here in the *Convivio* he tells us that the window lady not only has reason on her side, she represents philosophy itself. In her real meaning she is thus not a flesh-and-blood woman at all, but a quite different object of love, and "appetite" would have nothing to do with her.

It is never easy to interpret poems as musical and as suggestive as this *canzone* and the other poems about the window lady. They are subtle dramatizations of *some* change in the object of love, with the more or less remorseful delights and ambiguous rationalizations that accompany this phenomenon. It is always hard to see where reason is when love turns from one object to another. Dante certainly did turn to "reason" after Beatrice's death, and when he tells us (in chapter xiii) that he read Boethius for comfort, and then Cicero, and then the philosophers, we can believe him completely. Perhaps reason was on the side of the window lady even at the time of the *Vita Nuova*. But I think she was a real woman, and I cannot believe that *Voi che intendendo* was originally written to celebrate *philo-sophia*, the love of wisdom, genuine though that love was in Dante.

He planned, as he tells us (I, ii) to "reveal the true meaning" of all his love poems, in order to show that "not passion but virtue was the moving cause." The poems he particularly had in mind were probably the so-called *Pietra* group, numbers I, V, VI, and X in the Temple Classics *Canzoniere*. They certainly seem to be addressed to a real woman, who proves as stubbornly unyielding as a stone (*pietra*) to her passionate lover. Can we believe that *la Pietra* was not a woman at all? Or that Dante was innocent of the kind of passion he so powerfully expressed?

He says of these poems (I, i) that "to many their beauty was more in favor than their excellence"—"excellence" meaning sound moral teaching. That would not bother us, for we do not usually care whether a beautiful poem has an edifying moral or not; and these poems are as beautiful as any lyrics in our tradition. There is, for instance, the famous sestina (*Canzone* I in the Temple Classics *Canzoniere*) in which love's frustration is made into cold and quiet music. Here is the first stanza:

Al poco giorno ed al gran cerchio d'ombra
Son giunto, lasso! ed al bianchir de' colli,
Quando si perde lo color nell'erba.
E'l mio disio però non cangia il verde,
Sì è barbato nella dura pietra,
Che parla e sente come fosse donna.

(To little day, and the great circle of shadow,
Have I come, alas, and to the whitening of the hills,
When color is lost from the grass.
And my desire does not therefore change its green,
So rooted is it in the hard stone
That speaks and hears as though it were a woman.)

Or there is *Canzone* VI, in which the erotic imagery is much more violent. Stanza VI, just before the *tornata* is quoted here:

S'io avessi le belle treccie prese
Che fatte son per me scudiscio e ferza,
Pigliandole anzi terza
Con esse passerei vespro e le squille:

E non sarei pietoso nè cortese,
Anzi farei com'orso quando scherza.
E se Amor me ne sferza,
Io mi vendicherei di più di mille;

Ancor negli occhi ond'escon le faville
Che mi fiammano il cor, ch'io porto anciso,
Guarderei presso e fiso,
Per vendicar lo fuggir che mi face:
Poscia le renderei con amor pace.

(If I had grasped the beautiful tresses
That have been my lash and whip,
Seizing them before tierce
I should have spent with them vesper and evening bells:

And I should be neither pitying nor courteous,
  But like a bear when he plays.
  And if love thereby scourges me,
  I should take more than a thousand vengeance:
Still into those eyes whence issue the sparks
  That set on fire the heart I carry slain
  Should I look, close and fixed,
  To avenge the flight he made me take:
  Then should I give her with love peace.)

A modern reader must agree with Dante's contemporaries that the poems are beautiful, though the passion itself may be unedifying; but they have that relentless clarity (*la tête dans le coeur*) which makes Dante's greatness as a moralist, and as a dramatic poet. When he wrote them, his eye was on the struggles of his psyche, and he wanted to make music out of them without considering what sort of public figure he would cut. But when he wrote the *Convivio* he needed both to defend himself and to relate that passion to the passion for rationalized morality on which he was endeavoring to rebuild his life.

One wonders how he would have interpreted the *Pietra* poems in order to show virtue and *not* passion as their moving cause, if he had completed his plan for the *Convivio.* He might have reminded us that all frustrated loves, whatever their object, are analogous; and accordingly *la Pietra* might stand for philosophy (who is notoriously hard to woo), or even his beloved Florence (as some scholars have suggested), for Florence stubbornly continued to refuse him her favors. These poems, like *Voi che intendendo,* approach the condition of music: they reflect the movements of the psyche before they are specified by a particular object of love. But poetry is not music; it cannot do without specific objects, even though they may be merely metaphors to lead us to the underlying vision. One can imagine, therefore, that *la Pietra* might have been intended as a metaphor for philosophy, or Florence, or something else. But, even if one grants that, one cannot believe Dante when he tells us that he was guiltless of the passion the poems "seem" to represent. Good metaphor emerges from experience; and *la Pietra,* metaphor or not, shows that Dante, in speaking of violent passion, was speaking from experience.

There is a good deal of evidence from other sources that Dante's erotic life (like his political and philosophical aims) was for a time lost in the dark wood. Boccaccio says he had the reputation of being incontinent, and Dante's attempts here in the *Convivio* to defend his reputation seem to confirm this. There is also the very sad sonnet which the "best friend" of his youth, Guido Cavalcanti, addressed to him:

> I' vegno il giorno a te infinite volte
> e tròvote pensar troppo vilmente;
> allor mi dòl de la gentil tua mente
> e d'assai tue vertù che ti son tolte.
> Solevanti spiacer persone molte,
> tuttor fuggivi la noiosa gente:
> di me parlavi, sì, coralemente,
> che tutte le tue rime avea ricolte.
> Or non ardisco per la vil tua vita
> far mostramento che tuo dir mi piaccia,
> nè vegno in guisa a te che tu mi veggi.
> Se'l presente sonetto spesso leggi,
> lo spirito noioso che t'incaccia
> si partirà da l'anima invilita.
> (*I Rimatori del dolce stil novo*)

> (I come to you many times a day
> and find that you are thinking too vilely;
> then do I mourn for that noble spirit of yours,
> and for the great virtues that are taken from you.
> The great crowd used to displease you,
> you used to avoid the vulgar people:
> you spoke of me, indeed, most cordially,
> who had accepted all your poems.
> Now because of your vile life I do not dare
> to show that what you say could please me,
> nor do I come to see you face to face.
> If you read this sonnet many times,
> the vulgar spirit that is pursuing you
> will depart from your degraded soul.)

Neither the circumstances nor the date of this sonnet are known, though it seems certainly to have been written after the time of the *Vita Nuova*. It may possibly refer to Dante's political doings, but is usually supposed to refer to his erotic life. It obviously shows an important change of heart, which Guido regards as *vile*, after the turn from Beatrice. (It is, of course, also another painful sign that the friendship was darkened even before Guido's banishment.)

The most persuasive evidence on Dante's erotic life is to be found in two of his own writings. The first is the "Letter" (*Epistola* III in the Temple Classics *Latin Works*) which he wrote, between 1306 and 1308, to "lord Moruello, Marquis Malaspina," a member of one of the great families that most faithfully befriended him in his exile. He thinks he must explain to his patron that he has been taken captive; hence any neglect of duty of which he may be accused. His captor is Love, "returning after long exile to what is all his own! For he slew or banished or enchained all opposition in me. He slew that praiseworthy determination in the strength of which I held aloof from women, those instruments of his enchantment; and the unbroken meditations wherein I was pondering on things both of heaven and of earth, he relentlessly banished as things suspected; and finally, that my soul might never again rebel against him, he chained my free will; so that I needs must turn not whither I would, but whither he wills." The second bit of evidence is a poem that is thought to have accompanied the letter, the "Mountain Ode" (IV in the Temple Classics *Canzoniere*). It begins:

> Amor, dacchè convien pur che mi doglia,
> Perchè la gente m'oda,
> E mostri me d'ogni virtute spento,
> Dammi savere a pianger come voglia,
> Sì che'l duol che si snoda
> Portin le mie parole come'l sento.

> (Love, since I must perforce complain
> So people can hear me,
> And show myself bereft of all virtue,
> Show me how to wail as I would,
> So that the pain that is freed
> May be borne forth in my words just as I feel it.)

It goes on to depict the losing struggle of the rational will against passion, and to lament the servitude which the beauty of a pitiless lady has thus imposed upon him. This lady is probably not *la Pietra*, but a successor; she comes with the imagery of high mountain country: sun, snow, and sudden thunder, instead of stone. Moreover, in this poem the focus is not upon the lady, but upon the passion she inspires. As in the letter, it is precisely the writer's subjection to passion that is the point.

I think we have, in this letter and this poem, Dante's own record of a change of heart which made him abandon the *Convivio* before he had completed a third of it. For in both letter and poem he explicitly renounces the effort to present himself as a "temperate and virile" man, at one with the moral will, and impeccably obedient to reason only. And in the poem he resumes the attitude that underlies his *Pietra* poems, and indeed most of his lyrics: he accepts an experience as deeply as he can, imitates it in his song as faithfully as he knows how, and lets the work stand as prior to moralizing or personal apology.

Following the apologetic theme of the *Convivio* through the work itself, and on to its end in the "Mountain Ode" and the letter to Moruello, one can make out Dante's desperate effort to persuade his readers—and (what is much worse) himself—that when he turned from the love of Beatrice he embraced nothing but rational perfectionism. "Desperate" because the apology itself shows that he was driven by the need for a respected place in his tough world, and his own poems show him deep in worldly, glamorous, and extra-rational loves. Some of Dante's idolaters find this picture distressing, but I find it both heroic and touching: it enables one to appreciate, a little, the appalling difficulty of the road that would lead, after 1308, to the freedom and candor of the *Commedia*.

Dante must have thought, in this period, that his discovery of reason was the end of the road; but his enthusiasm and his impatience misled him. He found that reason could not free him from worldly loves, nor provide the ultimate satisfaction his spirit demanded. It could, however, reveal to him the majestic, ordered world of his tradition; and the picture of man, his history and society, his arts, and his cosmos, which is embodied in the *Convivio* and the *De Vulgari Eloquentia*, is a permanent achievement. In these two works one can study the many-storeyed setting that Dante finally used for the *Commedia*, and the conception of the human psyche, the protagonist of the great poem, which he learned from Greek psychology and ethics at this time.

Convivio II: The Cosmos in the Light of Reason

Treatise II is based on *Voi che intendendo* (Ode XV in the Temple Classics *Canzoniere*) and we have seen how dubious

Dante's account of the genesis of this poem is. But in order to explain the first line he must show what he means by the "third heaven" and those who move it; and thence he is led to expound the whole conception of the cosmos which had been built by the philosophers, astronomers, and poets of the long Classical-Hebrew-Christian tradition. One is likely to be put off at first by Dante's pedantic manner, and by the mixture of elements that we prefer to keep apart: Aristotelian philosophy, geometry, Ptolemaic astronomy, pagan myth, and Christian theology. But if one disregards the more puzzling details and the superannuated technicalities, one can "get the picture": the world as the cultivated men of Dante's time saw it.

In the astronomy that Dante inherited, the sphere of the earth is taken as the center of the universe. It is surrounded by nine physical "heavens" in the following ascending order: I, that of the moon; II, of Mercury; III, Venus; IV, the Sun; V, Mars; VI, Jupiter; VII, Saturn; VIII, the Stars; and IX, the Primum Mobile—an invisible sphere whose movement sets in motion all that lies below it. Beyond the Primum Mobile is X, the Empyrean, which is beyond both space and time, the "place" of God. This astronomical scheme was expressed mathematically and elaborated with enough refinement to account for the seasonal and diurnal movements of the heavenly bodies, as seen with the naked eye from our earth. Dante uses it in the *Purgatorio*, as a sailor or explorer might, to tell time; and in the *Paradiso* it is the setting of his visionary journey toward the ultimate human goal.

If Dante could use the visible heavens to represent the invisible goals of the human spirit, it was because, in his Mediterranean world, they had been used that way since the Psalmist and the early Greek poets and thinkers. And if he could present all of that here, as part of his feast of reason, it was because the most ancient poetic imagery had been slowly combined with Aristotle's sober metaphysics and with all the science and mathematics then available. The heavens were supposed to be moved by "intelligences," and the intelligences were assimilated in various ways to angels, pagan gods, essences, and (half-understood) Platonic ideas. Moreover, as he explains, the heavens represented the "sciences" in the following order: I, Grammar; II, Dialectic; III, Rhetoric (the Trivium); IV, Arithmetic; V, Music; VI, Geometry; VII, Astrology (the Quadrivium); VIII, Physics and Metaphysics; IX (the

Primum Mobile), Moral Science; and X (the Empyrean), Theology.

In the intricate consistency of this scheme, the multivalent analogical relationships within it, there is plenty to please the intellect, as the reader will see if he studies it out a bit with the aid of the notes in a good edition of the *Convivio*. But this order and harmony strikes us as poetry, *not* truth. For Dante, on the other hand, it was both truth and poetry: he points out that some of it is conjectural, and that his authorities disagree on certain details, but it never occurred to him, all his life long, to doubt its essential truth. This humanized cosmos (in its main outlines, at least) was the home of the European spirit until Shakespeare's time, as readers of Professor Tillyard's *Elizabethan World Picture*, or Professor Kernodle's *Symbolic Stage of the Elizabethans*, will recognize at once. It has, thus, both historic and esthetic significance in itself, and for Dante it was the permanent setting of his life and art. I shall return to it briefly in connection with the *Paradiso*, below.

Convivio III: Love According to Aristotelian Psychology

This Treatise is based on *Canzone* III (in the Temple Classics *Canzoniere*), *Amor, che nella mente mi ragione*, "Love, that in my mind discourses to me." The lady of this contemplative poem represents *philo-sophia*, the love which the beauties of rational knowledge may evoke, form, and satisfy. In order to locate and define this form of love—the ultimate *human* goal—Dante offers a classification of the many forms of love to which the psyche is subject in its perpetual quests for fulfillment. In Treatise II he had sketched the cosmic setting; now the protagonist appears: the insatiable human spirit, with its divine endowment of reason. Treatise III is written in the abstract terms of Aristotelian psychology and ethical theory, for Dante (as always in the *Convivio*) wants to be as rigorously logical and scientific as he can. But the underlying vision of the life of the psyche is the same as that which will eventually be incarnated in the countless particular lives of the *Commedia*, and in the mystical vision at its summit.

"Love, truly taken and subtly considered," Dante writes (III, ii, line 18) "is nought else than a spiritual union of the soul and of the loved thing; to which union the soul, in virtue of its own nature, runs swift or slow, according as it is free or impeded." In *Purgatorio* XVI (lines 85 ff.), he will present this fundamental conception in the pretty image of the guileless child:

> Esce di mano a lui, che la vagheggia
> prima che sia, a guisa di fanciulla
> che piangendo e ridendo pargoleggia,
> l'anima semplicetta, che sa nulla,
> salvo che, mossa da lieto fattore,
> volentier torna a ciò che la trastulla.
> Di picciol bene in pria sente sapore;
> quivi s'inganna, e retro ad esso corre,
> se guida o fren non torce suo amore.

> (Issues from His hand who loves her
> before she is in being, like a small girl
> crying and laughing as she plays,
> the simple little soul that knows nothing,
> save that, moved by a joyful maker,
> she turns all willingly to what intrigues her.
> A minor good, at first, she tastes;
> with it she is beguiled, and runs after it,
> if guide or curb do not divert her love.)

In *Purgatorio* XVIII (lines 19 ff.), it is put more abstractly:

> L'animo, ch'è creato ad amar presto,
> ad ogni cosa è mobile che piace,
> tosto che dal piacere in atto è desto.
> Vostra apprensiva da esser verace
> tragge intenzione, e dentro a voi la spiega,
> sì che l'animo ad essa folger face.
> E se, rivolto, in ver di lei si piega,
> quel piegare è amor, quello è natura
> che per piacer di nuovo in voi si lega.
> Poi come il foco movesi in altura,
> per la sua forma, ch'è nata a salire
> là dove più in sua materia dura:
> così l'animo preso entra in disire,
> ch'è moto spiritale, e mai non posa
> fin che la cosa amata il fa gioire.

Or ti puote apparer quant'è nascosa
la veritade alla gente ch'avvera
ciascuno amore in sè laudabil cosa;
però che forse appar la sua matera
sempr'esser buona; ma non ciascun segno
è buono, ancor che buona sia la cera.

(The mind, which is made to love immediately,
is movable by everything that pleases,
as soon as pleasure quickens it to action.
Your perceptive power draws from a real thing
an impression, and unfolds it within you,
and so makes the mind turn toward it.
And if, so turned, it inclines toward it,
that inclination is love; that is your nature
bound within, once more, by pleasure.
Then, as fire moves upward
because of its form, which by nature rises
to where it lasts longest in its material:
so the caught mind enters into desire,
which is a movement of spirit, and never pauses
until the loved thing makes it rejoice.
Now may be evident to you how hidden
the truth is from those who assert
that every love is laudable in itself;
for perhaps its material may seem
always to be good, but not every seal
is good, even though the wax may be good.)

For Dante, *amor* = the movement of the spirit toward what it perceives as pleasant or good = "action" (in Aristotle's terms).

He proceeds to show us the psyche, with its divine gift of reason, seeking the objects of love that its nature needs (III, ii, line 57):

> . . . it naturally desires and wills to be united to God, in order to fortify its own being. And because it is in the excellences of nature and of reason that the divine excellence manifests itself, therefore the human soul naturally unites herself with them in spiritual fashion, the more swiftly and the more mightily in proportion as they appear more perfect. And they so appear in proportion as the soul's power of recognition is clear or obstructed. And this union it is which we call love, whereby the inner quality of the soul may be recognized by examining outwardly the things which it loves.

The psyche by its nature needs the "divine" objects of intellectual perception, but Dante firmly places its actual life in the world of nature: in the body, and in the objective world we see and hear and feel about us. In chapter iii he explains, indeed, that all the energies of nature may be understood as *amor*, and therefore as analogous to what moves the human psyche: gravitation, heat, light, and the lives of plants and animals. The human creature, being also body, is subject to gravitation, and being a living organism, it shares the plant and animal forms of *amor*. But the intellect enables it to perceive the true order of the countless forms of love, and thus to find its way upward to the fulfillment of its own rational nature. It is very much like the Platonic vision of Eros, ascending the scale of loves toward the ineffable object which the intellect may learn to see.

Dante has greatly expanded and objectified his understanding of *amor* since his efforts to deal with that mystery in the *Vita Nuova*. Love first dawned upon him in the romantic context of Courtly Love, and we have seen how he then joined the poetic dialogue of the Tuscan *fedeli d'amore*, subtly considering the nature and genesis of that wonderful passion. The *Vita Nuova* already shows that he was learning to use philosophy and theology to understand *amor*; but that work is necessarily limited to the love—wonderfully significant as it was—which Beatrice had awakened in him. Now he wants to form a conception of love in general, in order to understand all its forms. One can see why he had to free himself completely from the attachment to Beatrice before he could fully accept, and work out, the wider vision.

The vision of the *Convivio* which reason revealed to him, and which he served as faithfully as he could, may be described as Christianized Aristotelianism. Dante knew some of Aristotle's works in Latin translations: the ones he mentions most frequently in this part of the *Convivio* are the *Nichomachean Ethics, De Anima,* and the *Metaphysics*. He also relied on commentaries by the Arabic philosopher Averroës, and the Christians Albertus Magnus and Thomas Aquinas; and Greek concepts reached him less directly through religious writings all the way back to the early Fathers of the Church, who had begun very soon to absorb Plato and Aristotle. He was firmly grounded in Aristotle—but Aristotle related to the Christian creed, and rethought in the light of subsequent cultures. He sees the life of the psyche as

Aristotle had seen it, and his *amor*, the perpetual movement of the psyche toward the objects it perceives as pleasing, is Aristotle's *energeia*, "action" in the most general sense. In Dante's tradition *amor* is also the romantic love of the lyric poets, and the Christian mystics' love of a personal God; and Aristotle had never encountered, and therefore never explored, those foci of the psyche's life to which Dante will return in the *Commedia*. But here in the *Convivio* Dante has resolutely turned away from the romantic focus of his youth, and he makes as yet no effort to approach the ultimate mysteries of his faith. It never occurs to him to question the Creed; but his eye is upon the psyche in the world of nature, seeking the fulfillment which reason offers there, just as Aristotle's was.

What, then, *is* the ultimate fulfillment that reason offers? Having understood the hierarchy of loves to which it is subject—mineral, vegetable, animal—and having perceived "the excellences of nature and of reason," what does the psyche find to love at the summit of its ascent? It finds a mode of its own action, just as Aristotle had: "Life consists of action, and its end [or goal] is a mode of action" (i.e., intellectual contemplation), as Aristotle puts it in the *Poetics*. In Treatise III, chapter xi, line 51, Dante writes, "*philos* and *sophia* are as much as to say 'lover of wisdom,' . . . Hence is derived the word for the proper *act* of such a one, 'philosophy'." In Treatise IV, chapter ii, line 155, he describes the action of *philosophia*, or intellectual contemplation, as follows: "the philosophizing soul not only contemplates the truth, but also contemplates its own contemplation and the beauty thereof, turning upon itself and enamouring itself of itself by reason of its direct contemplation." Other subtle lovers of reason in our tradition have had this same vision of their goal. In our time Paul Valéry uses the legendary figure of Narcissus, the man who was lost in the loving contemplation of his own reflection, to represent the paradoxical *mystique* of reason. The mind rises from the chaotic world of sense to more and more general, and therefore more and more abstract, truths, until it reaches the final abstraction, the principle of the whole movement, and gets itself into focus in the *act* of intellection.

Thus Dante explains the true meaning of the Lady of Canzone III: she represents the love of the truths of reason; ultimately, the psyche's love of its own highest life, or action. He will never lose his vision of human life as Aristotelian "action," the spirit's movement toward what it perceives as good. But he will decide, before he gets to the *Commedia*, that philosophic contemplation is not the ultimate, or finally satisfying goal of man's amorously seeking spirit.

Convivio IV: The Rational Order of Human Society, and of Individual Life from the Cradle to the Grave

In the *canzone* on which this Treatise is based (XII, in the Temple Classics *Canzoniere*) Dante turns away from Lady Philosophy herself, because, as he explains, he is finding her hard to woo. While waiting for her to restore her favors to him, he will defend her from her enemies in the human community, and accordingly he labels this poem *Contra gli erranti*, "Against those in error." In his account of the writing of the poem (chapters i–iii) he presents himself in a new way: not as the contemplative, marveling lover of wisdom, but as a moralizing orator in a public forum—like Cicero, for instance, castigating Catiline and exalting the imperiled, ideal *Res Publica*. He then sketches the ideal human society implied in the poem (chapters iv–xxix), the political philosophy which he will develop much more subtly and completely in *De Monarchia* and in the *Commedia*.

Dante does not devote much attention to the poem itself, for in writing it, he explains, he had abandoned both his love-music and all poetic "figures": the poem is to be taken literally, and requires no interpretation; it is a straightforward attack on those who identify "nobleness" with wealth. If one gets the picture that Dante sketches—of himself angrily addressing a circle of reason's snobbish enemies—one can see the poem as dramatic, like one of the great rationalizing speeches in a Sophoclean agon. But the poem in itself is not a lyric, but a composition based on rhetorical principles.

In chapters iv–ix, starting his long political-philosophical digression, Dante shows how reason itself reveals the need of a single, universal ruling power to keep mankind in order: i.e., an emperor. If one remembers his own experience of political and social chaos—civil war in his beloved Florence, wars between the

Italian cities, wars between the Pope's allies and his enemies in various parts of Europe—it is easy to sympathize with Dante's demand for the supra-national government of the Empire. But his defense of the Empire here in the *Convivio* has little connection with actual Ghibelline party-politics. In the search for light in the dark wood of politics his thought had moved from Florence to all Italy, and thence to the ultimate problem: Is there *any* rational way to order human society in accord with nature, and with the needs of man as a rational animal? That is the way Socrates, Plato, and Aristotle had investigated human society, and it is in Aristotle that Dante again finds the light he needs.

Dante's general theory is straight from Aristotle's *Ethics* and *Politics*, and Dante tells us that Aristotle is to be taken as the authority in politics because it was he who had seen that art most clearly. It is based upon the "art of life"—the regulation of all the modes of human action with reference to the highest of all, the life of reason. The aim of political and social life is the fulfillment of the human creature, and accordingly the art of the ruler consists in ordering and regulating the various elements in the community in accord with the art of life itself: the *Politics* is based on the *Ethics*. Because man is a political (as well as a rational) animal, the art of politics is crucial; man can fulfill himself only in society. The principles of Dante's politics are Greek, and the recovered classical picture of the truly human society which he here sketches is basic in European political thinking through Shakespeare's time and beyond.

But there is one all-important element in Dante's political philosophy which is not to be found in the Greeks: the Empire. Greek political theory was based on the short life of the city-states; it did not consider either history or international order. But for Dante the need of a universal ruler was crucial. He could, and did, demonstrate it by reason, using Greek principles; but when he demanded a real, concrete ruler, sanctioned by history, he was quite outside the spirit of Greek thought. In his time the proper ruler of mankind—if there was to be one—could only be Rome, and the Empire (or the Papacy) as the heir of Roman authority. He gradually convinced himself (as he tells us) that God, who had permitted Rome to acquire dominion over all the civilized world, must have designated Rome for the task of rule. "And herein," he says (IV, iv, line 114) "doth Virgil agree, in the first of the *Aeneid*, where, speaking in the person of God, he says: 'To them (to wit, to the Romans) I assign no limit of things nor of time. To them have I given empire without end.' " But though Rome was the most august and historically valid symbol of empire, the question of its proper heir, Emperor or Pope, and of the relation between secular and ecclesiastical authority, was incredibly thorny. It involved legal technicalities, questions of faith, the interpretation of sacred and profane history. Dante does not fully mature his thought on this matter until *De Monarchia* and the *Commedia*.

Here in the *Convivio* he is rejoicing in the achievements of reason, and he presents the Empire primarily as the guardian of the life of reason in human society. One of the chief signs of Rome's Imperial mission is Roman law, which was sometimes called "written reason"; and the Emperor's first duty is to rule in accord with Law. Moreover, since the art of the ruler depends on the art of life which philosophy reveals, the Emperor is subject to reason. In Dante's ideal society, the authority of reason is final, even though he recognizes our actual need of power incarnate in a ruler, and sustained by religious piety.

The "erring ones" that Dante specifically wishes to refute in his *canzone* are those who maintain that human *gentilezza*, "nobleness," is a matter of wealth, or of family and social position based on ancient wealth. To show how utterly wrong they are, he has been obliged to sketch the whole notion of a rational society; having done that, he returns to the argument of the poem in chapters xii–xv, and then devotes the rest of the Treatise to showing what *gentilezza* really is.

He maintains that true nobleness is a God-given quality of spirit which may be found in anyone, without reference to wealth or social status. But nobleness is not virtue, for we see that women and children may be *gentili* even though they lack the moral and intellectual virtues as the Greeks defined them. The mature male may be noble, but if he also has *virtue* it is because he has acquired it through effort and instruction. Nobleness—that quality which precedes reasoning, and which reason cannot account for—is manifested in a different way at each stage of life; Adolescence; Youth (by which he means what we call maturity); Age; and Decrepitude. Dante's description of the nobleness of the four Ages of Man evokes a beautiful dream of the generalized human being, the "humane," as one might call it. At this point he abandons the service of strict rationality, to rejoice in the full nature of man when the grace of "nobleness" is granted to it.

This Eden-like vision is akin to the inspiration of Dante's youth, that of the *dolce stil nuovo*: *Al cor gentil ripara sempre Amore*, as Guinizelli put it, "To the gentle (or noble) heart Love ever comes." And it anticipates many subsequent visions of earthly felicity, the Golden Age—a characteristic theme of Renaissance Humanism. For example, Dante's description of *gentilezza* in Adolescence (chapter xxv) could be applied exactly to the amoral young lovers of Shakespeare's Romantic Comedies, with their graces of body and of spirit—though Shakespeare is more inclined to associate the nobleness of the young with noble blood than Dante is. In these chapters of the *Convivio* Dante is very close to his final freedom of spirit, when he will see classical reason as only one mode of understanding and will accept his own direct sense of life, in all its mystery and diversity, as the source of his poetry. But he is still guided by Greek philosophical thinking; still focused upon the *idea* of man, or the definition of the species, so that "youth" or "age" seem to him more true, more significant—even more real—than young or old individuals. When he writes the last half of the *Purgatorio* he will know how to dramatize the paradoxical relationships between classical and Christian modes of understanding. But the Fourth Treatise was broken off unfinished, while he was still convinced that the light of Greek philosophy was the end of the road for him.

De Vulgari Eloquentia: The Project of a Science of Language

Dante was probably working on *De Vulgari Eloquentia* ("Concerning Vernacular Speech") during the first years of his exile, concurrently with the *Convivio*. They seem clearly to be companion pieces: both are based on the *canzoni*, and both are devoted to immediate problems of Italian culture. In both he regards the question of the Italian language as crucial; but in the *Convivio* he defiantly uses Italian to expound philosophy, while in the *De Vulgari Eloquentia* he writes in the recognized language of the learned, Latin, in order to defend the vernacular and to explain the properties of the language-medium itself.

Dante intended to make this book a complete "science of the vernacular language," as he tells us; a task which no one had ever attempted before. The little book is indeed far ahead of its time, not only in its scientific aim, but in the objective, scrupulous spirit of the inquiry. Dante was emulating Aristotle's rational and empirical *methods*. But since his topic was new, he could not rely on Aristotle's results, or on his authority, blindly; and for that reason he is much closer not only to Aristotle's own practice, but to modern science, than the more literal-minded "Aristotelians" of his own and later generations. Thus *De Vulgari Eloquentia* affords us another glimpse of Dante as he rejoices in the unfolding potentialities of the intellect. But like the *Convivio*, it is unfinished business: all we have is Book I, on the genesis and nature of Italian; and Book II, a severely technical exposition of the rules governing the art of the *canzone*.

De Vulgari Eloquentia: Italian as the Medium of Civilized Life

He starts, as always, with careful definitions. The "vernacular" is the language that all men learn as babies, and use all their lives to communicate with their fellows. All language is both sensuous (i.e., audible) and rational; and it is this double nature that makes it our basic human means of communication, for we are rational *animals*, and our minds can be in touch only through the common world of sense perception. Language is therefore the basis of common human life, whether in the family, in society, or in the arts and sciences. Dante was very proud of his professional status as a master of language. At the end of Book I and the beginning of Book II he suggests that he and his fellow poets of the vernacular (as makers of the language) are constructing Italian civilization in a more fundamental way (poor and helpless as they are) than the powerful leaders of church and state; and it would be difficult, in the light of subsequent history, to say that he was wrong.

In Book I Dante is in search of standard Italian, but he begins with a sketch of the whole history of language, from Adam, through the Tower of Babel, down to his own time. He knew, of course, much less than modern anthropologists do about prehistory, and was willing, perforce, to rely on Old Testament legend. His speculations about Adam's language are merely quaint; but the closer he gets to the languages he knows, the more he sounds like a modern philologist. His classification of the languages of Europe into northern, eastern and southern, is not so much wrong as crude. He sees that the "southern" group, which he knew best—French, Spanish and Italian—had evolved from a common root-language, but he does not identify it, as we do, with Latin. His elaborate discussion of Italian dialects is a matter for the experts, but the layman can see that it is full of shrewd observations on the ways in which spoken language is always evolving or degenerating. He does not find the perfect Italian he is seeking in any of the regions or cities of Italy; but he says that he can "smell" it in several of them. He concludes that standard Italian must be extracted from the dialects by a process of selection and purification; and that is the task in which he and his fellow poets are engaged.

In chapters xvi–xix, Dante describes the highest form of Italian as "illustrious, cardinal, courtly and curial." He seems to have in mind a language like Dryden's English: refined, rational, and neoclassic. It must have some of the stability of the "grammars," Greek and Latin, in order to provide a standard. It must be a medium, not for everyone, but only for the educated and intelligent; it must be suitable for the courts of princes, the courts of justice, and the most dignified forms of prose and verse. It is the language of the kind of man Dante wished to be in this phase of his life: the mature citizen, serving the *res publica* in obedience to reason and moral virtue.

De Vulgari Eloquentia: Poetry as Rhetoric and Music

Book II, continuing the study of perfected Italian, is devoted to the *canzone*, for Italian prose writers, he says, take verse as their model, and the *canzone* is the highest form of vernacular poetry.

It includes "the whole art of vernacular verse," i.e., the lesser forms like the ballad and the sonnet. It alone is suitable for the great human themes: "Safety," by which he means warlike heroism; "Love," and "Virtue." The *canzone* is tragic, for (chapter iv, line 39) "By tragedy we bring in [sic] the higher style, by comedy the lower style, by elegy we understand the style of the wretched." Dante's generation did not have any Greek tragedies, nor did it have Aristotle's *Poetics,* and for him the "tragic" was not a complete dramatic or narrative form, but simply a kind of *language.* In chapters iv, vi and vii he tries to describe tragic language: its syntactical and rhetorical structures, the kinds of words that must be chosen for it, the kinds of classical models (Virgil, Ovid, Lucan) which writers of tragic Italian should imitate. In these chapters one can see quite clearly what Dante thought the highest style of poetry should be, in the years between the *Vita Nuova* and the *Commedia.* He sought an eloquence subdued by the manners and the decorum of an elite, disciplined by reason, and refined by long familiarity with the ancient masters. More than three hundred years later Racine showed what could be done with a thrice-purified neoclassic style of this kind. But that style proved to be not quite adequate to Dante's wider vision of the human psyche—and the rigid formal ideal could not quite account for his actual practice as the poet of the *canzoni.*

Dante's study of Italian poetry is Aristotelian in spirit, though it stops short of a full theory of poetry. Thus he seeks to discover what poetry is empirically, by studying the most highly developed form he knows, the *canzone,* just as Aristotle sought the nature of poetry in the most highly developed form he knew, Sophoclean tragedy. In the beginning of chapter viii, Dante defines the *canzone* as "the action of the poet," and at that point he seems to be on the verge of Aristotle's basic theory of poetry as the mimetic *action* of the poet or maker. But he had neither the *Poetics* nor any other recognized theory of poetry as an art. He had Horace's *Ars Poetica,* which assumes poetry, and offers bits of professional advice to beginners, some of which Dante quotes; but he did not find Horace very illuminating. He had the practice of his own school of lyric poets, and he had the medieval science of Rhetoric, which was supposed to include all that could be said of the art of poetry, and these are the two sources of his exposition on the art of the *canzone,* which occupies most of Book II.

In chapter iv Dante offers a definition of poetry which throws a good deal of light on his view of that art at this time (line 19): "poetry, which is nothing else but a rhetorical composition musically composed," (*fictio rethorica musice composita*). Dante knew Aristotle's *Rhetoric* as well as many subsequent treatises based upon it. Aristotle defines rhetoric as "the art of persuasion," and he shows how language may be used both logically and emotively for that purpose. In the *Convivio*, where Dante is trying to bring out the intellectual content of his *canzoni* he analyzes them according to the principles of Rhetoric: he shows both their logical coherence and the rhetorical figures whereby he makes them pleasing and persuasive. Here in the *De Vulgari Eloquentia* he is interested not in the content of the poems, but in the medium of Italian and the forms for which the medium is suitable. In Book II he considers the second part of his definition, the "musical" form of the *canzone*, i.e., the rules governing its prosody.

Dante's account of the musical forms of the *canzone* is singularly abstract: "music" is here understood as "numbers." He says that the Provençal singers had originally devised their poems to be sung, and the Italians took their prosody from Provence, even though they now write *canzoni* that are not sung. It was Dante's lifelong habit to attach an almost mystical significance to "number" in every sense of the word, and some of the formal elegance of his poetry is due to his respect for meter. Book II may be described as a handbook on the rules of the *canzone*—an austere little treatise of great but very specialized interest.

In the *De Vulgari Eloquentia*, as in the *Convivio*, Dante writes in the confidence that he has reached the end of the road. But neither work was completed, and a deeper vision awaited him in the final phase of his life.

Convivio: Rhetoric to Allegory to Poetry

Since one of Dante's purposes in writing the *Convivio* is to show that in the poems he wrote after the *Vita Nuova* he was moved by reason, not passion, he needs a theory of allegory in order to explain those poems which, as he candidly says, appear to be love poems addressed to a woman. In the case of *contra gli erranti*, the *canzone* which is the basis of Treatise IV, no allegorical interpretation is needed: the meaning is all presented directly, without "figures," as he tells us—and we might add that it is all clearly the utterance of Dante in his rationalistic *persona*, the Ciceronian moralizing orator. But the other two *canzoni*, as well as many of those which he planned to discuss and never got to, must be interpreted if they are to be read as praise of philosophy, not of a woman.

What Dante says about allegory in the *Convivio* is much less satisfactory than his discussion of it in his letter to Can Grande, which he wrote years later, when the *Commedia* was finished and all his ideas were in order. The text itself of the crucial passage (*Convivio* II, i) is corrupt, and Dante's meaning is still disputed by experts. The most significant paragraph however, is quoted below:

> The first ["sense" or meaning] is called the literal, and it is the one that extends no further than the letter as it stands; the second is called the allegorical, and is the one that hides itself under the mantle of these tales, and is a truth hidden under a beauteous fiction. As when Ovid says that Orpheus with his lyre made wild beasts tame and made trees and rocks approach him; which would say that the wise man with the instrument of his voice maketh cruel hearts tender and humble; and moveth to his will such as have not the life of science and art; for they that have not the rational life are as good as stones. . . . It is true that the theologians take this sense otherwise than the poets do, but since it is my purpose here to follow the method of the poets I shall take the allegorical sense after the use of the poets.

This passage sounds very much like that simple-minded moralizing or rationalizing of poetry which was common in Dante's time and for four or five hundred years thereafter. Both the classical poets and the Old Testament narratives were "moralized," much as Dante here moralizes Ovid's tale of Orpheus; and the poets who wrote in this rationalistic tradition simply "clothed" the commonplaces of moral philosophy with their pretty (but too often lifeless) imagery. But Dante's own *canzoni* are not like that: they are not mere illustrations of abstract concepts, but what we think of as true poems, each with a unique life of its own. In order to understand what Dante meant by his "poets' allegory" one must see just how he uses it to interpret his own *canzoni*.

The *canzone* that Dante considers in Treatise II is *Voi che intendendo* (XV in the Temple Classics *Canzoniere*). It was pointed out earlier that when he interprets the *donna gentile* (who in this poem replaces Beatrice) as originally philosophy, and not a woman, he contradicts what he says about her in the *Vita Nuova*. Moreover in allegorizing her in this way he seems to be reducing his own beautiful poem to the most hollow, tiresome, and unconvincing moralizing. But it is doubtful that this was his intention: he did not think he was destroying the poem whose beauty he was frankly proud of. As part of his apologia for his abandonment of Beatrice, he wants to persuade the reader (uncandidly, I believe) that he had imagined the *donna gentile* originally *merely* in order to represent what really moved him: philosophy. But for this purpose he does not have to deny her womanly reality *in the poem*. On the contrary, in his lengthy analysis of what he calls the "literal meaning" of the poem (in chapters ii, viii, ix, x, xi, and xii) she appears as that very woman who looked pityingly out of her window in the last part of the *Vita Nuova*. What, then, did he include in the "literal meaning" of the poem?—The question is crucial for the understanding of his notion of allegory, both here and in the *Commedia*.

In Dante's view, the "literal sense" *contains* all the others, and that is why he always makes sure that it is clear, in his analyses of his poems, before he proceeds to the allegorical meaning, or meanings: "And in thus expounding, the literal sense should always come first as the one in the meaning whereof the others are included" (II, i). The literal *sense* is, of course, not the words, but what the words mean. Thus when Dante expounds the literal sense of *Voi che intendendo*, he leads us, by carefully elucidating the words of the poem, to imagine the troubled psyche as it moves now toward the memory of Beatrice, who had died, now toward the present vision of the *donna gentile*. He thought of such an analysis as rhetorical, because it is concerned with the words and figures that the science of rhetoric describes and classifies. But it is very much like a modern "poetic" analysis, which leads us to grasp the unique life of the poem. A modern critic would stop with what Dante calls the literal sense and content himself with remarking that this moment of the inner life, this wavering *moto spiritale*—the content of the poem which analysis reveals—suggests many meanings. Once we have recognized the concrete, variously suggestive life of the poem itself, it is not difficult to accept the "allegorical" meaning that Dante insists upon—the painful and tentative turn from Beatrice and her Courtly Love, to philosophy—as at least one meaning that may be found in the poem.

When Dante (in Treatise III) analyzes the literal sense of *Amor che nella mente mi ragiona* (III in the Temple Classics *Canzoniere*), he devotes most of his attention to the meaning of *amor*. I have already said that what Dante says about *amor* here clearly shows how he conceived the life of the psyche, from this time until the end of his life. *Amor* is defined as the movement of spirit (*moto spiritale*), and that concept is basically Aristotle's *energeia*, "action" in the most general sense. I now wish to point out that this concept is crucial also in Dante's deepening conception of poetry. His analysis of the literal sense of *Voi che intendendo* and *Amor che nella mente* amounts to demonstrating the "action" they "imitate." Dante never read the *Poetics* of Aristotle and was not familiar with Aristotle's basic definition of poetry as the imitation of an action, but when he examines his own poems, here in the *Convivio*, it is their action, or *moto spiritale*, which he sees as their essential content: the "literal sense" that includes all the other meanings.

This is all especially clear in his analysis of the literal sense of *Amor che nella mente*, which is scattered through the first ten chapters of Treatise III. The literal analysis reveals the abashed but delighted spirit "moving" toward the contemplative enjoyment, and the praise, of his lady's overwhelming beauty. When he comes to the allegorical meaning, he has only to tell us that the lady represents (or, from the point of view of the writer of the poem, "imitates") the highest form of the psyche's life, *philo-sophia*, when the psyche not only contemplates the truth, but contemplates its own act of contemplation. The psyche moves timidly toward this ultimate earthly fulfillment, the beauty of which makes it fearful and confused. But if we are to get this meaning, the lady of the literal poem is not to be thought of as unreal: on the contrary, we must believe in her first of all, for the life of the poem is in the analogy between the enjoyment of the woman's beauty, which the eyes take in, and the enjoyment of the forms which only the intellect can perceive.

The "literal sense" of a poem is always a movement of spirit, an action, whether the spirit "moves" toward an object of sense or an object of intellect. But the spirit itself is not sensuously perceptible; indeed, to call its life "movement" is only a spatial metaphor for what is not spatial at all. How, then, can a poet imitate an action? In chapters v, vi, vii and viii of Treatise III, Dante considers this problem in the light of his own realistic view of the spirit in the body, and in the world that the senses apprehend. In his efforts to expound the meanings of his poems, he has been led beyond poetry as rhetoric and prosody and moral philosophy, to an Aristotelian theory of poetry as an art in its own right.

Dante had pointed out, in *De Vulgari Eloquentia,* that language itself can be a medium of communication between minds only because of its double nature, which is at once sensuously perceptible (audible) and rational. The human body serves (he explains here) in a way analogous to language-as-audible: to make one spirit perceptible to another; for the spirit (or psyche) is "the form of the body." In our earthly life, at least, body and spirit are one, and so we divine the quality of a man's spirit by "what he does outwardly" and by noting the objects of his attachment. We can also learn to "see" the spirit through the countless tiny changes it makes in the body, especially in the responsive eyes and mouth, as it "moves," now toward one object, now toward another, forming and reforming the body moment by moment in accord with its restless life.

The spirit may be attracted by what the senses present to it; or by the abstract concepts and logical concatenations of the rationalizing mind; or by "objects" like certain axioms which only the contemplative intellect perceives. It has countless modes of perception, it perceives many kinds of objects, any of which may determine its action. But the spirit, one must remember, is one, and its modes of perception are analogous. What the light of the sun reveals to the eye is analogous to what the "light of truth" reveals to the mind. Because the human creature is body-and-spirit, and lives in a real world which sense and intellect reveal, the poet may avail himself of analogies of many kinds in order to represent the unseen movements of the spirit.

When, in the discussion of *Amor che nella mente mi ragiona,* Dante elaborates at great length the analogies between the "body" of the lady and the "body" of philosophy (i.e., the particular sciences), his ingenuity gets the better of him, and he fails to persuade us that so much science and philosophy is really in the poem. Analogizing, like any other good thing, may be abused. The irresponsible multiplication of analogies is the besetting sin of Dante's time, and even he had to learn, slowly, how to control it with judgment and common sense. But his discussion of the revelatory properties of his beautiful *donna*'s face is extremely important, for it is a central theme in the whole long course of his poem-making.

It is his lady's eyes and mouth that overwhelm him, for it is through them, as he explains, that the life of her spirit is most clearly "visible." He felt that also when, in the *Vita Nuova,* he first saw Beatrice clearly and wrote *Donne, ch'avete intelletto d'Amore,* "Ladies, who have intelligence of Love," and the wonderful sonnet, *Negli occhi porta la mia donna Amore,* "In her eyes my lady carries Love." He will feel it again when, in the garden at the summit of Mount Purgatory, Beatrice unveils her eyes, and then her smile. In the *Vita Nuova* he thinks it is *Amor* that Beatrice's face reveals. Here in the *Convivio* the beautiful *donna della mia mente* reveals the ultimate action of philosophy, the soul "turning upon itself and enamouring itself of itself by reason of its direct contemplation." In the *Commedia* Beatrice's eyes and smile reveal the life of the spirit more deeply still, as we shall see. It took Dante all his life to explore the meanings of the *moto spiritale* which the spirit of the beloved *donna* revealed to his spirit, thereby forming it anew. But it is here in Treatise III that he explains the poetic *art,* whereby he sought to represent that fundamental and recurrent experience.

We have come a long way since the brief exposition of the allegory of poets in Treatise II, i. At that point "allegory" looked like the rationalistic, moralizing allegory which our modern taste rejects as a dead, mechanical simulacrum of real poetry. But when Dante reveals the "literal sense" of his two *canzoni,* it is clear that he thinks of them as poems first and moral philosophy second. He does not think of the poet as taking the "allegorical meaning" from the abstract schemes of moral philosophy and then illustrating it in his poem: the poet perceives a movement of spirit directly, and imitates it in the imagery, words, and music of his poem. The moral meaning is there—in Dante's view every tiniest shift of the psyche's focus is morally significant—but other meanings also may be found within the "literal sense," which is the particular movement of spirit, the concrete unique life of the poem. So there emerges a view of poem-making as neither rhetoric, nor prosody, nor moral philosophy—though the poet makes use of those arts—but a unique and irreducible way of apprehending and representing the life of the spirit.

Dante as the Faithful Lover of Reason

Io mi son un che, quando
Amor mi spira, noto, ed a quel modo
che ditta dentro, vo significando.

(I am one who, when
love breathes in me, take note, and in that mode
which he dictates within, go signifying.)
—*Purgatorio* XXIV, line 52

Dante's final definition of his poem-making applies to his rational maturity as well as it did to his romantic youth. He still presents himself as lover, obedient in his *poetando* to what love tells him, though it is now the life of reason that he passionately loves. The key word in the formula is *amor*: the inspired content of the poem. And we have seen that he now understands *amor*, just as he will in the middle of the *Purgatorio*, as the "movement of spirit," which we know in countless "modes," that is, "actualized in varied ways as it forms attachments to varied objects." His new mistress, Greek reason, has shown him much more than Beatrice had about human life and poetry. And yet he will not realize the full meaning of his definition, in his own practice as poet, until he returns to Beatrice in the *Commedia*.

Dante's middle period is rightly called his rationalistic phase, but that does not necessarily mean that he rejected the Christian Creed and the teachings of the Church. It simply means that he was devoting his attention to worldly philosophy and science instead of the mysteries of the faith. When he comes to the *Commedia* he will see human reason itself in a wider context, that of a "world it never made"; but while writing the *canzoni*, *De Vulgari Eloquentia*, and the *Convivio* he is all inside what reason sees, and he feels sure that he will never need more than his new mistress offers him. He rejoices in all the parts of her "body," as he puts it: the sciences of government and linguistics, prosody and astrology; rhetoric, logic, astronomy. His faith (his actual faith as distinguished from the "habitus" of the Creed) is that the life of his lady's "spirit," the self-regarding love of the contemplative intellect, will prove to be the ultimate and sufficient satisfaction of the needs of his own amorous spirit. Even when he finds her difficult, and turns away to attack her enemies, *gli erranti,* he is completely faithful. His spirit even at that moment is formed by hers: he shares her mode of being; he loves what she loves and hates what she hates.

Because Dante feels that the discovery of reason is the end of his road, he often anticipates the attitudes and the refined, if rigid, taste of later Rationalism and Neoclassicism, which assume that civilized man, his society, and his arts have been fixed once and for all in the steady light of classical reason. When he describes the "tragic" high style of the *canzone* he anticipates the taste of the age of Racine and Dryden. And when he defends his own mature virility against passion, he reminds one of a hero of Baroque tragedy, perpetually defending the citadel of reason and the moral will against the assaults of sense and emotion. This somewhat conventionalized mask—a *persona* in Pound's sense of the word—is no more dishonest than the *fedele d'amore* of the *Vita,* but it also does not quite suffice. Dante's wider perceptions and more flexible feelings keep showing through the official image, as has been suggested. This is most evident, perhaps, in *Convivio* IV.

It is there (chapter xii) that he offers us the image of the soul's life—the *moto spiritale,* the content of poetry—which most clearly foretells the underlying movement of the whole *Commedia*:

> And like a pilgrim who is travelling on a road where he hath never been before, who believes that every house which he sees from afar is the hostel, and finding that it is not directs his belief to another, and so from house to house until he comes to the hostel; even so our soul, so soon as it enters upon the new and never-yet-made journey of life, directs its eyes toward the goal of its supreme good, and therefore whatever it sees that appears to have some good in it, it thinks to be it. And because its knowledge is at first imperfect, through having no experience or instruction, little goods appear great to it. . . . And so we see little children intensely longing for an apple, and then going on further, longing for a little bird, and then further on longing

> for fine clothes, and then a horse, and then a mistress. . . . And this comes to pass because in none of these things does he find that for which he is ever searching. . . . But in truth we may lose this way in error, just as we may lose the paths of earth.

In this passage reason's vision is more Greek-classical than French-classical: it opens out into the world, where the soul moves in response to countless attractive things that are more or less good, more or less true. The *Commedia* looms on the mental horizon, with its many individual journeys; but as yet Dante cannot realize it poetically and dramatically.

If he cannot, it is not because he fails to understand the concrete, dramatic portrayal of individual lives: on the contrary, he explains it in chapter x of the same last Treatise of the *Convivio*. He quotes, and then glosses, a line of *Contra gli erranti*:

> Poi che finge figura,
> Se non può esser lei, non la può porre . . .
>
> (Further, whoever paints a figure,
> Unless he can *be* it, cannot set it down . . .)
>
> Wherefore [he explains] no painter could set down any figure unless he first become in intention such as the figure is to be.

This is a technically accurate description of the poet's mimetic action when he brings a character before us: in his own inner being he acquires the character's motive; his spirit moves as the character's does, and thus he gestures and speaks in, or through, that character. But Dante never ventures upon dramatic (or histrionic) creation of this kind until the *Commedia*. We may feel that the girls in the *Vita Nuova*, or the women he loves in his *canzoni*, are real; but we are told *about* them, they do not move and speak before us in their own beings. There is no doubt that Dante, even when he was trying to be reason's most faithful lover, could *see* the many modes of love in the people around him, but he could not allow his own spirit to move except in response to a rational object. And as poet he must not listen to what any love, except the love of reason, "dictates within."

The *Commedia* replaces the *canzoni* in Dante's *poetando*, and his reasoned prose works, *De Vulgari Eloquentia* and *Convivio*, are broken off before they are half completed. Did his own thinking lead him gradually to see through the schemes of reason, as a careful reading of *Convivio* IV suggests? Or was it the Mountain Lady of the famous *canzone* who separated him from reason, as he says in his letter to Moruello? Or was it the sudden appearance of the idealistic young emperor, Henry VII, that turned him from the motionless light of reason to the perilous actualities of his immediate time and place?

There would be no point in trying to choose one of these factors to account for the sudden end of Dante's classical-rational phase. Probably they all have some validity: there are many "reasons" for what a man does, especially a man who lives as deeply as Dante did. Certain it is, however, that the brief time of Henry VII's reign marks the second and final turning-point in Dante's career. It was then that he made his last attempt to intervene in practical politics; then that he suffered most intensely the dark course of history, learning the hard way that "the will of God" in human affairs is not to be fathomed by reason alone. It is necessary to have in mind the main facts of his tragic relation to Henry VII in order to understand what he wrote when he emerged from that ordeal.

«« IV »»

Political Catastrophe and the Final Years, 1308–1321

European Politics: Destruction of Dante's Hopes for the Empire

IN 1266, at the famous battle of Benevento, Charles of Anjou, acting for the Pope, defeated Manfredi of Sicily, the bastard son of the Emperor Frederick II, and seized the kingdom. As we have seen, that was when the Guelfs gained their firm control of Florence, ushering in the time of prosperity and comparative peace which Dante knew in his youth. Benevento also marked the end of the Emperor's real power in all Italy. For the next fifty years the Empire showed few signs of life, and its formidable enemies, France and the Papacy, had everything their own way. The Guelf-Ghibelline feuds continued, but they were confused power-struggles, with little general significance, in spite of the steady hatred between the Ghibelline princes and the Pope.

When, at the turn of the century, Guelf Florence was split by the fight between the Blacks and the Whites, and Dante fled into exile, he depended upon the enlightened patronage of such Ghibelline magnates as the della Scala family of Verona, but there is no evidence that he ever identified himself with the Ghibelline party, or parties. He withdrew from party politics and devoted his energies to making his own diagnosis of the Italian anarchy. We have seen that, when he wrote the *Convivio*, his political thinking had moved from Florence to all Italy, and from Italy to the problem of secular order in all Christendom. Hence the political theory of the *Convivio*: if there is to be a human society in accord with reason, a universal secular ruler, an Emperor, is required; and the monarch himself must be subject to reason. History (through which God speaks) confirms this reasoning: it designates Rome, the universal lawgiver, for the task of secular rule, and therefore the Empire as Rome's heir. Actually, the Empire was slumbering beyond the Alps, and no proper Emperor was in sight. But through his reading of political philosophy and of history Dante had, so to speak, deduced him: an ideal figure in his anxious and lonely thought.

In 1308 the *de facto* Emperor, Albert of Austria, died, and the following year Henry of Luxembourg was elected Emperor as Henry VII. The sudden advent of that vigorous and idealistic young man, after so many years of helpless torpor, was attributed by Dante, and by many others, to Divine Providence. Henry seemed, at least at first, to be an incarnation of the very "Monarch" of Dante's austere meditations. According to the contemporary chronicler Villani, Henry was "wise and just and gracious, strong and accomplished in arms, and though of small estate in his inheritance [he was only the Count of Luxembourg], magnanimous of heart, feared and respected; and if he had lived longer he would have done great things." His first public pronouncements confirm Villani's impression: he proposed to be above all regional, national, and party interests; to mediate all quarrels; to restore the political exiles to their native cities; to seek only justice in his rule. Moreover, when he was first elected, he enjoyed the blessing of Pope Clement V. There was thus reason to hope that Pope and Emperor would end their destructive feud at last and devote themselves to their proper tasks, those, respectively, of spiritual and secular guidance.

In 1310 Henry entered Italy to assume the Imperial authority that had been so long forgotten in that country. He was met by enthusiastic crowds of simple people who believed, as Dante did, that he had been sent by God to restore order and dispense justice. Dante went to Milan, where Henry was receiving the iron crown, to offer him his personal allegiance. His impassioned "Letter to the Princes and People of Italy" (*Epistola* V in the Temple Classics edition), bidding them accept Henry with gratitude to God, shows clearly what he felt and thought at the time. It opens in a Biblical tone of prophetic exaltation: "Lo, now is the acceptable time wherein arise the signs of consolation and peace."

It proceeds to rehearse, briefly but cogently, the *Convivio* argument, tracing Henry's authority to Rome, and Rome's authority to the will of God. And it ends with a reference to Clement's support, which must have struck Dante as truly miraculous: "He it is . . . whom Clement, the present successor of Peter, doth illuminate with the light of the apostolic benediction."

The Utopian dreams of the people, Dante's own thought and faith, even (at that moment) the Pope, all pointed to the attractive figure of Henry as the predestined political redeemer. One can see that Dante could not possibly have resisted the fervor that overcame him at that time. But, knowing what we do, it is also evident that Henry was doomed in advance. His election itself was the fortuitous result of the faithless game which those who held real power in Europe were always playing behind the scenes. The most important of these powerful intriguers were Philip the Fair of France, and Pope Clement V.

Philip the Fair was an extremely able king, engaged in the familiar project of building up the wealth, power and prestige of France. He had inherited the cynical French alliance with the Papacy, which was precariously based on their common hatred of the waning Imperial power. We have seen how Philip's brother, Charles of Valois, assisted Pope Boniface VIII to undermine the government of Florence at the time of the Black rebellion. But not long after that, Philip and Boniface started quarreling over the Pope's authority in France, especially his claim to the rich revenues of the French church. That ended when Philip's troops brutally seized Boniface, and the old, ill, and bitterly humiliated Pope died, perhaps "murdered." Boniface was succeeded by Benedict, who ruled as Pope less than two years; and then Philip forced the election of Clement V. Clement was a Frenchman, he made his headquarters at Avignon, and Philip must have thought that the Pope, thenceforth, would be completely obedient to him.

Clement, however, was almost as devoted to the aggrandizement of Papal wealth and power as Boniface had been. And in spite of his weak position he proved to be a most slippery antagonist for Philip. When the Emperor, Albert of Austria, died, Philip wanted to make his brother, Charles of Valois, Emperor, and Clement pretended to accept that plan. But he had good cause to mistrust Charles, and he must have realized that if the House of France controlled the Empire too, its power would be supreme in all Europe. Accordingly he betrayed Philip, secretly used his influence to procure the election of Henry, and then, as we have seen, "illuminated" him with his benediction. That was the moment when Henry's prospects and Dante's hopes were brightest.

Dante did not know this story when he hailed his Emperor in Milan, but eventually he learned all the facts. The sinister doings of Boniface, Charles, Philip, and Clement are referred to in various parts of the *Commedia*. In the *Purgatorio*, breaking into the beauty of Eden with poisonous virulence, is the nightmare vision of the relations between the Papacy and the House of France (XXXII, line 142):

Trasformato così il dificio santo
  mise fuor teste per le parti sue,
  tre sopra il temo, ed una in ciascun canto.
Le prime eran cornute come bue;
  ma le quattro un sol corno avean per fronte:
  simile mostro visto ancor non fue.
Sicura, quasi rocca in alto monte,
  seder sopr' esso una puttana sciolta
  m'apparve con le ciglia intorno pronte.
E, come perchè non gli fosse tolta,
  vidi di costa a lei dritto un gigante,
  e baciavansi insieme alcuna volta;
ma, perchè l'occhio cupido e vagante
  a me rivolse, quel feroce drudo
  la flagellò dal capo infin le piante.
Poi, di sospetto pieno e d'ira crudo,
  disciolse il mostro, e trassel per la selva
  tanto, che sol di lei me fece scudo
alla puttana ed alla nuova belva.

(So transformed, the holy structure
  sprouted heads through its parts,
  three over the pole and one at each corner.
The first were horned like an ox,
  but the four had a single horn at the forehead:
  such a monster never yet was seen.
Secure, like a fort on a high hill,
  a loose whore sitting on top of it
  appeared to me, her eyes quick around.

And, as though to keep her from being taken from him,
  a giant I saw, erect beside her,
  and sometimes they kissed each other;
but because her greedy, wandering eye
  she turned toward me, that fierce lover
  whipped her from her head down to her feet.
Then, filled with suspicion and cruel with anger,
  he loosed the monster and dragged it through the wood
  so far that with it alone he screened from me
the whore and the strange beast.)

The sacred edifice is the corrupt church sprouting all seven sins; the harlot is the Papacy, and her brutal lover the House of France.

There is no need to follow in detail poor Henry's doomed venture among the perils of Italy. In the north were the Ghibelline princes, enemies of France and the Pope, but soon mistrustful of Henry too. In central Italy the Guelf cities, led by Florence, which was still firmly held by Corso Donati and the Blacks, were frankly hostile. In the south was the French Kingdom of Naples, under Robert of Anjou. Henry moved southward from Milan, but his own forces were inadequate, and the support of his Italian "subjects" leaked away, especially when Clement—frightened, perhaps, by the popular enthusiasm for Henry—quietly withdrew his support and encouraged the Guelf cities to resist him. In 1312 Henry was in Rome, where he had intended to be crowned in Saint Peter's; but the forces of Robert of Naples held that part of the city, and he had to be content with a substitute ceremony across the river in Saint John Lateran. He could no longer maintain his idealistic position above the parties; he had to recognize the enmity of the Guelfs and get what help he could from the Ghibellines. In 1312 he laid siege to Florence, but had to raise it in a couple of months and fall back on Pisa. For there he turned southward again, intending to attack Robert in Naples. He died on the way there, on August 24, 1313.

We do not know where Dante was or what he was doing during these few sad and desperate years. But two of his *Letters* survive, which show clearly how he felt about the stubborn resistance of his own Florence, and how hard he tried to maintain his faith in Henry.

Epistola VI (in the Temple Classics edition) is addressed to the recalcitrant Florentines. It begins with a brief but majestic sum-mary of his political creed: that the Providence of God "hath committed human things, for governance, to the Holy Roman Empire," and, moreover, that "antiquity, leaning only on the support of reason, beareth witness thereto." He adds that the present state of Italy unmistakably demonstrates the need for Imperial authority. As he continues, his passion increases: How can the Florentines be so blind and so presumptuous, and how do they expect to resist the might of the Empire? His hope that his own unjust banishment may soon be avenged is evident. The last part of the "Letter" shows Dante in the heat of battle, and the passions of all-out strife are never very pretty.

Epistola VII, dated May, 1311, was written to Henry while he was still based at Milan: "And I too, who write for myself and for others, have seen thee, as beseems imperial Majesty, most benignant, and have heard thee most clement, when that my hands handled thy feet, and my lips paid their debt." But after hailing Henry as the political savior ordained by God, Dante explains that Henry's delay in asserting his authority in all Italy has already led some to doubt him, and he beseeches him to make haste. It is a great *Letter*, both in its spirit and in its eloquence. It ends with a touching reaffirmation of the faith he shared with Henry.

Dante is completely lost to sight during the next two or three years. But we know that Henry's death did not change his belief that a just ruler, armed with the authority of Rome and obedient to Law and reason, was required for the peace and order of Christendom. *De Monarchia*, his tightly reasoned treatise on political theory, is the monument of that faith.

De Monarchia: The State, the Church, and the Course of History

There is no way to determine the exact date of *De Monarchia*, but it must be later than the *Convivio*, for it presents the same political doctrines in a more complete and final form. We cannot tell, however, whether it was written during the reign of Henry VII or after his death, for that tragic figure is never mentioned. It is as deeply partisan as the great political letters written in support of Henry, but the passion takes the form of austerity. It is scrupulous, even pedantic, in its use of formal logic, and in its careful marshaling of all the recognized evidence; Dante apparently meant to settle the question of secular authority once and for all.

As soon as one learns to see through the scholastic methods of inquiry to the structure of the thought, it is evident that *De Monarchia* has that combination of strength, concision, formal beauty, and suggestiveness which we call "Dantesque." It is in three Books. Book I expounds the rational human community as it would be in any time and place; it is a more beautifully ordered exposition of the doctrine we have already glanced at in connection with the *Convivio*. Such a society requires a monarch to rule it, and the monarch is the servant of reason, of law, and thus of the welfare of the community as a whole. Book II sets forth the view that the Emperor was designated by God to rule all mankind. Dante supports this view with a Virgilian reading of Roman history culminating in the time of Augustus, which was also the time of the Incarnation. In Book III he argues that even after the Incarnation the authority of the Pope, the Vicar of Christ, does not supersede that of the Emperor, in secular matters, at least. Thus he maintains that mankind, in his time, must recognize one secular monarch, the Emperor, as well as the Pope, whose authority (he assumes) is supreme in religious matters.

We have seen that neither the Popes, nor the House of France, nor Corso di Donati's Florence shared this vision which, Dante thought, was certified by both faith and reason. Europe was not moving toward political or religious unity, but toward nationalism and the breakup of the Church. Dante was not "in tune with the times" nor riding "the wave of the future"; but we must not therefore conclude that he lacked insight into human government or the course of history. In *De Monarchia* he was not studying the actual disorder of Europe—he pays his respects to that in the *Inferno* and the *Purgatorio*—but rather what was *needed*, at that moment, to compose the disputes within Christendom. His hopes were cruelly mocked by the destruction of Henry VII; but his analysis of the perennial requirements for a civilized society, and his efforts to get his bearings in history, can help one to understand the norms of Classical-Christian Europe for the next five hundred years.

Book I is the easiest for the modern reader, because it is a clear, economical statement of some of the great commonplaces of Western political theory. It is founded on Aristotle's politics, but its defense of human freedom, especially intellectual freedom (the basis of Dante's resolute separation of church and state) and its reliance on both reason and law, would have been approved by the framers of our own Constitution. The analogies that Dante sets forth between the healthy individual and the well-ordered state, and between social and cosmic order, may look merely "poetic" now, but they were standard in Renaissance political theory. Readers of Shakespeare's Histories and Roman plays will remember how often the organic and cosmic analogies are used, both explicitly, and implicitly in the metaphysical and moral structure of the plays.

If the ideal and timeless order is to become actual in our temporal world, one real authority we must have, one "standard to which the wise and honest may repair," and in Book II Dante argues that the Emperor, Rome's heir, is that authority. He does not conceal the difficulties of this thesis (Book II, chapter i):

> Time was that I too, marvelled that the Roman people had been raised to supremacy on the terrestrial globe, with none to resist. For it was my thought, as I looked upon the surface only, that they had gained it by no right but merely by force of arms.

That, of course, is the way we look at Roman history, and very much the way Saint Augustine had looked at it in *The City of God*. But when Saint Augustine wrote, Rome and its civilization were disintegrating, and it appeared that the true City must be outside the saeculum altogether; while in Dante's generation, a thousand years later, the Day of Judgment seemed more remote, and the secular classical culture—Greek science and philosophy, Roman law—seemed plainly necessary. It was part of Dante's faith that God must have provided the means for a rational and natural human society, and in this faith he reread Roman history:

> But now that I have pierced with the eyes of my mind to the marrow of it, and have seen by most convincing signs that it was divine providence which effected this, my wonder has vanished, and a certain derisive contempt comes in its place when I understand how the nations muttered against the pre-eminence of the Roman people . . . when, moreover, I see the grievous sight of kings and princes agreeing in this alone, to oppose their Lord and his anointed Roman prince.

Granted the need for world government, and the goodness of God, it now seems evident to Dante that God had willed the power of ancient Rome and the authority of the Emperor. But he knew that "the will of God is in itself invisible," and must be studied out by way of the visible events of history. That he proceeds to do in Book II, again with more order and thoroughness than he had when making the same argument in the *Convivio*.

The belief that God speaks through the events of history was as old as the Bible itself, and Dante assumes it; it is an essential part of his Christian faith. But men had been seeking to read God's will in history since the compilers of the Old Testament, and that religious tradition of historiography had developed its own critical sophistication, and its own rigors of method. In Book II Dante is careful to distinguish between what reason can see in history, and what only faith can make out. He considers what unusual signs, portents, miracles, may be taken to reveal God's will. He explains how, under what circumstances, and in what sense, the warlike rivalries of nations, and the ritual "ordeal by combat" of individuals, may be used to determine God's will. So he leads the reader, by converging paths, and in full awareness of the nature of his evidences, to his view of the Empire.

Dante's Roman monarch of all mankind was to have no future in Europe, but the builders of the national states—Spain, France, England—had the same Hebraic-Christian belief in history as Divine Providence, and they too felt the need of a monarch sanctioned by history. The chronicles that interpreted English history as culminating providentially in the Tudor monarchy, for example, are in this tradition. They are the main source of Shakespeare's Histories. Book II of *De Monarchia,* where Dante discusses the will of God in history, may be used to gloss Shakespeare's plays about the English monarchy, with their dramatic interplay between reason and religious loyalty to the anointed King; their more or less ritual ordeals by combat; their assumption that God's will in history is the ultimate arbiter of political conflict. The particular monarch that Dante demanded—the universal "Roman Prince"—was less and less accepted after his time. But his recipes for *making* a monarch, his careful combination of reason with faith, of the timeless principles of law with historic (and therefore Divine) sanction, lasted in the kingdoms of Christian Europe until the "Age of Revolutions."

But, of course, Dante's whole effort was to defend *Rome*, not only because of its super-national authority but because it represented, for him, all that human reason could do before, or apart from, Revelation. He fully accepted the Pauline interpretation of sacred history, according to which the Old Law of the Jews had been "a schoolmaster to bring us to Christ." But Dante thought that Greek philosophy and Roman law also served as teachers to bring us to Christ. And so he saw the history of the pagan world also as leading to the Incarnation: a divinely devised preparation, like Old Testament history in Saint Paul's interpretation of it. He had Virgil's *Aeneid*, which (providentially, as he believed) offered him the clue he needed: the mission of Rome was to pacify the world, in order to establish the rule of justice and reason, and this mission was accomplished in the time of Augustus. In the *Purgatorio* Dante will dramatize his own discovery of this vision of history. The path he takes up the purgatorial Mountain is marked by examples from Scriptural history, and from the history of the classical-pagan world, in alternation. Virgil is his guide, and the climax is reached at the top of the Mountain when the freedom and the rational clarity of man's earthly fulfillment is interrupted by the mysterious appearance of Christ. In Book II Dante makes much of that moment of history, when the Pax Romana and the Revelation of God coincided. He maintains that Christ Himself sanctioned the authority of Rome by choosing to assume human nature under it; by counseling his followers to give Caesar his due; and finally by dying on the Cross in obedience to the legitimate agent of Roman justice.

At the end of Book II (xiii) Dante maintains that the universal authority of Roman justice under Augustus and his successors was necessary in the Divine plan of Redemption itself:

> If, then, Christ had not suffered under a qualified judge, that suffering would not have been a punishment. And the judge could not have been qualified had he not had jurisdiction over the whole human race; since it was the whole human race that was to be punished in that flesh of Christ, who, as the prophet saith, was bearing or sustaining our griefs. And Tiberius Caesar, whose vicar Pilate was, would not have had such jurisdiction unless the Roman empire had been of right.

This startling way of conceiving the paradoxical relations between rational human justice and the extra-rational love of God is probably original with Dante. It is an essential part of his thought, and appears in its final form in *Paradiso* VII, the best place in which to study the subtle and manifold meanings that Dante saw in it. Here in *De Monarchia* it puts in boldest terms Dante's basic contention: that the effect of the Incarnation is not to supersede human reason, but rather to confirm its authority in its own sphere, that of nature, the Empire, and the civilization of the classical world.

Book III is devoted to history from the Incarnation to Dante's own time. In that whole period the relation between the Empire and the Christian Church was crucial: "We are to ask whether the authority of the Roman monarch, who is monarch of the world by right . . . is then dependent on God, or rather . . . on the successor of Peter, who in very truth bears the keys of the kingdom of heaven." Dante knew that to argue that the Emperor's authority was independent of the Pope put him in conflict with the actual power of the Church. (Boccaccio tells us that a few years after Dante's death, at a time when a new Emperor was being chosen, the Cardinal Bishop of Ostia publicly burned *De Monarchia* and endeavored to do as much for Dante's bones.) And it put him more immediately in conflict with the learned and agile defenders of Papal authority. No wonder he sees his task in warlike terms (chapter i):

> I will enter upon the present wrestling ground, and by the arm of him who delivered us from the power of darkness by his blood, in the sight of all the world will I hurl the impious and the liar out of the ring.

One can learn a great deal about Dante by noticing how coolly and carefully (in spite of his pugnacity) he conducts the dispute of Book III, assessing the alleged Scriptural bases of the Pope's claims, and the historic evidences, and at every point catching his opponents in the crushing holds of formal logic. But the questions at issue can mean little to a modern reader, unless he is a specialist in church history, and it is better to devote most of one's attention to the latter part of the Book, especially chapter xvi, in which Dante sets forth some of his basic views of man in the world and in eternity.

The passage quoted here clearly explains the philosophy which is behind the whole doctrine of *De Monarchia* and will be incorporated in the structure of the *Purgatorio*:

> . . . providence, then, has set two ends before man to be contemplated by him; the blessedness, to wit, of this life, which consists in the exercise of his proper power and is figured in the terrestrial paradise, and the blessedness of eternal life, which consists in the fruition of the divine aspect, to which his proper power may not ascend unless assisted by the divine light. And this blessedness is given to be understood by the celestial paradise.
>
> Now to these two as to diverse ends it behooves him to come by diverse means. For to the first we attain by the teachings of philosophy, following them by acting in accordance with the moral and intellectual virtues. To the second by spiritual teachings which transcend human reason, as we follow them by acting according to the theological virtues; faith, hope, to wit, and charity. Now albeit these ends and means are made plain to us, the one by human reason (which the philosophers have wholly brought to our knowledge), the other by the Holy Spirit (which hath revealed the truth that is beyond our nature, but yet needful to us, by means of the prophets and sacred writers and by Jesus Christ the Son of God co-eternal with the said Spirit, and by his disciples), yet would human greed cast them behind were not men, like horses going astray in their brutishness, held in the way by bit and rein.
>
> Wherefore man had need of a twofold directive power according to his twofold end, to wit, the supreme pontiff, to lead the human race, in accordance with things revealed, to eternal life; and the emperor, to direct the human race to temporal felicity in accordance with the teachings of philosophy.

This is the conception of order in Christendom which Dante had sketched in the *Convivio*, and which Henry VII seemed on the very verge of realizing when he first appeared, hailed by the people and blessed by Pope Clement V. Here in *De Monarchia* he reaffirms it, either during, or just after, Henry's failure. It is characteristic of Dante that so complete a calamity should not have made him abandon his vision of human society and its history, but, instead, made him deepen it and define it still more exactly. He was never more sharp in controversy, more "engaged" in actual issues, than in Book III; but he also feels that he is bearing witness to truths far transcending the immediate scene in Italy: "in the warmth of that coal which one of the seraphim took from the celestial altar and touched the lips of Isaiah withal," as he puts in it Book III, i. *De Monarchia* is regarded as a classic of political theory because it does, in fact, deal with perennial needs of the political animal. At the same time, it helps us to understand classical-Christian Europe because Dante, never satisfied with general ideas, insisted on working with the knowledge, the beliefs, and the powers, secular and religious, of his time.

De Monarchia is the best place to study Dante's political thought in itself. But one would get a false impression of his habits of mind if one did not go on to see how his political ideas appear in the *Commedia*. In the *Purgatorio* and *Paradiso* he brings them out in many stages, as part of the whole effort of understanding, and in many different contexts. Only in the great poem can one see how much—and how little—the doctrine means in Dante's vision of human nature and destiny.

Dante's Last Years

The course of events after Henry's death justifies Dante's gloomy warnings to the Florentines, and the visions of chaos in church and state which appear in the *Commedia*, especially the *Purgatorio* and *Paradiso*.

Pope Clement died in 1314, but he was succeeded two years later by John XXII, who proved to be no better. John, too, was famous for his avarice; he was a Gascon, completely under the control of the House of France, and under him the "Babylonian capitivity" of the Papacy at Avignon looked permanent. Robert of Naples was made Imperial Vicar, and the power and authority of the Empire continued to decline. Dante might have been encouraged momentarily by the revival of the Ghibellines in northern Italy. Under Ugoccione della Faggiuola they decisively defeated the Guelfs, headed by Florence, at the battle of Montecatini, in 1315. Dante's patron, Can Grande della Scala of Verona, became the leader of the Ghibellines. In 1316 Florence offered amnesty to the White exiles, including Dante, but he refused it, on the ground that its conditions were impossible. By that time he had turned away from practical politics altogether, to become completely absorbed in the writing of the *Commedia.*

Three *Letters* of Dante, written after Henry's death, survive. One of them is the famous "Letter to Can Grande," dedicating the *Paradiso* to him. It is a very important little work, essential for understanding his poetic and allegorical methods in the *Commedia.* The other two are the "Letter to the Italian Cardinals" (VIII in the Temple Classics edition), and the "Letter to a friend in Florence."

The Cardinals whom Dante addresses had met near Avignon in 1314 to select Clement's successor. By this time Dante knew of the intrigues which had resulted in Clement's election nine years before, and he scolds the cardinals for their part in that, as well as for their irresponsibility, avarice, and worldly ambition, their neglect of theology, and their failure to learn the lessons of history. He blames them for the utter eclipse of Rome: he is directly concerned with the desperate plight of the exiled Roman Church, but he does not forget that Rome also stands for Imperial authority and its historic (and therefore Divine) sanction. It must have taken great courage to defy the ecclesiastical authorities so directly, but Dante speaks as the prophet rather than the political partisan. "He who alone is eternal," he writes in the introductory part, "looking down from the lofty watchtower of eternity, did through the Holy Spirit impress the same by his command upon the mind, worthy of God, of a man who was a prophet"; and he too, he says, must "wail with Jeremiah." The combination of detachment with passionate concern for the world reminds one of the moments in the *Paradiso* when he looks down from the stars and sees the round little earth, far below, like a bloody threshing-floor.

Letter IX was written, most probably, in 1316, to a friend in Florence who had urged him to accept the amnesty which the city was then offering to its exiles. He refuses the conditions, that he "pay a certain sum of money, and be willing to bear the brand of oblation." He will never return unless a way should be found "which hurts not Dante's fame and honor." He is careful to thank his friend for his solicitude, but it is clear that his scorn for his enemies is as hard as ever. The Florentines remained hard too: they reaffirmed his banishment, and condemned both Dante and his son to death if they should return; just as they had in 1311, when Dante, in Letter VI, bitterly denounced them for resisting Henry. But one can feel, in Letter IX, that Dante is speaking with a new serenity, in spite of the pain and anger which the thought of Florence causes him—and will continue to cause him until his death.

Dante's whereabouts after he was in Milan to greet Henry are uncertain, and there seems to be little point in going over the more or less plausible conjectures of experts on the period. Verona, Assisi, and Bologna are perhaps the places most frequently discussed as probable places of refuge; he was a most distinguished man of letters by that time, and seems to have had plenty of friends and willing patrons in regions where the Florentine power did not extend.

It is known that about 1316 Guido da Polenta, Lord of Ravenna, invited him to that city, and he spent the rest of his life there in comparative security. His children, but not his wife, are generally thought to have joined him there. The works that survive from this period include a scientific work, *Quaestio de Aqua et Terra* (whose authenticity is sometimes questioned), and his correspondence, in the form of Latin Eclogues, with the Bolognese teacher of rhetoric, Giovanni del Virgilio. Scholars who have studied all the available evidence—including the somewhat conflicting testimony of the early biographers—usually tell us that the years in Ravenna were peaceful for Dante, and that he was receiving at least some of the honors due to one of the very greatest poets of mankind.

In 1321 Guido da Polenta sent an embassy to Venice, in the effort to avert war with that powerful neighbor, and Dante was one of the ambassadors. He is supposed to have caught "a fever" as he was returning from this mission; he died in Ravenna on September 14, 1321. He was only fifty-seven years old; but fortunately for us he had completed the *Commedia.* In that poem his spirit continues to live with unparalleled vitality—in our time, and, so far as we can tell, on into the far distant future.

PART TWO

The *Commedia*

«« I »»

The *Commedia:* Dante's Fulfillment

The Final Change of Heart

> Io mi son un che, quando
> amor me spira, noto, ed a quel modo
> che ditta dentro, vo significando.
>
> (I am one who, when
> love breathes in me, take note, and in that mode
> which he dictates within, go signifying.)

THERE IS no way to determine, on objective evidence, just when Dante started to write the *Commedia*. But he could hardly have done so before he stopped writing *canzoni* and broke off work on the *De Vulgari Eloquentia* and the *Convivio*. Between those works and the *Commedia* we must assume a crucial change of heart if we are to account for the new vision of man and of poetry which suddenly unfolds in his masterpiece. Of course he had been moving toward that culmination, and half-consciously preparing for it, all his life. In retrospect the *Vita Nuova* looks like a tiny, dreamy premonition of the *Commedia*. After that he turned to the sciences of language, and to the cosmic and moral schemes which were to serve as blueprints for the *Commedia*. But in his rationalistic phase he did not know that another phase was in store for him; he thought he had reached stability, the end of his road. The author of the *Commedia*, with its sustained movement, its freedom of style, its unparalleled wealth of concrete perceptions, is a new Dante.

It was always his habit to try to assume full responsibility, as a man, for what he uttered as poet; that is why, through his whole career, changes of heart and changes in his conception of *poetando* are cognate. In the narrative of the *Vita Nuova* his youthful image of himself as man-and-poet does change, as we have seen; but all occurs within his cult of the love of Beatrice. In each major phase he feels the need to project a public image, or *persona*: first the *fedele d'amore*, then the champion of reason and the moral will. Each of these figures embodies his values and beliefs at the time—his *amor*—and is thus answerable for whatever he is then writing. When he comes to the *Commedia* he feels more strongly than ever the obligation to account for himself as author. But he knows and accepts himself far more completely than ever before, and a stylized mask, an artificially simplified *persona*, will no longer serve the purpose.

Dante presents himself in the *Commedia* (as he had in the *Vita Nuova*) in two ways: as the protagonist, the man who made the visionary journey beyond the grave; and the poet, who now records it as he finds it again in memory. But this stereoscopic effect reveals far more than it did in his youthful work, for all that Dante had seen and suffered in the course of his life is reflected in the changing scenes of the journey. Everything gradually falls into place: his follies, defeats, and infidelities, as well as his intellectual triumphs; the passions of youth and the different passions of maturity; the light of reason and the different light of grace. As reflected in the *Commedia*, Dante's whole career looks predestined, as though planned as a paradigm for everyman. Shakespeare's career also has this look, in the perspective of his final plays. Perhaps a very great poet must be defined simply as one who can live through all the common human phases consciously, and digest the whole sequence at the end.

We hear Dante's unmistakable voice in all the *Commedia*, and see him in all the varied situations of the trip. But in several places he presents himself with special emphasis, as though to offer the reader his exact credentials. One of the most significant of these is in the prologue (*Inferno* II, line 31). He and Virgil have started from the dark wood to the world beyond the grave, and he suddenly cries to Virgil:

Ma io, perchè venirvi? o chi'l concede?
Io non Enea, io non Paolo sono;
me degno a ciò nè io nè altri'l crede.

(But why should *I* come here? or who permits it?
I am not Aeneas, I am not Paul;
Neither I myself nor others think me worthy.)

He is weak and lost, the more so when he reflects that only the founder of the Roman Empire and the codifier of Christianity had come, as living men, to this point, the beginning of the most stupendous of all journeys. The Dante we see here has little in common with the "mature and virile" citizen he claimed to be in the *Convivio,* his feet firmly planted on the earth, his eye recording all things in the tranquil natural light. He sees himself now as far less, and yet far more, than he did then: in his own strength next to nothing, but by the grace of God (as Virgil explains to him in the next lines) following the ancient course of the supreme pilots of the race. It is his faith (unreliable as he knows himself to be) that God has marked out for him a special destiny as seer and poet. In the time of the *Convivio* he tried to play the sober role that any rational creature can see for man on earth; now he is *umile ed alta più che creatura,* "more humble and more high than any creature," as Saint Bernard says of the Virgin Mary, pattern of the Christian life, in the very last canto of the *Paradiso.*

It is this faith that he relies on in writing the *Commedia,* and offers to the reader, in the prologue, as his credentials for the huge task. In the light of this faith, the formula for his *poetando* (which I have quoted above for the third time) acquires its full meaning. He offers it to Bonagiunta (*Purgatorio* XXIV, line 52) ostensibly as the secret of his early *dolce stil nuovo*: to follow the dictates of *amor* as closely as possible, instead of relying on the mechanical ingenuity of Provençal prosody, as Bonagiunta had done. We have seen that it applies to his middle phase also, when *amor* means the love of reason. It applies *a fortiori* to the *Commedia;* but now *amor* means nothing less than God's love, which (in Dante's philosophy) is the life and movement of all creatures, including those human spirits that missed their way and landed in the dead-ends of hell. His job as poet is now not only to "signify" the life of reason, but to signify *all* the modes of love: apprehending each by the sympathetic and mimetic response of his own spirit; "becoming in intention" the being he wishes to portray, as he puts it in *Convivio* IV; obeying love in whatever mode it dictates, as he puts it here. If he can imitate these movements of spirit accurately in his *poetando*, he believes, he will represent that bit of God's truth which the destiny of each embodies.

It is proper to describe Dante's change of heart between the *Convivio* and the *Commedia* as a turn to a religious view of man and his fate. But one must understand (Dante's religion being what it was) that this meant freeing him as poet to represent the human with a subtle, many-sided realism that had no parallel in his time, and has not been surpassed since. Freed from the strait jacket of "reason and the moral will," he can, for the first time, fill his poem with many spirits and many voices besides his own, and with all the sights and sounds and smells of "God's world." We cannot possibly believe what Dante believed; but the human life and experience he unrolls within his religious framework requires no efforts of faith on the part of the reader: it reaches us directly the moment we open the book.

The Rebirth of Poetry in the Full Aristotelian Sense

In Limbo, where the sages of pagan antiquity have their eternal dwelling, Virgil introduces Dante to Homer, Horace, Ovid, and Lucan, who receive him with honor as "a sixth among such intelligences." So he recognizes, with no false modesty whatever, what subsequent generations have confirmed: that with the *Commedia* poetry in the fullest sense of the word is reborn in Europe. He had brought about this renaissance in full awareness of what he was doing: representing or "imitating" every mode of action. He knew what was required technically to embody *amor*'s new dictation in one hundred cantos of *terza rima*; and he knew how his poetic stratagems differed from those he had found adequate for his *canzoni*.

In the "Letter" he writes dedicating the *Paradiso* to his patron, Can Grande (*Epistola* X in the Temple Classics edition), he explains the new flexibility of his verbal style in two ways. He has rejected (he says) the "tragic" high-style which, in *De Vulgari Eloquentia,* he prescribed for the *canzone*—a purified language suitable for the hero of reason and the moral will on public occasions—in favor of a more informal speech which he associates with comedy: "lax and humble," as he puts it, "for it is the vernacular speech in which very women communicate" (paragraph 10). His second explanation shows that, humble though it may be, this language must serve every purpose: "poetic, fictive, descriptive, digressive, transumptive; and likewise proceeding by definition, division, proof, refutation, and setting forth of examples" (paragraph 9). The exact meanings of these terms are disputed by experts. They apparently are derived from rhetoric, and intended to cover both emotive and metaphorical uses of language (the first five terms) and conceptual and logical uses (the second five). They also remind one of what Aristotle says, in the *Poetics* (XIX, 2) of the poet's means of presenting what his characters think or perceive: "every effort which has to be produced by speech, the subdivisions being—proof and refutation; the excitation of the feelings, such as pity, fear, anger and the like; the suggestion of importance and its opposite."

The speech we hear in the *Commedia* does indeed serve every purpose: that of the author, as he tells the story, or interrupts it to address the reader directly or to scold Florence in a grieving, angry tirade; that of the spirits who tell their stories; that of Virgil or Beatrice when they unfold philosophical or theological thought in passages which are at the same time musical and logical. But prior to the words are the characters that speak them, and the characters emerge from the carefully contrived settings and dramatic situations of the long journey. In composing the *Commedia* Dante used all the poet's resources for imitating action, not only words but character-portrayal, plot-making, spectacle, and music, just as though he had read the *Poetics.*

I have pointed out that in the *Convivio* Dante presents the literal meaning of his *canzoni* as the singer's *moto spiritale,* or action. As poet he is limited to his own voice, and (for his theme) to the love of reason; but as psychologist and philosopher he sees, even then, the whole Aristotelian vision of human life as action, the psyche's "movement" toward the objects it perceives as desirable. And (in the passage quoted on page 67) he elaborates this conception in the metaphor of the journey from the cradle to the grave, the "journeys of earth" with their many possible paths, some right, some mistaken. Now, in the *Commedia,* he takes full possession, as dramatic poet, of the whole vast theme: "Man, as by good or ill deserts, in the freedom of his choice, he becomes liable to punishing or rewarding justice," as he puts it in his "Letter to Can Grande" (paragraph 8).

In the *Commedia* Dante sees the spirit's life unfolding and meeting its destiny in the classical world of nature, as he had in the *Convivio,* but now he also sees the world as God's, according to the Christian faith. In that vaster and more mysterious setting, the spirit has two goals, as he had explained at the end of *De Monarchia.* The first, which he now regards as true but insufficient, is earthly felicity, and reason shows it to us; the second, "the blessedness of eternal life," can only be apprehended by faith in the Christian Revelation. In writing the *Commedia* he must show the life and destiny of the human spirit in this widest of all perspectives, and so he places the metaphorical "journey" not on earth but beyond the grave, where all the countless goals, true or false, that men pursue, may be seen in the final light of God's judgment.

This otherworldly theme might seem, at first sight, to demand a conception of poetry quite different from Aristotle's—sober biologist and empirically based philosopher as he was. Especially in the *Paradiso* Dante explores religious experiences which only Old Testament prophets and Christian mystics had described before him. Aristotle had, of course, never heard of the Trinity, which Dante approaches as he rises through the ten heavens of the *Paradiso.* But the poem "imitates" that action just as Aristotle had said that poetry must: in the six stages of the poet's *poetando.* The *Poetics* is therefore essential for understanding the art of the *Commedia*: it is the connecting link between Dante's inspiration, action in all its forms, and the poem we read.

Allegory as a Function of Dramatic Narrative

It is by means of "allegory" that Dante leads his readers to the moral and religious meanings he sees in human life. But the basis of his kind of allegory is realistic or experiential: life comes first—the changing life of Dante as he travels beyond the grave, the infinitely varied lives of the spirits he meets there—and the allegorical meanings come second, they emerge from the concrete dramatic situations of the unfolding narrative. As he had explained in the *Convivio*, the literal meaning of the poem, in this case the story with all its scenes and characters, *contains* the allegorical meanings.

In the *Convivio* Dante rejected the "allegory of theologians" in favor of the "allegory of poets," and proceeded to interpret his *canzoni* according to Greek moral philosophy. But in his "Letter to Can Grande," explaining that the *Commedia* is of "more senses than one," he adopts the religious or Scriptural type of allegory, which, of course, he needed in order to represent his religious vision. The example he offers is a passage of Scripture interpreted according to the theologians' four senses (Letter X, paragraph 7):

> And this mode of treatment, for its better manifestation, may be considered in this verse: "When Israel came out of Egypt, and the house of Jacob from a people of strange speech, Judaea became his sanctification, Israel his power." For if we inspect the letter alone, the departure of the children of Israel from Egypt in the time of Moses is presented to us; if the allegory, our redemption wrought by Christ; if the moral sense, the conversion of the soul from the grief and misery of sin to the state of grace is presented to us; if the anagogical, the departure of the holy soul from the slavery of this corruption to the liberty of eternal glory is presented to us. And although these mystic senses have each their special denominations, they may all in general be called allegorical, since they differ from the literal and historical; for *allegory* is derived from *alleon*, in Greek, which means the same as the Latin *alienum* or *diversum*.

The theory of this "theologians' allegory" was that God spoke, not in words, but in the events of history which the writers of the Bible were inspired to record truly. The "literal" living event—the donkeys and camels, the dust, the banging pots and pans, the squalling children, and Moses with his immediate motive, to lead his people out of Pharaoh's bondage—*contained* the three allegorical meanings. Philosophers might see a moral meaning in Moses' motive: to separate the psyche from its material servitudes. Only a believer could see the *allegoria*, which is defined as *quid credas*:

i.e., Christ, who is the actual Way for all humanity. In the *allegoria* Moses is seen as a "figure," or sign, whose full meaning is clear only when we see Christ. The *anagogia* also depends on religious faith; in this case faith in the future life, where God's glory may be seen; the ultimate goal, the "meaning" that includes all the rest. The literal narrative of Dante's trip beyond the grave contains these moral and religious meanings.

Dante's ultimate purpose in writing the *Commedia,* he tells Can Grande (paragraph 15), is "to remove those living in this life from the state of misery and lead them to the state of felicity." That he can do only as a divinely inspired *poet*; i.e., by revealing human actions of all kinds in such a way as to bring out all three allegorical meanings. He built these meanings, or "perspectives" as one might call them, into the cosmic setting, and into the temporal sequence of incidents, of the great poem.

The setting of the *Inferno* is the confined darkness below the surface of the earth, "the bottom of the universe"; that of the *Purgatorio,* a mountain rising from the ocean shore to a point high above our earthly weather, a plateau at the top, the "earthly paradise"; that of the *Paradiso,* the ten heavens which Dante had described in *Convivio* II. In constructing this many-storeyed setting, the cosmos of his tradition, he used all the recognized authorities—Aristotle, the astronomers, Scripture—as he explains at length to Can Grande (paragraphs 20–33). But what we see and hear in these realms as we travel through them is perforce imaginary; and the setting, as in any good drama, is there, not for its own sake, but in order to reveal the movement of spirit and its meanings, by the vastly elaborated metaphor of spatial movement and sensory perception.

Dante the traveler is the protagonist of this drama, or journey, of enlightenment, as Dante the young poet was in the *Vita Nuova.* The function of this figure is the same as that of one of Henry James's sensitive heroes or heroines: his "consciousness is the center of the composition." By sharing successive experiences of the traveler we learn, first, what happened (the "letter") and then what it means (the "allegory"). In the *Inferno* we meet the lost spirits and hear their stories. Neither moral nor religious truth availed them to find their way through life, and as we share their experiences in the confinements of hell, we, also, fail to place them in God's wide world; we get the "letter" with unparalleled impact, but not the meaning. In the *Purgatorio,* back in God's world, guided by Virgil, and by many signs along the path, we meet the spirits who are finding their way; and on the second day Virgil explains action, and its *moral* meanings. He accompanies us to the top of the Mountain, the terrestrial paradise in which, as Dante had explained in *De Monarchia,* earthly felicity, the goal of the classical moral philosophers, is "figured." There the scene of earthly beauty is invaded by the pageant of historic Revelation, from the Prophets of the Old Testament to Christ: the *allegoria* in literal, visual terms. Virgil is gone, and Beatrice takes his place as guide. In the *Paradiso* we meet the spirits who have reached the goal which includes and transcends all the rest, and share their delectation as the traveler's spirit, moving toward *its* fulfillment, perceives the glory of God in many contexts. The *Paradiso* thus shows man "as" supernaturally satisfied, the *anagogia.* It is in this way that Dante, following the allegorical mode of Scripture as he understood it, built the three allegorical "meanings," or ways of understanding action, into the successive scenes of the journey. The process of enlightenment is dramatized; the journey and its interpretation unfold together.

It is most important to notice that Dante himself keeps reminding us, throughout the *Commedia,* that it is a *poem* we are reading. He does not wish his readers to suppose naïvely that, like the writers of Scripture, he is recording historic events—that in a few days, around 1300, he had made the round trip beyond the farthest stars. He means the *Commedia* to be literally true, not as Scripture, but as *poetry,* is: by presenting what God had "dictated to him within"—a mode of love, a movement of spirit. When we read Juliet's words (in Shakespeare's play) we sense the movement of her awakened spirit and recognize it as "true" without inquiring whether Shakespeare had been in Verona and overheard her monologue in the moonlight. In the same way the truth of Francesca's lost spirit (in *Inferno* V) reaches us the moment we understand the literal story. To get that we do not have to believe that Dante was "there" in hell, or even that there is such a place. We may, if we like, take all the scenes of the *Commedia* as "imaginary gardens with real toads in them," Marianne Moore's famous recipe for all poetry. In *Purgatorio* IX, line 70, we read:

Lettor, tu vedi ben com'io innalzo
la mia materia, e però con più arte
non ti maravigliar s'io la rincalzo.

(Reader, you plainly see how I am elevating
my material: therefore, if with more art
I sustain it, do not be surprised.)

This is only one of many places in which Dante interrupts the story to remind us of his labors as poet. He does not intend to destroy the drama he had been creating, or to make us doubt the truth of its *moto spiritale,* which we have just shared by sympathetic perception. He merely intends to detach us momentarily from the action, real though it is, so that we may consider its place in the vast cosmic setting in which the *moralia,* the *allegoria,* and the *anagogia* are embodied; and consider, also, Dante himself, noting love's dictation, and then by his art finding the proper mode to signify it in this passage of the poem before us. He wishes to make us aware of *all* the aspects of the visionary journey, in which enlightenment and *poetando* are cognate. The *Commedia* is poetry in the classic sense; but it is at the same time more technically self-conscious, more sophisticated, than any other poetry in our tradition.

II

The *Inferno*

From the Midst of Life to the World of the Dead (Cantos I and II)

THE FIRST two cantos of the *Inferno* are the prologue of the entire poem. They serve to introduce the author, who is also the protagonist; to foreshadow the story to follow; and to lead us to the point where the actual narrative of the supernatural journey can begin. Dante speaks to us, in the opening lines, of his crucial night of terror:

> Nel mezzo del cammin di nostra vita
> mi ritrovai per una selva oscura
> che la diritta via era smarrita.

> (In the middle of the journey of our life
> I found myself in a dark wood,
> where the straight way was lost.)

He tells us of his deathly fear "in the lake of the heart," of the sunlit "delectable mountain" he wants to climb, of the nightmare beasts that drive him back into the darkness. These elements combine, as in a modern lyric, to give us an intense moment of the inner life, whether we attempt to interpret the dreamlike visions or not.

But as one mulls over the canto it appears that the dark wood, with all that Dante finds there, the good as well as the bad, reflects the experience he actually had in the period which I have called his rationalistic phase. It was then that he suffered both his own passions and the enmity of the powers that divided Italy. The handsome leopard is probably intended to suggest both earthly pleasures and Florence; the lion, ambitious pride and the House of France; the famished wolf, greed and the Papacy. The "delectable mountain" is a figure of the earthly felicity he aspired to; and at the moment of his deepest despair the spirit of Virgil appears, as Greek philosophy had when he wrote the *Convivio*, to show him that a way out is possible.

The spirit of Virgil will make the wisdom of Greece and Rome available to the traveler, but he is not "wisdom," or any other abstraction. He is a real, individual being, the very man who lived under the good Augustus and wrote the poem from which Dante had learned to write. Pagan poet as he is, he will rescue Dante from the despair created by the greed of the Papacy. But he cannot lead him directly back to the "delectable mountain"; if he restores him to the world of the living and its felicity at all, it must be by a very long detour. Virgil explains in vague terms that he will lead Dante through two of the three realms of the dead, hell and purgatory; that he will then leave him, and that Beatrice (whom he does not yet name) will guide him the rest of the way. So he starts off, and Dante follows.

In Canto II we see Dante, as night falls, trying to pull himself together for the trip *che ritrarrà la mente che non erra*, "which memory that does not err will restore," and also for the task of recording it:

> O Muse, o alto ingegno, or m'aiutate!
> O mente, che scrivesti ciò ch'io vidi,
> qui si parrà la tua nobilitate.

> (O Muse, O high ability, now help me!
> O memory, that wrote down what I saw,
> here shall be shown your quality.)

What his memory recorded is "love's dictation"—the movement of his own spirit, and the movements of the spirits of the dead. It will require the help of the muses and all his art to "signify" the life he "noted within" as poets do: in the sensuous imagery of the literal journey.

It is then (line 10 ff.) that he confesses his terror to Virgil, and his inadequacy to undertake the journeys of Aeneas and Paul. Virgil's reply gives him his true credentials: no one expects him to accomplish the tasks before him in his own strength; the grace of God is behind their meeting here and the whole journey that lies ahead. It was the spirit of Beatrice that moved Virgil to come to his aid; Lucia who moved Beatrice, and the Virgin Mary who moved Lucia. The assurance of divine aid, descending through these intercessors—women moved by love, not justice—revives Dante, and the two start off again on the "steep and wild" path to hell.

The effect of Virgil's explanation is to foreshadow the dramatic interplay between Dante, Virgil, and Beatrice which reaches its climax and turning point at the end of the *Purgatorio*. The elaborate Thomistic doctrine of the interplay between grace and human effort is one clue to the meaning of this plot. But it will take most of the trip for Dante the traveler, and for the reader who moves and learns with him, to understand the story in Christian terms. At this point, the end of Canto II, we have not yet entered the setting of the supernatural journey; we are somewhere between the life we know and the visionary realm. The narrative movement has begun; the chief *dramatis personae* have been mentioned at least; but the doings of the heavenly ladies are recounted as though for the sake of the literal story only, like a conference of gods in a classical epic. When Dante tells Virgil that he has learned his style from him, he is not offering idle flattery. The *Commedia* is, among other things, an epic; and when it serves his purpose, Dante can use the glamour of distant voyaging as Virgil does, or even Homer, whom he knew only indirectly.

The Inscription on the Gate of Hell (Canto III)

We realize that we have reached hell proper when we read the inscription with which Canto III abruptly begins:

"Per me si va nella città dolente;
  per me si va nell'eterno dolore;
  per me si va tra la perduta gente.
Giustizia mosse il mio alto Fattore;
  fecemi la divina Potestate,
  la somma Sapienza e il primo Amore.
Dinanzi a me non fur cose create,
  se non eterne, ed io eterno duro:
  lasciate ogni speranza, voi ch'entrate."

("Through me is the way into the suffering city;
through me the way into eternal pain;
through me the way among the lost people.
Justice moved my high Maker;
I was made by the Divine Power,
Supreme Wisdom, and primal Love.
Before me were no created things,
except the eternal, and eternal I endure:
abandon all hope, you who enter.")

These words have dismayed many generations of readers, and they dismay Dante the traveler when he sees them: "Master," he says to Virgil, "their meaning is hard for me." Virgil does not try to explain them:

"Qui si convien lasciare ogni sospetto;
ogni viltà convien che qui sia morta.
Noi siam venuti al luogo ov'io t'ho detto
che tu vedrai le genti dolorose,
ch'hanno perduto il ben dello intelletto."

("Here must be abandoned all mistrust,
all cowardice must here be dead.
We have come to the place where I told you
that you would see the miserable people
who have lost the good of the intellect.")

Virgil is giving Dante his marching orders for the whole descent to the bottom of hell. He must simply accept it with the unwavering faith that it is the will of God; summoning what courage he can, but not trying to understand or digest it.

The literal meaning of the inscription is, of course, that God made hell: God as Justice—therefore there are rational explanations of it—but also God as Power, Wisdom, and Love, the Trinity. But the traveler will not consider the mystery of the Trinity, or the unfathomable relations between divine Justice and Love, until he gets to paradise, and the reader is not supposed to either. The inscription, with its theological shorthand (like a wordless set of traffic signals), is a set piece such as Dante often places at the boundary between two realms of experience.

But, of course, Dante the *author*, planning the sequence of his poem, knew just what the inscription meant; and in the literal story to follow he makes the reader *feel* what it means. The infernal setting, the actions of the spirits he meets, and the experience of the traveler, all represent with extraordinary consistency "Man," not as we know him in this life, but in the one sharply defined perspective: man as totally lost. By noticing how the main points of the inscription are represented, one can get a preliminary notion of the *Inferno* as a whole, and of the controlled and conscious art required to make it.

Eternal I endure; abandon all hope, you who enter. The doctrine that the human spirit can be lost forever is unpalatable to us, and there are modern theologians who tend to mitigate it. Dante the traveler also finds it "hard" in every sense; but the theological problem is not the concern here. What must be pointed out is that Dante represents the "eternity" of damnation chiefly by keeping his *Inferno* outside time as we know it. By placing it under the earth he deprives it of all the sights and sounds that serve to give the living their bearings in time. Enclosed, and dark or artificially lighted, hell has neither the cycle of day and night nor the cycle of the seasons; and changes of weather are unknown there. The lost, as Farinata will explain (Canto X, line 100) can see dimly "the things that are remote," but their intellects are unable to apprehend events near in time, or present. They are confined to the "world" which their mistaken movement of spirit has created, an unchanging present, "a circle closed on the outside," as Bradley puts it in the passage quoted by Eliot in his notes to *The Waste Land.*

Here on earth the objective world of nature—*il dolce mondo,* "the sweet world," as Dante often calls it—breaks into our private worlds with the changes that time brings, suggesting possibilities beyond our immediate state. That is why we may hope here on earth: hope depends on change. Outside time, hope is gone; and by accurately excluding change from the infernal scene Dante has deprived the movements-of-spirit of the lost of all hope.

Many other writers since Dante's time have pictured the experience of being utterly lost, and they too represent it as "timeless." Shakespeare's Macbeth, once committed to his criminal aim, loses his sense of the real world of nature, and finds himself in a dissociated realm that never changes, no matter how fast he runs to murder. Pirandello's six characters can never find their way into time; Sartre and Brecht have consciously imitated some of

Dante's devices in making their images of hopeless, and therefore timeless, frustration. Dante's vision of the human spirit as lost is amply confirmed by other writers of candor. What makes the *Inferno* unique is its variety within the strictest consistency; in short, the completely conscious technical control of the poet who made it.

Justice moved my high Maker. The *Inferno* is famous for the imaginative variety of its torments. Sometimes Dante himself boasts about it, interrupting the course of the story to address his reader, with irony and bitter relish, as the ingenious poet who invented it all. Sometimes he gives other writers part of the credit, as he does in Canto XXV, jokingly claiming to have outdone Lucan and Ovid. He is thought to have used Mohammedan tales of the other world also—to say nothing of sources which have not been identified—for many details of the hellish masquerade. But we are to see Divine (as well as poetic) justice in the carefully devised and psychologically convincing relation between the evil motive and the timeless plight it ends in. The lost make their own hells; and that, according to the inscription, is "just," appalling though it is.

I was made by primal Love. But the *life* of the masquerade is to be understood in Aristotelian terms: as action, the movement of the spirit toward what it perceives as desirable. Dante (as he explains as early as *Convivio* III) thought of the love-driven human psyche as having been created by a loving God and needing God (unseen though He is) as the only object adequate to that love. The spirits in hell have lost their way toward God, but "primal Love" still drives them through their unavailing gestures and attitudes. It is this tormented love which is Dante's inspiration: the "dictation" within; what his "unerring memory" brings back; what he "signifies" in the phantasmagoria of the literal journey. Hence the human vitality of the *Inferno,* and the sympathy with which Dante the traveler, and the reader who accompanies him, explore the timeless scenes where the lost have their being. In hell, as on earth, it is the God-given love of the human spirit that makes the wheels go around.

I was made by the Divine Power. In the prologue, as we have seen, Virgil encourages Dante by telling him that not his strength, but the power of God, accounts for the journey beyond the grave. At various points on the downward climb the keepers of hell challenge the travelers, and Virgil always overawes them by invoking the omnipotent and unfathomable will of God: "It is willed, there where what is willed can be done; ask no more," he says to Charon (III, line 94). When Minos the bull-monster tries to stop them, he gives him the same formula, and adds, "Do not impede his fated going."

It is the metaphor, or symbol, of gravitation that Dante chiefly relies on to make us feel the irresistible power that makes hell, and especially his own journey through it. In Dante's cosmos the earth was at the center, and so all the weight of the universe converged at the mid-point of the earthly sphere. In each of the various circles on the way down the travelers share the "life" of the lost, but when they continue their descent, their "fated going," it is the will of God that moves them, and the transitions in hell are accomplished by a wonderfully varied series of fallings, sinkings, and dizzy downward rides. They obey the dark will of God by obeying the pull of gravity. At the "bottom of the universe," all movement, including heat and light, is supposed to cease: the perfect image of the total frustration of human love, which is "movement of spirit." And as we pass that mid-point, going down surprisingly (but inevitably) turns into going up.

People who have lost the good of the intellect. Virgil's brief charge to Dante, after Hell Gate, indicates both the condition of the lost, and the condition which the traveler must accept when traversing hell.

According to Aristotelian psychology, action has two causes: the character of the psyche, and what it perceives as desirable. That is why (as Dante explains in *Convivio* III) we can judge the quality of a man's inner life by noting the objects toward which his spirit moves. The spirits in hell may be defined as those whose intellects have not discerned those good things which can truly nourish and fulfill them. That does not necessarily mean that they have lost the intellect itself: on the contrary, hell is full of very intelligent spirits. Often they are learned, too, in philosophy and religion, things which should have availed to guide them. But knowledge may lie unused in the back of the mind, and the intellect, nimble though it be, may be pushed off the track by forces both inside and outside the psyche; and then it gyrates futilely in the void. Virgil is not saying that the damned have lost the intellect—only the *good* of the intellect.

Dante the traveler also loses the good of the intellect—or most of it, at least—while he is in hell. That is because there is nothing good in hell which he can *actually* see. Virgil provides him with maps, and with classifications of the sins, and reminds him of what he is supposed to have learned in ethics. But none of this true knowledge avails to save him from passion when he meets the lost lovers, or from treachery when he finds himself in the cold city of those who have betrayed. Dante is not talking *about* being lost, but re-creating that condition, with all the arts of the dramatic poet.

From the point of view of Dante's allegorical scheme, hell may be described as that realm in which the traveler, and the reader who accompanies him, *actually* understand only the "letter." The paradoxical "life" of the lost reaches us directly, and with unmitigated sharpness; but we do not really see the moral, allegorical, and anagogical meanings until hell is left behind. The only explanation of hell really available while we are there is "the will of God." Our knowledge of moral and religious truths (if we have any) is unused, "potential" only, until we creep out the other side of hell, and the light of God's world of nature, and that of Virgil's human intellect, begin to make the wider perspectives actual. Dante the traveler is neither dead nor alive as he passes the low point, "For the letter killeth, but the spirit giveth life"; and Dante the poet has constructed a series of unchanging scenes where the intellect, powerful though it may be, can see only what is literally there.

Amor as the Beginning of Hell (Canto V)

The story of young Paolo and Francesca, who in their heedless passion give themselves to each other and are thereupon murdered by Gianciotto, Francesca's hunchbacked husband, dominates Canto V. No one can miss its pathos and power, even in translation, and a lengthy analysis is not needed here. But it is the first realm after Limbo (Canto IV), the entrance to hell proper, and thus a very important part of the structure of the *Inferno*, and can be considered from that point of view.

In Canto III (line 112 ff.) we see the lost spirits gathering from every country by the great river that bounds hell and casting themselves from the bank one by one, like dead leaves in autumn, to be ferried across the brown water; and we learn that on their way to their timeless torment *la tema si volge in disio,* "fear is turned into desire." It is one of the moments when we directly glimpse "primal Love" as the motive-power of hell.

In the opening sequence of Canto V we meet the lost throngs again as they gather before Minos to confess and learn their final destinations: *dicono e odono, e poi son giù volte,* "they tell and hear and then are whirled downward." Virgil has to give Minos Dante's credentials too, and warns him, *non impedir lo suo fatale andare,* "do not impede his fated going." Dante, like the damned, is moved by what he can neither understand nor control.

In the second sequence (lines 25–51) this unwilled motivation is suggested by the setting, which is "mute of all light" and loud with storm, and then in the image of the spirits as flocks of birds—first starlings, then cranes—streaming downwind; and the traveler learns that in those spirits "reason is subject to lust." Virgil names some of them, ladies and cavaliers famous in Biblical and Classical legend or in medieval Romance, "whom love separated from our life." When Dante wants to speak with two who "seem so light upon the wind," Virgil tells him that he must appeal to their love; and when Francesca hears the love in Dante's cry she and her Paolo come. Virgil has just told his pupil the moral meaning of their plight—reason subject to lust—but he knows that here, where his own Dido is, the truths of moral philosophy are powerless and therefore irrelevant. Only lost *amor* avails; human communication can be only on its terms.

Having spent his youth as a *fedele d'amore,* Dante knows the language, and Francesca's story brings back the incomprehensible glamour of the world of *amor cortese:*

> Amor, che al cor gentil ratto s'apprende,
>   prese costui della bella persona
>   che mi fu tolta, e il modo ancor m'offende.
> Amor, che a nullo amato amar perdona,
>   mi prese del costui piacer sì forte,
>   che, come vedi, ancor non m'abbandona.
> Amor condusse noi ad una morte;
>   Caina attende chi vita ci spense.

(Love, which in the gentle heart is quickly learned,
seized him of the handsome person
that was taken from me, and the way still hurts me.
Love, which excuses no loved one from loving,
seized me with pleasure in him, so strongly
that, as you see, it still does not leave me.
Love led us to one death;
Caina waits for him who put out our life.)

Francesca's first line, above, echoes the first poem of the *dolce stil nuovo* (Guinizelli's), which Dante himself had echoed in his sonnet, *Amore e'l cor gentil son una cosa*, "Love and the gentle heart are a single thing." But the song of love brutally and unexpectedly ends, in the third tercet, in death. We have seen that Dante felt the pull of the love-death theme when he was love's subject, but (as he shows in the *Vita Nuova*) he slowly learned to distinguish the life-giving from the deathly solicitations of the *dubbiosi desiri*. Paolo and Francesca had no time for that: "one moment alone it was" that overcame them, as they read of Lancelot, "how love constrained him":

Quando leggemmo il disiato riso
esser baciato da cotanto amante,
questi, che mai da me non fia diviso,
la bocca mi baciò tutto tremante.

(When we read that the amorous smile
was kissed by such a lover,
he, who shall never be divided from me,
kissed my mouth all trembling.)

This moment, as Francesca relives it, overcomes Dante too: "and I fell as a dead body falls." So the canto ends, in a movement of sympathy closely analogous to the *amor* that led Paolo and Francesca to one death.

Much of the power of this canto is due to the miraculous figure of Francesca. Her delicate, generous and unthinking spirit reaches us through every little word and gesture, constraining us also to love. In *Convivio* IV Dante says that when he loved his Lady Philosophy his spirit moved as hers did: he loved what she loved and hated what she hated. He was very responsive to women, and all his life he found it natural to represent his inner life objectively in a feminine figure that moved him. Francesca is the first of a series of such figures, placed at the beginnings of new realms of experience, who serve to reveal the quality of the traveler's *moto spiritale* at various stages of the journey of enlightenment. At this point she shows the way into hell, the easy descent into Avernus. She is the most seductive embodiment possible of the *primo Amore* that makes the life of the lost.

The Canto as the Imitation of One Action

Canto V is very clearly the imitation of an action in Aristotle's sense of the phrase. This action, or motive, is "to obey the love that moves one without thinking, or questioning it." The canto as a whole is built like a short but complete tragedy. The first sequence (lines 1–25), the prologue, introduces the action in general terms, as we see the lost souls of all kinds on their way into the abyss, and Dante the traveler moving downward in an analogous way. When we then enter the circle of the lust-driven on their dark wind, and learn some of their names, we understand the action more concretely; and when Paolo and Francesca are called from the throng, the action is made as "actual" as possible, in individual character and destiny. Francesca's story (like that of many figures of tragedy) is plotted into two simultaneous movements, that of the love that led her and Paolo to one death, and that of the love that now leads her to recount their catastrophe to Dante; and he, as he hears, responds analogously. All six of Aristotle's poetic arts are employed, in this canto, to represent the one action. The plot is of the type that Aristotle calls "simple": it presents the action moving toward its black end without peripety or any new recognition, and all the characterization, imagery, and verbal rhythms spring from that ill-fated movement of spirit.

I think that each of the one hundred cantos of the *Commedia* is planned as one action. Dante explains in *De Vulgari Eloquentia* (II, viii) that a *canzone* is the action of the poet who composed it; the cantos of the *Commedia* are poetic units analogous to *canzoni*: at the beginning of each one Dante takes breath for a new song, which will present a different part or aspect of the great theme. Sometimes we hear mostly the author's own voice, as in the *canzone*, in narrative or lyric utterance—especially in the transitions from one circle to another. But the cantos that show the travelers in one of the circles of the damned, hearing their stories and sharing their situations, usually have a fully developed dramatic form, like that of Francesca's Canto V.

These dramatic cantos are all composed on similar principles. The setting, and the visible plight of the lost, always suggest the real nature of the "world" created by their deluded motivation, and the travelers must spend some time there, seeing only the dreary scene around them. Moreover, like tourists here on earth, Dante and Virgil must obey the custom of the country: "In church with the holy, and in the tavern with the rascals," as Dante appropriately puts it in the realm of the agile barrators (Canto XXII, line 14). They often find that they cannot continue their journey at all unless they act very much as the damned do; they are perforce pulled into the eternally present "drama" of each circle, sharing by analogy that "mode" of love, as they shared the romantic tyranny of Francesca's *amor cortese.*

But there are countless ways in which love in the human creature may go wrong, and Dante displays it in an extraordinary variety of settings, characters, and stories. He shows "Dante the traveler" involved with the lost spirits all the way down; and the action of that figure is therefore always a significant version of the action of the canto as a whole. But the traveler does not always sympathize with the lost as he does with Francesca: he enters many realms of experience where sympathy of that kind is undreamed of. For example, he sees the crooked senators and clerics of Cantos XXI and XXII, and the busy demons that bully them, as a timid boy might see a gang of toughs in an industrial suburb; but he and Virgil are drawn into their agile and cruel intrigues, which are plotted like classical farce: a pattern of action endlessly and absurdly repeated. Part of the hellishness of that dangerous circle of hell is its triviality; but Canto XV, where he meets his beloved teacher, Brunetto Latini, among the Sodomites, is anything but trivial. Brunetto, with his cooked and scorched face, moving ceaselessly on his hot sand, would like to transcend his absurd plight as he converses with his former pupil. Dante, on a bank above the burning sand, has to walk along with his head bowed "as though in reverence" in order to converse with Brunetto. His plight is absurd too, for he is forced into that posture by his fear of the hot sand; yet the "reverence" in his bearing also expresses a wistful longing like Brunetto's—that things were different.

Perhaps the motive, at once grotesque and infinitely sad, which Dante shares with Brunetto in this canto, is most suggestively put in his speech of gratitude:

> "Se fosse tutto pieno il mio dimando,"
>   risposi lui, "voi non sareste ancora
>   dell'umana natura posto in bando:
> chè in la mente m'è fitta, ed or mi accora,
>   la cara e buona imagine paterna
>   di voi, quando nel mondo ad ora ad ora
> m'insegnavate come l'uom s'eterna."

> ("If what I wish were all fulfilled,"
>   I answered him, "you would not yet
>   be banished from human nature;
> for in my memory is fixed, and pierces my heart now,
>   the dear and good fatherly image
>   of you, when in the world, time and again,
> you would teach me how man makes himself eternal.")

"Exiled from human nature" is a cruel way to put Brunetto's post-mortem situation here among the lost Sodomites. Yet it was Brunetto who taught Dante to extend his "human nature" beyond time by communing, in study, with the spirits of the past. The whole canto is a most subtle study in human relations, in which we are made to feel hell, not as cheap and dangerous, but hopelessly painful, and infinitely mysterious.

The proper way to read the *Commedia* is to linger over each canto, until one sees its unique life, or action, in every detail. But that is beyond my intention: a few samples must suffice to suggest the wonderfully varied poetic-dramatic forms that Dante created in these basic elements of his composition.

The Rational Soul as Lost (Canto XXVI)

Canto XXVI is dominated by Ulysses' great narrative of his final voyage, a passage as powerful in its way as Francesca's story is in its very different way. Dante did not take it from a classic source, but invented it himself, and packed into it a great deal of first-hand experience of the intellect's boundless appetite. The canto as a whole is one of the best places in which to see what Dante means by the formula, "those who have lost the *good* of the intellect," for Ulysses has not lost his intellect, but only the proper use of it, which would have shown him his way in the world.

Ulysses is in the "Eighth Bolgia," the place of the false counselors, and he is supposed to have given false counsel more than once. But the immediate poetic power of the canto depends, not upon the abstract classification of Ulysses' sin, but upon the unique, daring, and tragic movement of spirit that led him and his followers to ruin. That action, or motive, may be defined as follows: "to satisfy the needs of the rational soul without reference to the circumstances of time and place." Home from his wanderings, but still unsatisfied, he tells his followers: *Fatti non foste a viver come bruti,/ ma per seguir virtute e conoscenza,* "You were not made to live like beasts, but to pursue virtue and knowledge." As Ulysses puts it, his motive is that of all rational creatures: Dante himself was burning with it in his middle phase, as we have seen, and now, traveling beyond the grave, he will reach "virtue and knowledge" at the top of the Mount of Purgatory. But that he will do by obeying Virgil and all the requirements of the long climb, while Ulysses sees only his human need, blind to his situation as son, husband, and father—blind to the fact that the world is governed, not by the insatiable human mind but by the unfathomable will of God.

As in Canto V, the first two movements serve to introduce the action, and then build the scene, in this case the black chasm.

In the first movement Dante breaks the narrative of his remembered journey, as though overcome by the evidence of Florentine thieving which he has just recorded in the preceding canto:

> Godi, Fiorenza, poi che sei sì grande,
> che per mare e per terra batti l'ali,
> e per l'inferno tuo nome si spande!

> (Rejoice, Florence, since you are so great
> that over sea and over land you beat your wings
> and through all hell your name is spread.)

His motive in this diatribe is to secure the punishment of the Florentine wrongdoers, a motive as natural as Ulysses'; but like Ulysses he cannot wait until God, in his good time, brings it about:

E se già fosse, non saria per tempo:
così foss'ei, da che pur esser dee!
chè più mi graverà, com' più m'attempo.

(And if it were already, it would not be too soon;
would it were so, since it must be:
for it will weigh on me more the older I grow.)

After the diatribe he returns to his narrative at the point where he and Virgil reach the edge of the chasm, but then he breaks out again with a direct address to the reader:

Allor mi dolsi, ed ora mi ridoglio
quand'io drizzo la mente a ciò ch'io vidi,
e più lo ingegno affreno ch'io non soglio,
perchè non corra, che virtù nol guidi.

(Then I grieved, and now I grieve again,
when I turn my mind to what I saw,
and hold my wit back more than usual
lest it run where virtue does not guide it.)

In his task of writing the poem the same mad impatience threatens to frustrate his efforts. In this whole opening sequence (lines 1–24) Dante imitates the tragic action in his own character—not as the traveler in hell, but as the poet who even now, remembering that part of the journey, shares once more the desperate motives of the lost.

In the second main movement Dante as author disappears behind the scenes, and Dante the traveler takes the center of the stage. He looks into the black valley, sees the flames moving there like fireflies, and learns that each one enwraps and burns a sinner. It is a wonderful visual image of the intense, selfish *moto spiritale*, wrapped in itself and out of touch with what surrounds it. Moreover, the flames that hide the sinners increase Dante's curiosity to the point where he nearly falls over the cliff:

Io stava sopra il ponte a veder surto,
sì che, s'io non avessi un ronchion preso,
caduto sarei giù senza esser urto.

(I was standing on the bridge, upright to look,
so that, if I had not seized a rock,
I should have fallen without being pushed.)

We feel his impatience in many subtle touches, as he demands information from Virgil, especially in the following repetitive passage:

"maestro, assai ten prego,
e riprego che il prego vaglia mille,
che non mi facci dell' attender niego,
finchè la fiamma cornuta qua vegna;
vedi che del disio ver lei mi piego."

("Master, I strongly pray you,
and re-pray, that my prayer may be worth a thousand,
do not forbid me to wait
until the horned flame comes here;
you see that with desire I bend me toward it.")

Virgil's reply is a definition of the action of the whole canto: the God-given thirst for knowledge which goes wrong by failing to be guided by the objective situation:

"La tua preghiera è degna
di molta lode, ed io però l'accetto;
ma fa che la tua lingua si sostegna."

("Your request
is worthy of much praise, and so I accept it;
but see that you restrain your tongue.")

The word *lingua*, "tongue," refers not only to Dante's impatient speech, but by implication to Ulysses' tongue, which argued himself and his companions into their fond voyage; and also to the towering tongue of flame, the heedless consciousness of need, which still enwraps Ulysses' spirit.

Virgil, though not himself an impatient character, is drawn into the drama (as usual) because he is obliged to handle both Dante and Ulysses. He will not allow Dante to question Ulysses and Diomed because, being Greeks, they "might disdain" Dante's words. He seems to assume, here, a curious snobbery, as though the legendary hero were a football champion in a boy's school. He does not share either Ulysses' or his pupil's headlong drive, but here in hell he is obliged to play their game, flattering Ulysses and indulging his pupil's frantic curiosity; and his little part in the drama throws an unexpected and ironic light on the action.

After the two introductory parts we are ready for Ulysses' narrative, which carries the *moto spiritale* of the canto to its climax and catastrophe. It is one of the summits of poetry, for Dante intends to make his readers share Ulysses' drive, and for this purpose he employs his full poetic magic to seduce us. One might say that in Ulysses' *folle volo,* "fond flight," across the ocean floor and past far islands, the Homeric spirit lives again in a wholly new context; or one might say (thinking of his fear of dying before he has experienced all there is) that he embodies a startlingly modern spirit of exploration—daring and faithless. However that may be, the reader must share the exhilaration of the voyage, believe with Ulysses that the Mountain which appears on the horizon in the empty sea means the triumph of his daring; and, when the boat goes down, know unexpected and incomprehensible grief. If we read on to the *Purgatorio* we learn that the Mountain is the Mount of Purgatory, a figure of that patient labor which Ulysses thought he could do without. But here in hell we are expected to know and share Ulysses' movement of spirit, just as Dante the traveler does, without placing it in the moral-religious scheme. Ulysses' story is plotted like Francesca's, as a modern or Euripidean type of tragedy, in which the action, without ever turning from ignorance to knowledge, proceeds to its end in an undigested catastrophe.

In this canto, as in many others, Dante has combined surprisingly diverse elements to represent the one action: the great tirade against Florence; the traveler's childish impatience; the mysterious fires that flicker in the black valley; the wonderful, mad westward flight, with the coasts of Sardinia and Spain dropping behind us, just as they do now when we take that flight by air. Each effect, as we read, has its beauty and its interest, but to enjoy the poetry fully it is necessary to linger over it until one sees the whole canto as *one* poem. That is also the only way to grasp the action Dante is presenting here: not Ulysses, for his own sake, nor the travelers for the sake of their involvement, but the *moto spiritale* they share by analogy, "Man, in the exercise of his freedom of choice," trying to satisfy the needs of his rational soul without regard to his situation in God's world.

"Fated Going": The Traveler's Descent through Hell

Dante arranged the sins in hell according to the best authorities he knew, Aristotelian and Christian. Virgil summarizes the scheme in Canto XI: the sins of incontinence are in upper hell; then come the heretics; then the violent of many kinds, then the fraudulent, and at the bottom of the universe, in Cocytus, the treacherous. The sins of incontinence, like Francesca's, are the easiest and most natural, and do least damage to the soul, while treachery is the most lethal of all.

This scheme has its own interest and sheds some light on Dante's conception of the life of the psyche. But in the structure of the poem it has merely the function of the floor plan of a theatrical setting: it is a framework for visibly spreading out the actions before us. The life of the poem is in the characters, who embody the human pathos in each realm, and in the travelers who descend from circle to circle until they reach the bottom. We never feel that Dante has *made* the infernal setting, even as the author of the poem that so imaginatively embodies it; he accepts it, rather, as philosophy and religion have described it, and as he has confirmed it in his own experience of evil. And so Dante, as the *traveler*, is free to react in many different ways to the objective reality of God's punishment: *al cominciar*, he says (Canto III), *ne lagrimai*, "at first it made me weep." He does not have to pretend to understand or endorse Francesca's punishment, or to be immune to Ulysses' proud passion. In every part of hell he may himself be drawn into the "life" of the lost; as is most evident, perhaps, in Cantos V, X, XIII, XV, XVI, XXXII, and XXXIII.

In those great cantos the traveler's motive is analogous to that of the lost spirits; but how are we to understand his movement from one circle to another, and from bad to worse? There is something a little paradoxical about pursuing evil, unless (as in cases like that of "saint Genet") the motive is frankly depraved and pornographic. It is interesting to see how Dante motivates the long descent, and how he holds the reader's interest and sympathy, without either wallowing in evil, or pretending to be immune to it.

Dante assumes that part of God's assignment, in requiring him to go through hell, was to see and to report. Sometimes, while on the way with Virgil, or while passing through a region whose inhabitants don't involve him intimately, this motive comes to the surface: we become aware of Dante as author, regaling us, like any traveler returned from far-off places, with tall tales of marvels he has seen or heard of. In this manner he reports Virgil's account of the legendary Old Man of Crete (Canto XIV) or of the witch who founded Mantua (Canto XX). This "epic" or narrative manner is varied in many ways, in order to express the *moto spiritale* of that part of hell. In Cantos XXIV and XXV, for instance, where he recounts the transformations of thieves into lizards and vice versa, he adopts the taleteller's manner, and mocks it at the same time (Canto XXV, line 91):

> Egli il serpente, e quei lui riguardava;
> l'un per la piaga, e l'altro per la bocca
> fumavan forte, e il fummo si scontrava.
> Taccia Lucano omai, là dove tocca
> del misero Sabello e di Nassidio,
> ed attenda ad udir quel ch'or si scocca.

> (He stared at the snake, and the snake at him;
> one through his wound, the other through his mouth,
> smoked strongly, and the smokes met.
> Now let Lucan be quiet, there where he treats
> of wretched Sabellus and Nasidius,
> and wait to hear what I utter now.)

In this passage the author's fascination with his own thief-inspired poetizing, mingled as it is with horror, carries us on down.

Virgil also accounts for a good deal of the motivation on the way down. He is like a trainer in the army or in a gymnasium, whose task is to get his pupil through his ordeals. When Dante faints, as he does twice near the beginning of the journey, Virgil silently carries him down to the next circle, but he does not usually approve of his pupil's indulging in too much pity for the lost. Sometimes he will warmly praise Dante's anger, notably in Canto XIX, when Dante scornfully assails the simoniac Popes, thus adding his mite to the castigation of God. But in the next canto he scolds Dante for weeping in sympathy when he sees the diviners, their heads turned backward on their shoulders, irrigating their buttocks with their tears (XX, line 28):

"Qui vive la pietà quando è ben morta.
Chi è più scellerato che colui
che al giudicio divin compassion porta?"

("Here pity lives when it is quite dead.
Who is more impious than one
moved to compassion by divine judgment?")

Sometimes Virgil demands an effort of the will and the muscles, usually when the only way to continue is to negotiate a cliff or a rock-slide; but he never tries to lure his pupil onward with the promise of anything good or pleasant. In general, his coaching always re-emphasizes what he said at the beginning, just as they passed Hell Gate: Dante must simply accept the will of God without question, and with all the courage he can summon.

The will of God is a much more important cause of the whole journey through hell than anything the travelers themselves might try to do there. We are made to feel the relentless power of God, and the helplessness of the lost humans, in every circle; and in the transitions from one circle to the next below, where the focus is on the travelers, we learn that they too are obeying what they can neither understand nor dispense with.

This is all made explicit—or as nearly so as such things can be in hell—during the first major transition, that from the upper hell of the incontinent to the far graver City of Dis. The demons on the city wall refuse to admit the travelers, and Virgil himself can do nothing: he and Dante can only try to conceal their dismay from each other until the "messenger of heaven" arrives and scornfully forces the demons to open the gates. The literal narrative of this episode (Canto VIII, line 64—Canto IX, line 106)—the evil city with its towers glowing through the misty dark; its "grave citizens" and vast throngs; Virgil's covering his pupil's eyes lest the Medusa come and turn him to stone; the arrival of heaven's messenger (preceded by storm), traversing the marsh with effortless speed while he languidly waves the foul air from his face—is as absorbing as the most wonderful of travelers' stories. But Dante also tells us (Canto IX, line 62) to "consider the doctrine hidden under the strange verses." It is not clear whether he expected his readers to extract an exact theological "doctrine"; if so, he has been disappointed, for the experts still eagerly dispute the fine points of this allegory. In any case, there is plenty of meaning to be found in the literal narrative. The changing relationships between Dante, Virgil, the evil spirits of pagan and Christian legend, and the heavenly messenger yield all sorts of psychological insights into this moment of despair, if one thinks them over. And even the frightened traveler, who sees only what is literally before him, can recognize that evil is not to be handled by human strength, or fathomed by human wisdom, alone; for he sees that a divine emissary was needed to rescue him and his beloved Virgil at this point in their fated journey.

The next important downward step is that from the realms of violence to the realms of fraud. The travelers accomplish it (Canto XVI, line 106—Canto XVII, line 136) by riding on the back of Geryon. This episode, like that before the walls of Dis, is full of signs that indicate the point we have reached on the downward path. Virgil fishes for Geryon in the darkness over the edge of the cliff, with a cord Dante wears around his waist: traditional sign of chastity. Does the cord represent a lure, as though to say that the badge of chastity is particularly tempting to fraud? The traveler knows, even then, that Geryon, with his face and bust of a mild father, his gaudily spotted reptile body, and scorpion-tail flickering in the void behind him, is an "image" of fraud; thus Geryon shows, like a traffic sign, how far they've come on their road. But his immediate poetic-dramatic function is not to enlighten us, but to give us the experience of deepening evil. His appearance alone, like that of a well-designed property on the stage (and like the usurers' purses stamped with armorial bearings that we see in the same canto) can give one the irremediable discouragement of artificial hideousness. But Geryon is also a practicable prop; and it is when we mount the scaly back, push off backward into the empty dark, and sink with a despair like that of Phaëthon and Icarus in their guilty falls from the sky, that we get the experience that Dante means his artifact-monster to give us.

The descent on Geryon is perhaps the most elaborate use that Dante makes of gravitation, his basic symbol of the fated motivation of hell. Dead weight is felt in the ruined cliffs and causeways that collapsed when Christ harried hell; in the rivers and waterfalls eternally seeking the bottom; and in many minor transitions made by Virgil and Dante. Every descent expresses not only the fatality of the whole journey, but the particular nature of the realm. To escape the perilous horseplay of the barrators and their attendant demons, Virgil has to seize Dante and slide down the face of the rock (Canto XXIII). To reach the lowest circle, Cocytus, the travelers have to depend on the dim giant Antaeus to swing them down—a simpler, colder and more mechanical version of the ride on Geryon. It is in Cocytus that the descent, and the falling of all heavy bodies, stop.

I have pointed out that the classification of sins built into the physical structure of hell has its moral and psychological significance, but that Dante, as he explores the realms of the damned, does not necessarily reflect the relative deathliness of each sin in his own reaction to it. "Hypocrisy, flattery, sorcerers, cheating, theft and simony, panders, barrators, and like filth," (as Virgil says in Canto XI) are much farther down than Paolo and Francesca, for their falsity "kills the natural bond of love," as Virgil puts it (Canto XI, line 55 ff.). But the traveler does not share their sufferings as he does Francesca's—no doubt just because such sins do kill love. He is afraid of the barrators (Canto XXI and XXII) and sickened by the stench of the flatterers (Canto XVIII), but his attitude is that of the scornful tourist, not the deeply involved fellow sufferer. Thus the infernal journey is plotted, not as a single dramatic action with a beginning, middle, and end, but rather as a series of actions, an episodic, boldly varied narrative, a traveler's autobiography. Much of the hellishness of the trip is due to this apparently unfathomable variety, and Dante the author is careful to allow his travelers (and his readers) no pause, no chance to digest the sharp, successive visions on the way down.

In the structure of the *Commedia* as a whole, the *Inferno* is analogous to the prologue of a tragedy. It is a long, sharply varied period of dismay, a "pathos" of uncomprehending terror, out of which the more conscious and self-motivated action of the drama proper will arise as soon as the protagonist gets the clue. Dante cannot begin to "get the clue"—see his own way—in hell. But the experience has a fundamental effect upon him, as one can see by noticing how he crosses icy Cocytus, the last leg of the trip.

The Making of Cocytus (Canto XXXII)

The last three cantos of the *Inferno* are devoted to Cocytus, the realm of treachery, which Dante (like Shakespeare) regarded as the deathly sin. Simple fraud *uccida/ pur lo vinco d'amor che fa natura,* "kills only the bond of love that nature makes," as Virgil says (Canto XI, line 55); but treachery, fraud of the worst kind, kills also the more intimate bond—which is trust—between members of one family, or city, or party; or between a protector or benefactor and the recipient of such kindness. For Dante, human "life consists in action," i.e., love, the movement of the spirit; and the spirit must have trust if it is to "move" toward the persons or the things or the ideas that would fulfill and nourish it. Treachery does not destroy love, for love is inherent in the indestructible human soul; but it destroys trust, and so isolates the soul, turning its love from a vital to a deathly and futile aim.

Cocytus occupies a crucial spot, not only in the *Inferno,* but in the morally significant cosmic setting of the whole *Commedia.* It is the hollow center of the sphere of earth, and therefore "the bottom of the universe," the point toward which all *gravezza* ("heaviness"), all heavy things, converge. All the rivers of hell find their way down to Cocytus, to form its ice; upon it "lean all the other rocks," as Dante puts it (XXXII, line 3). Weight is here, but as motionless pressure, not downward motion; and in this dead center Dante thinks of other forms of kinetic energy, especially heat and light, as having ceased also, in a kind of stalemate.

In *Convivio* III Dante explains that the tendency of heavy objects to move toward earth's center is a form of "love," analogous to what moves fire, and to what makes the life of plants, animals, and the human psyche. Man, as sharing vegetable and animal modes of life, and as a physical body, knows all the forms of love; but the rational love that makes him human aspires "upward" while the body perpetually pulls downward. "The soul," says Virgil (Canto XXIV, line 53) "wins every battle,/ if with its heavy body it sinks not down." In Dante's scheme the "heavy body" often represents what pulls the rational soul away from the path to its own fulfillment; as pointed out before, *gravezza* prevails during the whole downward journey. Dante will continue to feel it all the way up the Mount of Purgatory, especially at night, when weariness and "the old Adam" take over and he sinks to sleep, and then sees, in dream-visions, the possibility of sinking back into hell itself. Dante is freed from this mortal heaviness only when he gets to the top of the Mount of Purgatory, is miraculously lightened, and speeds upward toward his supernatural goal beyond the stars.

There are many subtle analogies between the conception of the physical Cocytus, where the downward movement of all the heavy things in the universe ends in cold paralysis, and the state of the human soul whose movement of betrayal perpetually betrays *itself* into frustrated solitary confinement. Cocytus is, therefore, a perfect setting for the final movement of the *Inferno*. We tend to forget that it is a product of Dante's *poetando*: it seems (like other classic formulations of human nature and destiny) inevitable, a discovery of fundamental and inescapable analogies, rather than an invention. It is, however, only the setting; Dante has still to find the character, incident and language which will make this realm perceptible.

The last three cantos represent essentially one action, in three stages; and at the beginning of this final sequence, Dante speaks out as the poet who will now attempt to bring both the setting and the paradoxical action concretely before us (XXXII, line 1):

S'io avessi le rime aspre e chiocce,
  come si converebbe al tristo buco,
  sopra il qual pontan tutte l'altre rocce,
io premerei di mio concetto il suco
  più pienamente; ma perch'io non l'abbo,
  non senza tema a dicer mi conduco:
chè non è impresa da pigliare a gabbo
  descriver fondo a tutto l'universo,
  nè da lingua che chiami mamma e babbo.
Ma quelle Donne aiutino il mio verso,
  ch'aiutaro Anfion a chiuder Tebe,
  sì che dal fatto il dir non sia diverso.

(If I had rhymes harsh and hoarse,
  such as would fit the sad hole
  upon which lean all the other rocks,
I should press out the juice of my conception
  more completely, but since I do not have them,
  not without fear do I bring myself to speak:

For it is not a task to undertake as a joke—
to describe the bottom of all the universe—
nor for a tongue that calls mamma and papa.
But may those Ladies help my verse
who helped Amphion to close up Thebes,
so that my words may not diverge from the fact.)

Dante admits with a rueful smile that he fears he is, as poet, a mere infant in this setting. But he will beseech the inspiration of the Ladies (the Muses) who enabled Amphion, with his song, to move rocks in order to wall up Thebes, a city Dante always associates with faithless cruelty; and he will try, in making his poem, to act as God had acted in making Cocytus itself, "pressing" his conception, "closing" the city of treachery. In the words of his formula, he will follow as closely as possible the terrible "dictation" of God's love, moved by justice, which he has "noted within," and now remembers.

After the short prologue and invocation, Dante the traveler comes into focus again as he looks about him in Cocytus. We soon begin to realize that as traveler, also, Dante is identifying his will with the punishing will of God. The man who made the hellish journey has now come very close to the man who remembers and records it. The traveler who wept, at first, has now been so toughened that he can not only endure, but endorse, the desolation before him, just as the poet coldly and willfully reaffirms it in all the knowing acts of his art.

It is, I think, chiefly by means of the cold that Dante (entering Cocytus) unifies our impressions of the place of the lost spirits we meet there, and of the condition of his own inner being. One can hardly read about the lake (line 22) frozen too hard to creak without a chill. We learn what the cold does to the damned when we read (line 46):

gli occhi lor, ch'eran pria pur dentro molli,
gocciar su per le labbra, e il gelo strinse
le lagrime tra essi, e riserrolli.

(their eyes, that before were only wet within,
gushed upward at the lids, and the cold squeezed
the tears between them, and closed them up again.)

The spirit that has done the coldest thing cannot be thawed even in its own grief. In this imagery the act of treachery and its fate is perfectly represented, and Dante repeats it, with slight variation, in the next canto. As the traveler proceeds, "shivering in the eternal shade," he kicks the head of one frozen in the ice, without regret; and when that spirit won't tell who he is (though Dante pulls out several tufts of his frozen hair), he takes advantage of the fact that another spirit betrays his name. Treachery is the deathly custom of this country, and the closer the traveler comes to "the center/ at which all *gravezza* unites" (line 74), the closer his own motive comes to the mode of love which (as God wills) makes this cold prison for its eternal dwelling.

Ugolino (Cantos XXXII and XXXIII)

Ugolino's story of his death, in which the destiny of the spirit's movement of treachery is fully dramatized, dominates Cantos XXXII and XXXIII. It begins at XXXII, line 124, when the travelers come upon Ugolino frozen in the ice with the Archbishop Ruggieri and desperately gnawing his skull.

Ugolino, Conte di Donatorico, was a great lord in the region of Pisa—at the beginning of his career a leader of the Ghibellines. In the course of the savage struggles between Guelf and Ghibelline, Ugolino betrayed the Ghibellines to the Guelfs when the latter seemed to be winning. When the Ghibellines regained the upper hand, he betrayed the Guelfs to them, and, for good measure, one of his own sons. He accomplished this last treachery with the connivance of his supposed ally, Archbishop Ruggieri, who then betrayed *him* to the angry Pisans. Ugolino and his four young sons (as Dante mistakenly thought them) were left to starve to death in prison.

Ugolino does not tell this story, for he assumes that the Tuscan traveler will know it; it is, in fact, the kind of cruel and faithless intrigue that Dante had known in many instances, at first hand. Moreover Ugolino, like the other lost souls, has no wish to understand, or to repent, his treachery. He is still driven by the insatiate hatred that moved him on earth, before his death; and his purpose, as he tells the traveler (XXXIII, line 8) is "to breed infamy to the traitor I am gnawing." For this purpose he recounts only his end, remembering Ruggieri's betrayal but not his own.

There is nothing in Ugolino, as he wipes his mouth on the

wasted skull, to enlist our sympathy; and nothing in the desolate cell he describes, with the little hole through which the moon peers briefly, to warm us to his story, nor in his sinister and prophetic dream of the Archbishop, with his lean and eager hounds hunting down the wolf and his whelps. But when he wakes from his dream he hears his little boys asking for food in their sleep, and we realize that they are with him: "If you do not weep," Ugolino asks, at this point in his story, "at what are you used to weep?" We are, by now, ready and eager to weep, but the story continues in such a way as to deny us the release of tears. Ugolino can say nothing when the boys ask him for bread, for he has heard the key turn in the lock, and knows no bread will ever be forthcoming. The boys see his distress, but when they ask him what it is, he cannot tell them. When he gnaws his hands in agony, and the boys, thinking he is famished, offer themselves for food, he "quiets himself" not to distress them more. Little Gaddo dies, asking, "Father, why don't you help me?" but there is nothing Ugolino can say, and nothing he can say as the others die one after another. We might dissolve in tears when the story ends in Ugolino's death, as "fasting proved stronger than grief," were it not that he instantly turns back to the wretched head with "teeth strong as a dog's on the bone."

By means of the intricate and original plot of this brief story, Dante has presented exactly the same frustrated movement of spirit as he had in the image of the tears that are frozen before they can gush out. We are made to feel, in the hunger of Ugolino and the boys, and much more intimately in the boys' need to trust their father, and his need to respond to their trust, the *amor* that wells up perpetually in the human spirit, causing it to seek its natural fulfillments. This movement is then paralyzed in a series of crueler and crueler figures; and just as Ugolino can say nothing to his young sons, so the reader is too chilled by Ugolino's savagery to weep in sympathy. Dante uses the death of the little boys (which would have been a mere tear-jerker in the hands of a less controlled and scrupulous artist) to give us a hard, desolate experience as closely analogous as possible to that of the soul that has betrayed.

Ugolino's story is parallel to that of Paolo and Francesca, whom we met at the beginning of the infernal journey. Ugolino and Ruggieri, like Paolo and Francesca, are joined to each other for all eternity, but by cold hatred instead of warm and youthful lust. Ugolino, like Francesca, weeps and tells at once; like Francesca, he wants to pull the hearer into his plight. Francesca succeeds, for Dante the traveler is so overcome by her story that he is carried deeper into hell, but he apparently hears Ugolino as stonily as Ugolino has to hear his child's crying for food; for when the story is ended, he curses Pisa, "another Thebes," as though, like Amphion, he would wall up the whole city with his black incantation. Thus he is capable, here in Cocytus, of identifying himself almost completely with the will of God, that treachery should make for itself so bleak a world; while up above, entering hell, he could not accept Francesca's fate, and identified himself almost completely with her suffering.

In what is left of Canto XXXIII Dante enters the Tolomea, the lowest suburb of Cocytus. There he proves that he can not only take advantage of the treachery of the treacherous, as he had in his encounter with Bocca degli Abbati (Canto XXXII), but coldly and consciously practice treachery himself. He meets Friar Alberigo, who tells his story on the understanding that Dante will repay him by breaking the ice that seals his eyes. Having finished his story (line 148):

> "Ma distendi oramai in qua la mano,
> aprimi gli occhi"; ed io non gliele apersi,
> e cortesia fu in lui esser villano.

> ("But reach me your hand here,
> open my eyes"; and I did not open them for him,
> and it was courtesy to be mean to him.)

Dante the traveler does not digest hell as he descends through it. But the experience (like that of men who spent years in combat during the last war) hardens his spirit, and one can measure the change in him by comparing his reactions here in Cocytus with his reactions when he first meets the sights and sounds of hell.

Lucifer: The End of Hell in Two Senses (Canto XXXIV)

In Dante's Thomistic philosophy Evil has no independent existence; it exists only as an attribute of things that do have substantial being. A man is called evil when he loves what is harmful, but the loving soul, God's creation, is not originally evil in itself: it becomes so by mistaking its object, as Virgil explains in *Purgatorio* XVII and XVIII. That is why Dante had to represent Ugolino's *amor* (hunger for food and the love of his children), in order to show his being as a human spirit, and thus substantiate his evil and Ruggieri's. It is in Ugolino's famished hatred in the ice, and in his famished love for his children in their narrow cell—that is, in his lost movement of spirit—that evil is brought home to us. Yet his movement of spirit, a betrayal, kills the bond of trust, and so freezes our love; and evil, less nourished by our sympathy, begins to appear as mere paralysis, negation, the void.

Dante seems to have planned the last three cantos of the *Inferno*, the crossing of Cocytus and the passage out the other end, so as to dramatize these paradoxes of evil in the experience of the traveler. Leaving Friar Alberigo and Branca d'Oria, and pushing on in accord with God's appalling will, he loses all touch with human spirits: they are there, but like bits of straw in ice, silent and motionless. There is no movement but that of Lucifer, "emperor of the dolorous realm"; and he is an elaborate and horrifying artifact, a sign marking the mysterious *terminus ad quem* and *terminus a quo* of the infernal journey.

The mythic Lucifer, as the brightest angel, God's fairest creature, could qualify as emperor of hell, for he betrayed God Himself, fell from heaven, pierced the earth, and, as the earth shrank away from him in revulsion, hollowed out this deepest pit. But Dante (much more skeptical and cautious than Milton) had no intention of dramatizing the story, or making Lucifer into a living, individual character: if one comes to him expecting another and (if that were possible) more intense Ugolino, one is disappointed. He refers to the myth merely to indicate the *notion* of the first and greatest sinner; and then he makes the visible Lucifer the keystone in the physical-moral structure of hell. His helplessly beating bat-wings make the wind that freezes the infernal streams that converge here. His huge bulk (as we gradually make out) pierces the earth's center, so that the middle of his body is the point where all weights tend. His bodily "edifice" as Dante calls it (line 7) signifies so many theological meanings that the experts are still discussing them. Suffice it to say that the three sinners he is chomping in his three sets of fangs represent treachery toward order both human and divine, for Brutus and Cassius betrayed the empire, and Judas betrayed Christ Himself; and that his three faces—red, yellowish-white, and black—suggest a negative simulacrum of the Trinity, such as malice, impotence, and ignorance.

The style that Dante employs for representing Lucifer, or Satan—clear only visually, "like a Satan in a fresco in Siena," as Eliot put it—is the style he used for the Old Man of Crete (Canto XIV) and the monster of fraud, Geryon (Cantos XVI and XVII). More theology is signified in the ugly parts of Satan than in the metallic body and clay foot of the huge Old Man, or the fatherly bust and reptile tail of Geryon, but the poetic-dramaturgic principle is the same in all three images. They are not *dramatis personae,* for we are not put in touch with the spirit (if any) that moves them; they are like stage properties, or ecclesiastical iconographs: unspeaking signs of much philosophy and theology. Dante's purpose in adopting this style (as he does from time to time until the end of the *Purgatorio*) is to present an unfathomed mystery, the "letter" without the "spirit." He presented the unfathomable mystery of evil in the uninterpreted inscription on Hell Gate, and now, at the bottom, he presents it again in the visible but speechless body of Satan.

The poetic-dramatic effect of this canto is to be found not so much in Satan as in the traveler, just as it was when Dante saw Hell Gate with its "hard" words. But what happens to the traveler when he sees Satan can only be suggested (line 22):

> Com'io divenni allor gelato e fioco,
> nol domandar, lettor, ch'io non lo scrivo,
> però ch'ogni parlar sarebbe poco.
> Io non morii, e non rimasi vivo:
> pensa oramai per te, s'hai fior d'ingegno,
> qual io divenni, d'uno e d'altro privo.

> (How frozen and faint I grew then
> do not ask, reader, for I do not write it,
> since any speech would be inadequate.
> I did not die, and did not stay alive:
> think now for yourself, if you have a bit of wit,
> what I became, deprived of both alike.)

We can take it that he has a moment of "suspended animation," for here love, the spirit's life and movement, is utterly denied; but Dante does not try to find metaphors to make us feel that state, he gives us the fact only. So we reach the *terminus ad quem* of the *Inferno,* a pole of experience beyond the resources of art.

After this moment, Satan is described with scrupulous accuracy, so that we can see him with literal clarity. But, like Geryon, he is not only a visible but also a usable property, and must serve as "stairs" for the final descent. The descent on Geryon gave us the sickening and frightening sensation of falling, for we were approaching deeper evils; but here, as soon as Virgil says (line 68) "night is reascending, and now/we must depart, for we have seen it all," our attention is entirely focused on the physical feat of Virgil's climbing, with Dante clinging around his neck, down Satan's shaggy flank. We forget Satan as the bottom of all evil; he might be any cliff tufted with frozen herbage. When Virgil, passing the center of gravity, laboriously turns his head where his feet had been, we are struck mainly by the ingenuity of this device for signifying the turn of the spirit away from heaviness and/or evil. And when we finally dismount at the edge of a rocky opening, and look down at the "emperor of the dolorous realm," we see him absurdly suspended, upside down in the dark void. So he signifies the *terminus a quo,* evil from which we are released, and from which, therefore, we may turn away almost with indifference. After a few geographical explanations by Virgil, the travelers start their long climb back to the "bright world" where they can "see again the stars."

It is impossible to understand what Dante does with the end of the *Inferno* unless one considers the last three cantos as a dramatic unit, the imitation of a single action. One can, as usual, notice Dante the singing-narrator taking breath at the beginning of each canto for a new poetic effort; and each canto does mark a stage of the trip from Caina to Tolomea. But the setting is one, representing the basic situation of the lost spirits that have betrayed, and the traveler's action, like that of the recording poet, follows closely the eternal punishing act of God, until the mysterious point where guilt and punishment "end" in Lucifer. Only by following this action as revealed in relation to the frozen spirits can one see how "right" the deathly artifact of Satan is: the sign that the descent through Cocytus and through all hell ends here.

Because this sequence represents a pole of human experience, it is a good place to study Dante's virtuosity as dramatic poet, and also his undeluded honesty. The two qualities go together: he does not pretend to understand what is beyond him, nor to give his reader adequate images of what the reader himself has never experienced. But what the resourceful art of poetry can do, he does here.

III

The *Purgatorio*

The *Purgatorio* as the Center of the *Commedia*

In the first lines of the *Purgatorio* Dante tells his readers just what his new motive is, as poet:

> Per correr miglior acqua alza le vele
> omai la navicella del mio ingegno,
> che lascia retro a sè mar sì crudele.
> E canterò di quel secondo regno,
> dove l'umano spirito si purga
> e di salire al ciel diventa degno.

> (To course better waters now hoists sail
> the little bark of my native talent,
> leaving behind it a sea so cruel.
> And I shall sing of that second kingdom
> wherein the human spirit is made clean,
> becoming worthy to ascend to heaven.)

His motive as poet is, as always, analogous to the motive that he had as traveler, when he first made the long climb up the Mount of Purgatory, to Beatrice and the Terrestrial Paradise. But the traveler (and the reader who follows his experience) will understand the action and passion of purgation in many ways as his moral sophistication grows: the journey is a journey of change and enlightenment.

In the dramatic form of the *Commedia* as a whole, the *Inferno* may be regarded as prologue, the *Purgatorio* as the development of the main action, the *Paradiso* as the final vision that emerges from the whole experience. The vision of the lost, so close to the dark wood of this life, presents the initial situation out of which the traveler's more positive action will arise, much as the plague in Thebes, sign of the gods' wrath, starts Oedipus on his investigation; or as the Ghost's revelation, in the prologue of *Hamlet*, impels the Prince to try to set the times right. Hell, as we have seen, is essentially a pathos, especially for Dante the traveler, with his "fated going." Purgatory shows how he revives in response to the beauty of the real world, and then slowly begins to move toward what he himself can see as good.

The dark wood, and then hell itself, reflect the evil Dante knew in his middle period, but the *Purgatorio* shows the good he found there: the Christianized Aristotelian philosophy that showed him the theoretical possibility, at least, of order in the human psyche and, analogously, in human society. While writing the *Convivio* and *De Vulgari Eloquentia*, Dante thought (as we have seen) that the classical vision of human life on earth was sufficient for him, but by the time he came to write the *Commedia* he saw man as having two goals, the earthly and the supernatural, as explained in *De Monarchia*. The *Purgatorio* shows how the traveler reaches the first goal, that of earthly fulfillment, which is "figured," as Dante puts it, in the garden at the summit. But when he gets there he finds that the whole climb—the moral and intellectual effort under Virgil's guidance—has been merely preparation for the Christian Revelation. And Revelation points beyond the earth and earthly reason altogether, to that ultimate object of faith and hope which will be explained in the *Paradiso*.

Dante, when he wrote the *Commedia*, believed that man is fulfilled, finally, only in the supernatural vision of God. For that reason the ultimate understanding of man—that is, of the entire journey of the *Commedia*—is to be found only in the *Paradiso*, where the spirit's movement reaches its goal. But Dante tells his patron Can Grande that the subject behind the whole fictive journey, including that of the *Paradiso*, is "Man as by good or ill deserts, in the exercise of the freedom of his choice, he becomes liable to rewarding or punishing justice" (*Epistola* X, 11). Even in the *Paradiso*, as we shall see, the human spirit is always the immediate subject, as it moves in countless ways in response to the beatific vision: so we see it enjoying its ultimate "reward"; but it is in the *Purgatorio* that we see both the nature of the spirit's life itself and the process whereby it "becomes liable to rewarding justice."

The *Purgatorio* must be thought of as the "center" of the *Commedia* in more ways than one. It occupies the arithmetical center, never an unimportant consideration in Dante's writings, for he attributed mystical significance to number. For us, however, it means more to note that it is the answer to hell; that it contains Dante's final vision of the nature of man's earthly fulfillment; and that it sets forth the spirit's life which will be the basis of the beatific vision of the *Paradiso*.

The proper way to read the *Purgatorio* is canto by canto, for the canto is the dramatic-poetic unit of composition, just as it is in the *Inferno*. My intention here, however, is not to offer a close reading but rather to show how the *Purgatorio* fits into the grand scheme of the *Commedia*, and to provide the general observations which I think essential. General considerations of form or structure are more important here than in the *Inferno*, for the movement is double, that of the literal story, and that of the traveler's growing awareness. And in the course of the *Purgatorio* the drama which was briefly suggested in *Inferno* I and II, that of the subtle and poignant interplay between Dante and his two guides, Virgil and Beatrice, moves to its climax and turning point at the top of the Mountain.

The Setting and the Time Scheme of the *Purgatorio*

The framework of the purgatorial journey is designed to show continual change: moral growth, and the widening of vision. The time scheme, three days and nights on the beach and the Mountain plus a final morning in the Terrestrial Paradise, contrasts with hell, which is as "timeless" as the subway. The nine scenes of the journey—the foothills of the *Antipurgatorio* (Cantos I–IX), the seven terraces on the steep flank of the Mountain, where the seven sins are repented (Cantos X–XXVII), and the meadowy plateau at the top (Cantos XXVIII–XXXIII)—also contrast with hell, where the scene of each circle is closed and changeless; for the pressures of hope and suffering are figured in the design of each scene in purgatory, and also in the upward path which connects them all.

The setting of the first day is the beach and the foothills at the base of the Mountain, and though there are a few supernatural signs of the grace that prevails in "the second kingdom," the scene is essentially that of earth as we know it. After hell it is freshly attractive (I, 13):

> Dolce color d'oriental zaffiro
> che s'accoglieva nel sereno aspetto
> dell' aer puro infino al primo giro,
> agli occhi miei ricominciò diletto
> tosto ch'i'uscii fuor dell' aura morta,
> che m'avea contristati gli occhi e il petto.

> (The tender color of the eastern sapphire
> which was gathering in the clear sight
> of pure air, as far as to the first gyre,
> restored to my eyes once more their delight
> as soon as I emerged from the dead air
> that had so saddened both my eyes and heart.)

This first scene, delicately suggested at various times of day in the first eight cantos, is familiar enough. But when the travelers pass through the gate of purgatory proper (Canto X), and the guardian angel marks seven P's, for the seven sins, on Dante's forehead, they enter the ancient path to freedom and knowledge which modern readers find more strange and difficult.

The first terrace is that of pride, a rocky ledge between the Mountain wall and a sheer drop on the other side. On the Mountain wall they see carved figures representing acts of humility, the Virgin Mary receiving the Annunciation, David dancing before the Ark, the Emperor Trajan yielding to the poor widow: figures taken (as always in the *Purgatorio*), from both Biblical and Classical literature. Proceeding a little farther they meet the repentant proud, bowed under heavy burdens of stone, like caterpillars bent into their pupa-cases to await the maturation that will release them as butterflies. Some of the humbled proud tell their stories; and then the travelers, leaving them behind, see at their feet thirteen carved images of the proud of history and legend, beginning with Satan himself. Then they meet another guardian angel, who removes one of the P's from Dante's forehead and invites them to the next ascent.

The basic pattern is repeated (though with continual variation in the mode of representation) in each of the seven terraces: Professor De' Negri has explained this clearly in his illuminating "Tema e iconografia del *Purgatorio*," and the following diagram is adapted from his study:

A				A
N	Examples	Souls	Examples	N
G	of	Repenting	of	G
E	Virtue	Their Sin	Sin	E
L				L

Considered in this way, abstracted from the temporal sequence of the climb, the symmetrical design of the path reminds one of a piece of ecclesiastical iconography, a painting or a bas-relief. But, as Professor De' Negri explains, one must think over both the movement across each terrace, and the relation of each terrace to the next above, in order to sense the meanings Dante has built into the intricate setting.

Virgil briefly suggests the meaning of the sequence *within* each terrace, when Dante hears voices recounting acts of loving generosity at the beginning of the terrace of envy (XIII, 37):

> E'l buon maestro: "Questo cinghio sferza
> la colpa dell'invidia, e però sono
> tratte da amor le corde della ferza.
> Lo fren vuol esser del contrario suono;
> credo che l'udirai, per mio avviso,
> prima che giunghi al passo del perdono."

> (And the good master said: "This circle scourges
> the fault of envy, and therefore
> from love are drawn the cords of the whip.
> The bit must be of contrary sound;
> I think you will hear it, so far as I know,
> before you reach the pass of pardon.")

Love of some kind is always the motive power of the psyche—the "whip" that drives it—but in purgatory, by the grace of God, we are made aware of the right form of love before we suffer, once more, the wrong form. The repentant proud have seen (in visible images) the humility they want, and those images define their motive, or drive. The "bit" is the cramping burden, the true condition of pride; it holds them back until they have suffered enough. Then they can move on, like the travelers, and see clear, classic instances of the fault which is now being left behind. The tension between "whip" and "bit"—the motive and what impedes it—produces the passion that purges. One can confirm the psychological accuracy of the formula if one remembers being painfully obsessed by some public mistake of one's own, until it has been "repented" long enough, and can be dismissed with a sigh of relief. The passions of hell are suffered to no further end; the passions of purgatory, on the contrary, are suffered in the light of better possibilities above and beyond.

One must also consider the relation between each terrace and those above, for in each one the "whip" and the "bit" are represented in a different medium, and the differences are significant. We have just noted that the examples of virtue and vice in the terrace of pride are represented plastically, as carved figures. In the terrace of envy (XIII and XIV) they are recounted by voices from an unknown source. In the terrace of anger (XV–XVII) they appear in the traveler's mind, like vivid daydreams or a poet's inspired visions. This sequence represents the continual growth in awareness of the ascending path, and also the more intimate *kind* of knowledge which the traveler acquires as he goes, learning to identify the truths of moral philosophy in his own psyche. But one must not jump to the conclusion that the design of the path points more and more inward, in this manner, all the way up; for new variations are introduced on the third day of the climb, when Dante begins turning from the erring psyche itself toward the goal above.

The examples of virtue and vice are, of course, appropriate to each terrace. The Virgin Mary is always the first example of the virtue we seek, and then come figures from the Bible, and from classical legend and history, in alternation. Because the Virgin appears each time, the episodes from her life that are represented may be studied as clues to the action of each part of the journey. Thus at the beginning of the climb (the terrace of pride) we see her humbly receiving the Annunciation; at the beginning of the third day (Canto XX) she appears in the stable giving birth, for during this day's climb the figure of Christ is, for the first time, faintly "born" in the traveler's awareness as he hastens upward.

These samples must suffice to suggest the nature of the nine-storey setting of the *Purgatorio*, but, of course, one might profitably study it all like a great religious painting of the period, noticing endless analogies between its "iconographical" parts, which suggest many subtle things about the process of purgation. As we read the poem, however, the setting serves, as in any drama, chiefly as a framework for spreading out the action: the traveler's changing and deepening quest for his own fulfillment. And, in the structure of the poem, the plan of the setting and the plot—the temporal sequence of incidents—are cognate.

There are two particularly revealing ways of describing the plot of the *Purgatorio*. The first is based on Bonaventura's *The Mind's Road to God*; the second, on the traditional four meanings of Scripture which Dante attributes to his poem.

Bonaventura's short work is one of the masterpieces of medieval philosophy, and it is very probable that Dante made conscious use of it in plotting the stages of his purgatorial quest. He puts Bonaventura in heaven, side by side with Aquinas, and Bonaventura's whole notion of the mind's "road" or "journey" is Dante's own conception of human life as *moto spiritale*. Certain it is that the spirit of Dante the traveler "moves" successively in the three directions that Bonaventura says the mind must take: outside ourselves (*extra nos*), then inside ourselves (*intra nos*) and finally above ourselves (*super nos*). These three "directions" are presented in the three days of the climb.

Thus during the first day (Cantos I–VIII) the traveler turns outward (as in the passage quoted earlier from the first canto) toward the delights of the natural world, and with an unpremeditated spontaneity like that of a child. The pretty natural world is also God's world, filled with signs of the Divine plan for man, if one could only read them. But at this stage the traveler does not know what is good for him; he cannot find the ascending path, and his aspiration remains unfulfilled.

When the traveler passes through the gate of purgatory proper (Canto IX), the questing spirit is turned "inside ourselves," to see itself as it moves away from the bad and toward the good. The traveler does not lose touch with the objective world of time—day, night, and change—as he was obliged to do in hell when exploring the private worlds of the lost. But as the path leads through the terraces where the proud, the envious, and the angry, in that order, resuffer the true nature of their vices in order to get rid of them, the traveler looks inward: he sees what the psyche is. The visible path itself, by God's grace, shows what is good and what is bad for the spirit: one may think of the examples of human vice and folly as cairns left by the early explorers of man's inner world. And as the day draws to a close Virgil can explain to his pupil, on the basis of all he has seen, the classic vision of the psyche's life as ceaseless "movement" toward its infinitely variegated goals, some good, some bad (Cantos XV–XVIII). This is the arithmetical center of the *Commedia,* and here the life of the spirit, *in itself,* is clearly seen.

During the third day (XIX–XXVII) the traveler's spirit begins to turn away from the psyche itself, and toward the unseen goal which is *super nos,* "above us." Dante continues to pass through terraces where vices are repented—the lighter vices of incontinence—but they are easy to understand after all we have seen below; and the traveler's interest shifts to signs, like the shaking of the Mountain (XX) and the appearance of Statius just risen from his long repentance, which indicate Christ, and thus point upward. This sequence ends in the *Paradiso Terrestre* with the pageant of Divine Revelation (XXX), the cumulative sign that directs the insatiate psyche *altogether* above ourselves: to heaven, where (we are to believe) the limitations of mortality are transcended, and the heart's deepest desire is objectively real and present to perception.

The journey from the beach at the foot of the Mountain to the meadow at its summit also represents the process whereby the traveler learns to see the moral, and then the allegorical, meaning of human life and action. In hell the traveler saw the literal reality of the lost spirits without perspective or detachment of any kind, sharing their recurrent movements of spirit by analogy; for neither he nor they had any *actual* sense of moral or religious truth by which to "place" the hellish experience. It is these two aspects of the human situation, the moral, and the beginning of the religious, that the traveler and the spirits he meets learn to see in purgatory—to see *actually,* i.e., in such a way as to determine the movement of their spirits.

During the first day of nostalgic wandering in the *Antipurgatorio* below the Mountain, the traveler and those he meets see only literally, as in hell, though of course *what* they see—ocean, foothills, sky—is in sharpest contrast to the infernal scene. During the second day, turning inward, the traveler acquires a double vision; he sees not only the spirit's ceaseless movement but the moral meaning of that movement; and Virgil outlines for him (Cantos XV–XVIII) the classification of the seven sins, the *moral* map of the whole trip. During the third day, turning outward again, being struck by signs of Christ, he is led up to the top, where the pageant of Revelation unrolls before his uncomprehending eyes the allegory, which is defined as *quid credas*, "what you must believe." That is as far as he gets, in purgatory, in his exploration of the four meanings of Scriptural exegesis. The whole *Paradiso* is devoted to the fourth, the anagoge.

The Traveler's Growing Awareness: The Poetry of Day and Night on the Mountain

> "And like a pilgrim who is travelling on a road where he hath never been before, who believes that every house which he sees from afar is the hostel, and finding that it is not directs his belief to another . . . even so our soul, so soon as it enters upon the new and never-yet-made journey of life, directs its eyes to the goal of its supreme good, and therefore whatever it sees that appears to have some good in it, it thinks to be it."
>
> —*Convivio* IV, xii

The passage on page 67 no doubt reflects Dante's own experience of growth and change, and the *Purgatorio* represents his final vision of the process. But instead of in the real world, he now places the pilgrimage in the second realm beyond the grave, where every detail of the nine-storey setting shows (by the grace of God) the true way. And instead of writing simply as the omniscient author, Dante now presents it all from the point of view of the traveler "who hath never been before"; and so "the center of interest is in his consciousness, and the drama is the very drama of that consciousness," as Henry James said of Rowland Mallet in his *Roderick Hudson.*

The general plan of the *Purgatorio* (pp. 138–139) indicates how different it is in form and motive from the *Inferno*. But the life and meaning of this *Cantica* is (as always) in the experience of the traveler, or rather in the poetry whereby Dante makes us share that experience. At each stage of the journey the traveler has a certain motive and a cognate mode of perception, just like the naïve but

DIAGRAM SUMMARIZING THE SETTING

Cantos	*Days of the Journey*	*Classification of Sins*	*Meaning of Visible Scene for Pilgrim and Reader*	*Pilgrim's* Moto Spiritale
I–IX	First	Saved but unable to begin work of growth	Illegible, like visible world of nature	Lyric aspiration and awareness
FIRST NIGHT				
IX–XIX	Second	Repenting pride, envy, anger, sloth	The condition of soul under particular sin, i.e., emptiness or darkness	Moral and intellectual effort leading to "soul's knowledge of itself"; Virgil's natural light
SECOND NIGHT				
XIX–XXVII	Third	Repenting avarice, gluttony, lust	Condition of sinful soul and Christ's sacrifice	Effort to transcend mortality or "time," i.e., slake natural thirst which nature alone cannot slake
THIRD NIGHT				
XXVII–XXXIII	Fourth: dawn to noon	Innocence regained	Human innocence in relation to Fall and Redemption	Immediate obedience to all he perceives

AND THE PLOT OF THE *PURGATORIO*

Pilgrim's Guide	*Fulfillment of Dante's Own Life*	Itinerarium Mentis in Deum	*Allegory of Theologians*
Virgil—as omniscient father	Childhood or potentiality of growth	Direction of soul's love is "extra nos"	Toward the Letter (*littera gesta docet*); exploration of scene of earth, short of grace of Revelation
Virgil—as coach and then as philosopher and teacher	Growth through abandonment of the *Convivio*	Love's direction "intra nos"	Toward the Trope (*moralia quid agas*); moral content of journey is brought to light
Virgil—as companion, plus Statius	Middle age, return to Beatrice from "Lady Philosophy"; Pilgrim approaches Author	Love's direction "super nos" via signs of *allegoria*	The allegory (*allegoria quid credas*); we move toward allegory of *Paradiso Terrestre*
Matelda	Vision of his own and (by analogy) humanity's purgation	"Super nos" but blocked by "letter" of allegory	Letter of Allegory, visible signs of *quid credas*

growing pilgrim Dante described in the *Convivio*. And Dante the poet, "noting" at each stage the "mode of love" that moved him then, "signifies" it in the appropriate mode of discourse. In making his plans for the *Purgatorio* Dante worked with blueprints of various kinds, but when he came to the actual writing he never allowed himself to lose touch with his poetic inspiration. And he counts on his *poetry* to lead the reader every step of the way.

Thus, during the first day, when the traveler cannot find the path, the verse is filled with such homesick music, and such imagery of different times of day in the natural world, as we know in countless romantic poems (VIII, 1):

> Era già l'ora che volge il disio
> ai naviganti, e intenerisce il core
> lo dì ch'han detto ai dolci amici addio;
> e che lo nuovo peregrin d'amore
> punge, se ode squilla di lontano,
> che paia il giorno pianger che si more.

> (It was the hour that turns backward the desire
> of travelers by sea, their hearts made tender
> by the day they told their sweet friends good-bye;
> and that pierces the new pilgrim with love
> if he hear, far off, chimes
> that seem to lament the dying day.)

The rhythms of action, and all the human relations, fall into Chekhovian patterns, for here in the *Antipurgatorio* Dante is (like Chekhov) imitating a pathetic, but not hopeless, motive. Some of the touching portraits in this style and mood are Buonconte, and La Pia (whom Eliot echoes in *The Waste Land*), both in Canto V; Sordello (VI and VII), and Nino (VII).

During the second day, as the mind awakens to itself, and the ancient splits between reason and passion appear, the poetic-dramatic style changes sharply. The moral conflicts in the soul and in the body politic are reflected by Marco Lombardo in Canto XVI, dialectically, and one may be reminded of the black-and-white world of French Baroque tragedy. The dominant imagery, especially at the end of the day (Cantos XV–XVIII) is, in fact, that of light and darkness—sharply contrasted in XV and XVI, an illusory premonition of the *Paradiso* in the moonlight of XVIII, when Virgil and Dante intuit the *moto spiritale* together.

This part of the trip reflects Dante's own rationalistic phase, the time of the *Convivio* and *De Vulgari Eloquentia.*

During the third day the traveler begins to feel (XXI, 1) that he is driven by:

> La sete natural che mai non sazia,
> se non con l'acqua onde la femminetta
> Sammaritana domandò la grazia,
>
> (The natural thirst, which nothing ever sates
> except the water which the little woman
> of Samaria begged for as a grace)

—i.e., by the need for an object of love quite outside Virgil's philosophy, true as it is; and the two travelers are joined by Statius, who is both an ancient Roman and a Christian. The imagery of this third day (bodily weight and lightness, eating and drinking, fattening and thinning, burning) makes us aware of the spirit as the perpetually fluctuating "form of the body." We become aware of high mountain country; and of the Rome of Virgil and Statius when their pagan culture was at its height and all was ready for Christ. Virgil, who never saw Christ, is very near the end of his road, and the swift and civilized intercourse between Dante, Virgil, and Statius may be described as high comedy against a sad background of unsatisfied longing—like *Le Misanthrope,* for instance, or *Love for Love,* or *The Ambassadors.*

Such, in very broad outline, is the traveler's experience by day as his moral sophistication grows. But the three nights he spends on the Mountain are also essential in the rhythm of purgation, for they bring understanding in a more mysterious way. By day the four stars the traveler saw, just before the dawn of the first day, are in the sky; and they are signs of the cardinal virtues—prudence, fortitude, temperance, and justice—which human reason had discovered before Christ. At night these four stars are below the horizon, and three different stars appear as signs of the attitude the psyche needs during the dark hours, when it lacks both the power and the vision to progress on its own. They signify faith, hope, and charity, "supernatural" virtues unknown before Revelation, and to be had, even now, only by the grace of God. In the theological terms of Dante's time, one may say that the alternation of day and night on the Mountain represents the interplay of "works" with faith, or of human effort in the light of natural reason with the unearned and unfathomable grace of God. Thomas Aquinas's treatise on grace, in which he traces its intricate interplay with human moral-intellectual effort, provides much insight into the day-night rhythm of the *Purgatorio*. But what I wish to call attention to here is the literal poetry of the three nights.

The first night (Canto IX) comes between the first day, filled with frustrated longing, and the second day, when moral-intellectual progress begins. It thus marks the fundamental reorientation of the traveler's spirit, and Dante gives a careful account of its three main stages: 1) sinking into sleep, 2) the sequence of dream images, and 3) awakening to a new vision of the situation.

1) On the evening of the first day, in the nostalgic valley of the negligent rulers (Canto VIII), the traveler sees, without really understanding, two signs of the grace that prevails here: the three stars of the night sky; and two birdlike angels, who frighten away a serpent that vaguely reminds us of Eve's old seducer. And then (Canto IX, line 10) he sinks to sleep as his weary spirit, having "something of the old Adam," accepts the recurrent truce with the heavy body, the *gravezza* that might, at any time, weigh us down to hell. Near morning he is ready for his dream (line 16):

> e che la mente nostra, peregrina
> più dalla carne e men da' pensier presa,
> alle sue vision quasi è divina,

> (when our pilgrim spirit, wandering
> farthest from the body and least caught in thought,
> is in her vision very near foreknowing)

To understand the detachment of the sleeping psyche according to Dante's psychology, one must reflect that when awake, the psyche is attached to the object which either the bodily senses or the thought of the waking mind discerns as good; and the objects of its attachment form or "actualize" it moment by moment. Separated by weariness or sleep from these objective attachments, the psyche is freer to respond to any solicitation that may reach it; its "potentialities" for both good and evil are wider. The moral passivity of night is dangerous, and were it not for the grace that prevails in purgatory, the psyche might be moved downward, back toward hell. But in this auspicious "second realm" night always turns the psyche upward, toward some truth it had not known how to see by day.

2) The dream that comes near morning presents the creative change which the psyche is suffering in such varied and ambivalent images as we all know in dreams. The traveler sees a gold-feathered eagle poised in the air above him and ready to swoop. He must be at that very place (he thinks in his dream) where Jupiter snatched up the shepherd Ganymede. The eagle swoops, carries him up in his claws, and they burn together in the fiery sphere: obvious, and consciously intended, erotic imagery. The burning wakes him, and as he comes to himself in terror he associates the experience with that of Achilles, whose mother, the immortal sea-nymph Thetis, carried him sleeping in her arms to the isle of Scyros, to save him from the Trojan war.

3) Fully awake, the traveler sees that the sun is already high and has been hot on his face. The faithful Virgil is beside him, and he says that a lady named Lucia (whom we last heard of in the prologue of the whole *Commedia, Inferno* II, as having moved Beatrice to move Virgil to help Dante) had carried the traveler up the Mountain while he slept. They are now in front of the Gate of Purgatory, which is brilliantly visible in the early light, and the work of the new day is cut out for them.

Both in Jupiter's rape of Ganymede and in Thetis' rescue of her son the dreamer plays a passive role, like a child: his eroticism is what Freud likes to call "polymorphous-perverse," for Dante is representing love unfixed by its habitual objects—open, like a child's, to good and evil. The eagle also has a number of possible traditional meanings besides that of the classical legend: the eagle is the symbol of empire, and of moral order, and also (in the medieval bestiaries) of "rebirth" through baptism. Both the eagle and Thetis carry the dreamer, who is frightened and at the same time honored, to a new place; and in the morning we learn that Lucia, who signifies "illuminating grace," has in fact literally transported the sleeper upward.

This elaborate iconographic and mythic imagery serves to place this first night within the vast symbolic setting of the *Commedia*, and one may profitably mull it over for a long time. But the basis of the whole episode is a familiar experience: a reorientation of the psyche during sleep, which brings fresh insight on waking. "Don't make a decision until you've slept on it," we tell each other when faced with a problem that looks insoluble. Many artists and original thinkers in science or mathematics tell us that the new inspiration, the unexpected angle of vision that cannot be deduced from what is consciously known, is an essential moment in the process of creative work. They learn how to prepare for it by thought and study, and then woo it with the proper mixture of longing, confidence, and humility. Dante's account of this propitious night, in its three stages, may be studied as an analysis of the extra-rational, or pre-conscious phase of the creative process—a most sophisticated analysis, because Dante (as we have seen) had been closely studying the workings of his own inspiration since the *Vita Nuova.*

The other two nights on the Mountain are less elaborately recounted, for they mark less important transitions. But the *sequence* of the three, and its relation to the daylight climb, throw a great deal of light on the traveler's growing enlightenment.

The second night is "in the middle of the journey," for it follows the great expositions of moral and political philosophy by Virgil and Marco, and reflects the time of Dante's own infatuation with *philo-sophia.* As the traveler approaches the hour of sleep (Canto XVIII), the light of the moon—and the light of Virgil's classic insights—makes the stars of faith, hope, and charity appear "more thin," and there is no other sign of grace. The traveler is still stimulated by his conversations, and by the swift passage of the repentant slothful, as he sinks to sleep (XVIII, 139):

Poi quando fur da noi tanto divise
  quell'ombre che veder più non potersi,
  nuovo pensiero dentro a me si mise,
del qual più altri nacquero e diversi;
  e tanto d'uno in altro vaneggiai
  che gli occhi per vaghezza ricopersi,
e il pensamento in sogno trasmutai.

(Then, when were so far parted from us
  those shadows, that they could no more be seen,
  a new thought was set within me,
from which various others sprang;
  and from one to another I so rambled
  that I closed my eyes in longing,
and thinking I transmuted into dream.)

Sleep is again associated with the heavy physical being, this time as earth, chilled by Saturn and the moon (XIX, 1); and the truth-telling dream again appears near dawn. The dreamer sees a hideous woman, but as he gazes at her, his gaze, like the sun warming night-stiffened limbs, makes her beautiful, "colors her pale face as love wills." She sweetly sings that she is the Siren; but a "holy and alert Lady" appears, angrily calling for Virgil. Virgil rips the clothes off the Siren's belly, without taking his eyes off the angry lady, and the stench of the belly wakens the dreamer. He finds that Virgil is, in fact, calling him, and they hurry upward in the new sunlight. Virgil notices that Dante is depressed, guesses that he has dreamed of the Siren and of her showing up, and like an experienced counselor in a boys' camp, tells his pupil not to worry about his erotic dream but to get ahead with the upward climb.

This dream is, of course, intended to be much clearer both to the traveler and to the reader than the first one was. Its eroticism is more like that of the adult male; the Siren is an easily legible figure of lust, or the unregenerate pleasures of the senses. Moreover, Virgil had told his pupil the night before that during the next day they would pass through the realm where the sins of incontinence are repented. The dream acts out the control of lust, as Virgil averts his eyes from the Siren, while making himself and his pupil aware of her stench. The dream is thus close to the traveler's waking awareness, both on the day before and the day after; no such inspired widening of vision is indicated as was shown in the first night. The identity of the "holy and alert Lady" is much discussed by experts, but she looks to me very much like the "Lady Philosophy" of Dante's rationalistic phase, who, as we learn in the *Convivio*, strongly disapproved of all his more earthly loves. At this stage in the traveler's progress the split between reason and passion, represented in the dream by the two contrasted women, is absolute; and Virgil cannot tell him how to heal it, but only how to control the lust that would pull the psyche from the path of reason.

By the evening of the third day (Canto XXVII) the traveler has passed through the terraces where avarice, greed, and lust are purged, and he himself has had to cross the wall of fire guarding Eden. He spends his last night on the Mountain sleeping between Virgil and Statius, like a goat between two shepherds; and in the morning Virgil tells him (XXVII, 115):

"Quel dolce pome, che per tanti rami
cercando va la cura dei mortali,
oggi porrà in pace le tue fami."

("That sweet apple which the care of mortals
goes seeking after through so many branches,
on this day will bring peace to all your hungers.")

He then certifies Dante, so to speak, as having learned his (Virgil's) wisdom:

Non aspettar mio dir più, ne mio cenno.
Libero, dritto e sano è tuo arbitrio,
e fallo fora non fare a suo senno:
per ch'io te sopra te corono e mitrio.

(No more expect my word, nor my signal:
free, upright and whole is your will,
and it would be a fault not to do as it says:
wherefore I crown and mitre you over yourself.)

We know that Dante is driven by the "natural thirst" which is never satisfied short of Divine intervention, and Virgil, of course, does not pretend to provide that. He means, I think, not that his pupil has transcended the mortal condition, or gotten rid of the body's appetites, but only that he has learned to understand the solicitations of the flesh and hold them at bay, as Virgil, with his unsatisfied longings, must do. The traveler knows how to live on earth; no priest or policeman is needed; he is at peace with himself and may now see the garden that "figures" earthly felicity.

This last night is, in fact, spent very near a threshold of experience more significant, even, than the one adumbrated in the first dream, on the night before purgation begins. For the traveler will soon meet Beatrice, lose Virgil, and enter a new and profoundly disturbing realm of experience. But he cannot know what that incomprehensible boundary between the human and the Divine will feel like until he crosses it; and this dream is the most peaceful of the three. Gazing at the three stars, "larger and clearer than their wont," he slides smoothly into sleep (XXVII, 91):

Sì ruminando, e sì mirando in quelle,
mi prese il sonno: il sonno che sovente,
anzi che'l fatto sia, sa le novelle.

(So ruminating, and so gazing at them,
sleep took me; the sleep which often,
before the fact may happen, knows the news.)

He dreams of Leah and Rachel as beautiful young women, traditional "figures" of the active and contemplative life, as Leah herself clearly says. This dream *does* know the news, for Leah and Rachel in their literal appearance are close to the two women Dante will see next morning in the Terrestrial Paradise: Matelda, singing and gathering flowers; and Beatrice, contemplating Christ. But they look, in the dream, as they might to Virgil: two modes of earthly fulfillment, the natural culmination of the purgatorial climb and of Virgil's rational explanations—*philo-sophia,* the contemplation of the truth; and active life *in accord* with truth. And the traveler will, in fact, see them first in this earthly perspective, only later in the awful light of Revelation.

We have seen that Dante, from the beginning of his career, thought that his inspiration as poet and seer came from the love that moved him: *amor cortese, philo-sophia,* and finally the love of God. The dreams on the Mountain represent the traveler's modes of love at various levels of the climb, and the cognate modes of vision. As usual, the mode of love is represented by a female figure. In the first dream, Lucia is unseen behind images foretelling ambiguously the two-day climb ahead; the traveler at that point cannot understand what moves him. In the second dream the Siren and the alert lady clearly show the split he feels in himself, the two opposite directions his love may then take; and in this conflict, the next day's double vision is foretold. In the last dream there are also two female figures, representing the love that moves the traveler, but they are in harmony, and closer than either of the other dreams to what the waking mind will literally see.

We know from what Virgil says in the prologue (*Inferno* I and II) that the spirit of Beatrice is the immediate cause of his appearance to Dante, there in the dark wood, and that Beatrice herself can only be accounted for as a mysterious grace that has come down from God. Virgil accomplishes his mission of guidance all through hell, and during the three days of the purgatorial ascent. But in the nights on the Mountain we are made to feel that Beatrice is not only the unseen goal of the journey, but a continuous, if hidden, *presence*. Dante will hear her bitterly say, when he finally meets her (*Purgatorio* XXX, 133):

> Nè impetrare spirazion mi valse,
> con le quali ed in sogno e altrimenti
> lo rivocai; sì poco a lui ne calse.

> (Nor did it avail me to beg inspirations,
> with which, in dream and in other ways,
> I called him back, so little did he care.)

The spirit of Beatrice must have been somewhere deep within Dante all his life, ever since its first appearance as recorded in the *Vita Nuova*—even though, in the middle of his journey it had seemed to split, into the lady of relentless passion one way (*la Pietra*, or the "Mountain Lady"), and Lady Philosophy the other way. One may think of the three women of the three dreams—Thetis, the "holy and alert Lady," and Rachel—as thinner and thinner disguises imposed by his spirit upon the disturbing spirit of Beatrice, as it gradually comes back into his consciousness.

Virgil

The spirit of Virgil accompanies Dante from the dark wood, through hell, and all the way up the Mount of Purgatory to the garden at the top—the Golden Age, Eden, the "figure," as Dante tells us, of man's earthly felicity. He is, therefore, a character of the greatest importance in the design of the *Commedia*; yet as we read the story we may get into the habit of taking him for granted, as Dante the traveler often does. Virgil is always modestly pointing away from himself, toward what his pupil needs to see and understand. One must make a point of noticing Virgil, in order to see that his role is developed with the greatest care, and embodies a great deal of the meaning and the pathos of the first two *cantiche*.

Virgil first appears in the dark wood, that strange realm (*Inferno* I and II) between this world, where Dante addresses us as the man and poet he is, and the fictive postmortem realm, where Dante takes his place, as traveler, among the spirits of the dead. Virgil is thus established as a character in the poem in the *proemio*, before the beginning of the *Inferno* proper. He himself says that the spirit of Beatrice is the immediate cause of his appearance here, but we soon see that Dante's own efforts have been essential also. When he first sees Virgil's ghostly figure, "hoarse with long silence" (*Inferno* I), he cries to him, "May the long study and the great love avail me/ which have made me search through your volume." Virgil comes out of his "volume," the *Aeneid*; the light of Dante's study, followed by the warmth of his love, must have brought Virgil's spirit to life before him, very much as his "gaze" gradually endows the Siren (in his dream in Canto XIX, *Purgatorio*) with her virulent voice and beauty.

We soon learn a good deal about the nature of Virgil's being, here in Dante's poem, written as it is more than thirteen hundred years after Virgil's death. It is a bad mistake to suppose (as we are sometimes told) that Virgil is a personification of reason. He is a master of classical reason, especially Aristotelian philosophy, but he is first of all the spirit of a real man (*Inferno* I, 67):

> Risposemi: "Non uomo, uomo già fui,
> e li parenti miei furon Lombardi,
> Mantovani per patria ambo e dui.
> Nacqui *sub Julio,* ancorchè fosse tardi,
> e vissi a Roma sotto il buono Augusto,
> al tempo degli Dei falsi e bugiardi.
> Poeta fui, e cantai di quel giusto
> figliuol d'Anchise, che venna da Troia,
> poi che il superbo Ilion fu combusto."

> (He answered: "Not a man, a man I was once,
> and my parents were Lombards,
> Mantuans both by country.
> I was born *sub Julio,* late though it was,
> and lived at Rome under the good Augustus,
> in the time of the false, deceitful gods.
> A poet I was, and sang of that just
> son of Anchises who came from Troy
> after proud Ilium was burned.")

All of these elements of his nature and destiny as an individual are important for his role in the *Commedia*: his mastery of classical poetry, his identification with the legend of Rome, his Mantuan origin, and his time—the Augustan age, when, as Dante believed, the world had reached its most civilized state and was ready for the Incarnation.

In Canto IV we visit the "eternal place" of Virgil's spirit: the quiet castle of the pagan sages under the hemisphere of light that separates it from the darkness of the rest of hell. They exist much as they did in their earthly life; "without hope we live in desire," as Virgil explains. In spite of the wonderful resonance of this formula, the traveler does not pause to explore its meanings; the pressures of hell constrain him to move on. The true scope of Virgil's mode of being—desiring what Christ revealed, but unable to hope for it—cannot be estimated until we reach a point high up on the purgatorial Mountain.

During the grueling descent through hell we come to rely on Virgil's courage, his familiarity with the rough terrain, and his resourcefulness in handling porters, ferrymen, crooked guides, and the like. When he is frustrated, as before the gate of Dis (Canto IX), we admire his candor and his concern for his frightened charge. And if we look closely we can see that he adjusts himself with wisdom and insight to the varied atmospheres of each part of hell, and to the needs of his pupil there. Virgil's knowing participation was pointed out in the brief dramas of Paolo and Francesca (page 105) and Ulysses (page 112). But Dante the traveler hardly tries to understand the subtleties of Virgil's motives in hell; it is all he can do to survive the journey itself.

With hell left behind, Dante begins to look about more freely, and Virgil to respond to the more salubrious realm and its sympathetic spirits. Purgatory, "where the human spirit is made clean,/ becoming worthy to ascend to heaven," is Virgil's own realm of experience, and in the context of each of the three days on the Mountain, Virgil is revealed in a new and wider, yet more familiar, light.

In the earthly scene of the *Antipurgatorio* Virgil is very much at home. And he can easily share the moods of the spirits who are compelled to pause there instead of proceeding straight to purgatory, those whom a violent death, or the church's excommunication, or merely their own dilatoriness, have prevented from finding the true path in life. Like Virgil, they "live in desire" for what they cannot have, though, of course, not "without hope" of reaching it at last. When Virgil meets the spirit of the poet Sordello (who lived in the first half of the thirteenth century), he explains his own situation in such a way as to bring out its similarity to Sordello's exile here in the *Antipurgatorio* (VII, 25):

Non per far, ma per non far ho perduto
di veder l'alto Sol che tu disiri,
e che fu tardi da me conosciuto.

(Not through doing, but through not doing, I have missed
seeing the high Sun whom you desire,
and who was known too late to me.)

The whole scene between Virgil and Sordello, with Dante as passionate spectator (Canto VI, 58—Canto VIII), is the high point of the first day's wandering. When Sordello embraces Virgil only because he hears that he is a fellow Mantuan, Dante is overcome by their generous love of country, which contrasts so painfully with the spirit of the Italy he knows; and he launches into the great tirade that occupies the rest of the canto (VI, 76): *Ahi serva Italia, di dolore ostello,* "Ah servile Italy! ah dolor's hostel!" Dante is an exile in this life, Sordello and Virgil are both exiles, in different ways, in the world beyond the grave; and all three are briefly brought together here in longing for the welfare of their common country.

During the second day, when the travelers are climbing up through purgatory proper, Virgil is at home in another way. The ancient path, as was pointed out earlier, is marked by some specifically Christian signs, notably the episodes from the life of Mary; but this part of the journey represents the turn "inside ourselves," the essential effort of the psyche to know itself; and Virgil is a master of that knowledge. He is not only endowed with extraordinary insight—for he is always seeing his pupil's desire before it is expressed—he is also an expert in Aristotelian psychology and moral philosophy. Here, during the afternoon and evening of the second day, as Dante begins to ask him the fundamental questions, he can expound the comprehensive vision of the life of the spirit which has enabled him to guide his pupil all the way from the dark wood.

These cantos in the middle of the *Purgatorio* (XV–XVIII) reflect Dante's own experience in the middle of the journey of his own life, when he discovered classical philosophy, and felt, for a time, that it had superseded the love of Beatrice and all it had meant. In connection with the *Convivio* (page 48) an attempt was made to summarize Dante's classical conception of the psyche's *amor* or *energeia,* the perpetual "movement" toward what looks good to it, the natural quest for the Summum Bonum which so often misses its aim. It is this conception, or vision, that Virgil expounds in his three great discourses in Cantos XV, XVII, and XVIII, and that Marco Lombardo presents, in the context of his experience, in Canto XVI. These four cantos are the best place to study Dante's notion of the "action" he was "imitating" in the whole *Commedia*—or, in terms of his formula, the *amor* which his poetry "signifies."

What should be considered here, however, is Virgil's role as he completes his long task, giving Dante the essence of his own wisdom, yet at the same time warning him not to suppose (as he once had) that this pagan light can supersede what Beatrice, somewhere far above them, will provide.

In Canto XV, Virgil explains what human life must be like, when completely freed from the envy we have just seen repented (lines 49–57):

"Perchè s'appuntan li vostri disiri
  dove per compagnia parte si scema,
  invidia move il mantaco ai sospiri.
Ma se l'amor della spera suprema
  torcesse in suso il desiderio vostro,
  non vi sarebbe al petto quella tema:
chè per quanto si dice più lì 'nostro,'
  tanto possiede più di ben ciascuno,
  e più di caritate arde in quel chiostro."

("Because the focal point of your desires
  is where each sharer lessens each one's share,
  envy impels the bellows of your sighs.
But if the love of the highest sphere
  twisted upward the longings which are yours,
  you would not have within your heart that fear:
for the more there are there who say 'ours'
  the more of good each one of them possesses,
  and the more charity in that cloister glows.")

And again, in response to another question of Dante's (lines 73–75):

"e quanta gente più lassù s'intende,
  più v'è da bene amare, e più vi s'ama,
  e come specchio l'uno all'altro rende."

("and the more folk, up there, who comprehend,
the more to love well, and the more love is there,
and each one mirrors back what others send.")

This is an extrapolation, by Virgil, from the process of spiritual growth as he knows it—a premonition of the *Paradiso* itself. It satisfies Dante, momentarily at least, but Virgil tells him, "You shall see Beatrice, and she shall free you from this and every other longing."

By the beginning of Canto XVIII Dante's awakened mind is ready for Virgil's final wisdom, and the "mirroring" of light and love which was abstractly described in Canto XV is now briefly staged between them (line 7):

Ma quel padre verace, che s'accorse
del timido voler che non s'apriva,
parlando di parlare ardir mi porse.
Ond'io: "Maestro, il mio veder s'avviva
sì nel tuo lume, ch'io discerno chiaro
quanto la tua ragion porti o descriva."

(But that true father, who perceived
the timid desire that was not disclosing itself,
by speaking put courage in me to speak.
Wherefore I: "Master, my vision is so quickened
in your light, that I discern clearly
all that your reasoning produces or describes.")

Virgil proceeds to give his great discourses on the nature of love and free will. Dante again thinks he is satisfied, and Virgil again points out the limits of the light they then enjoy (line 46):

"Quanto ragion qui vede
dirti poss'io; da indi in là t'aspetta
pure a Beatrice, ch'opera è di fede.

("As far as reason sees here
I can tell you; beyond that point wait,
simply, for Beatrice, for it is a matter of faith.)

These moments when Dante perceives the movement of spirit in Virgil's light refer to the same experience—"intellectual contemplation"—which he described in the *Convivio* (IV, ii): "The philosophizing soul not only contemplates the truth but also contemplates its own contemplation and the beauty thereof, turning upon itself and enamoring itself of itself by reason of the beauty of its direct contemplation." The difference is that now he does not find that the psyche can be the adequate object of its own love, even in its highest mode of action, that of philosophizing; and Virgil, with his sad clarity, is here to let him know in advance that he has a long way still to go.

Where Dante has to go is, of course, beyond Virgil, to the Christian Revelation in the Terrestrial Paradise. During the third day Dante and Virgil, joined very soon by Statius, are together in the classical culture they all share, and Virgil can come into his own as the poet he was, and is. But they are rapidly approaching the place where Virgil can no longer accompany them, and from the beginning of the third day we notice that there are things Virgil does not quite understand; and we begin to feel that he is receding behind us. The whole sequence (XX–XXVII) brings out Virgil in a new and more intimate way—there is space here only for a few illustrations.

The theme of Virgil as poet, and father of subsequent poets, was announced at the outset, in *Inferno* I, with his first appearance; resumed in the castle of the classical poets and sages (*Inferno* IV), and given a most painful twist when Dante tells Guido Cavalcanti's father that his son (illustrious poet and Dante's first friend) is not with him on this exalted journey because he held Virgil in disdain (*Inferno* X). We hear it again when Sordello hails Virgil as "glory of the Latins, by whom our tongue showed forth all its power" (*Purgatorio* VII). But it is left to Statius, speaking for all the other poets (especially Dante himself), to bring out Virgil the poet most fully, in the context of his imminent departure. Statius learns from Dante, in the course of a resonant but most delicate recognition scene, who Virgil is, and, like Sordello, he is overcome (XXI, 130):

> Già si chinava ad abbracciar li piedi
>   al mio dottor; ma egli disse: "Frate
>   non far, chè tu se'ombra, ed ombra vedi."
> Ed ei surgendo: "Or puoi la quantitate
>   comprender dell'amor ch'a te mi scalda,
>   quando dismento nostra vanitate,
> trattando l'ombre come cosa salda."

(He was already stooping to clasp the feet
of my teacher; but he said: "Brother
do not so, for you are a shadow, and a shadow you see."
And he rising: "Now the measure
you may see, of the love that warms me toward you,
when I forget our vanity,
treating the shadows as a solid thing.")

Their communion here is in essence brief and bodiless. But in the next canto Virgil suggests how the three may communicate at all, across so much deaf time and space (XXII, 10):

"Amore,
acceso di virtù, sempre altro accese,
pur che la fiamma sua paresse fuore."

("Love,
kindled by virtue, always kindles another,
if only its flame shows outwardly.")

One is reminded of Dante's love for the *Aeneid,* outward sign of Virgil's love-driven spirit, whereby those two were brought together far below in the dark wood. And Statius completes the sequence with his famous tribute (line 64):

"Tu prima m'inviasti
verso Parnaso a ber nelle sue grotte,
e poi appresso Dio m'alluminasti.
Facesti come quei che va di notte,
che porta il lume retro e sè non giova,
ma dopo sè fa le persone dotte,
quando dicesti: 'Secol si rinnova;
torna giustizia e primo tempo umano,
e progenie discende dal ciel nuova.' "

(He said to him: "You were the first who sent me
on to Parnassus' grottoes, to imbibe,
and then on the way toward God your light you lent me.
You did as one who, going through the night,
bears light at his back, and does not profit thence,
but makes those wise who follow on behind,
when you said, 'The world is renewed again;
justice returns, and the first human time,
from heaven a new progeny descends.' ")

Statius refers to Virgil's Fourth Eclogue, which "harmonizes" with the early preachers of Christianity, as he says, "when the whole world was pregnant with the true belief" (line 76).

In these sequences near the top of the Mountain we are seeing Virgil in the round: as the pagan Roman poet he was, and is, but in the perspective of the Christian saeculum—a light that brings him out against the darkness of his times. The late Professor Auerbach pointed out (in his essay "Figura") that the Virgil of the *Commedia* is closely analogous to the Moses of the New Testament: a historic character filled with meaning for his own time, but whose full significance appears only in the light of Christian Revelation. Saint Paul says the Mosaic Law is "a schoolmaster to bring us to Christ"—but we can see that only when Christ has appeared. In an analogous way Dante makes classical ethics, as taught by Virgil, a schoolmaster to bring us to Christ. All the way from the dark wood he has been lighting our way, just as he had Statius', with his Greek philosophy of the spirit's life. So he has led us to a point where we may begin to sense Revelation, and therefore to realize that Virgil himself is "for the dark."

Dante, like other great men of his time, was determined to make room in his Christian philosophy for that classical culture of which Virgil is the generous master. But he found the relation between man, as seen in the natural light of his own reason, and man according to the Creed, full of unfathomable mysteries and painful paradoxes. With his usual candor he shows himself, as traveler, quite out of his depth as he approaches the Faith in the Terrestrial Paradise; and as tormented still, in the *Paradiso* itself, by the thought of the great spirits of the pre-Christian world who, according to the accepted doctrine, are lost forever. In the third day of the climb, hurrying faster and faster toward Eden and Beatrice, Dante the traveler has little thought for Virgil—no more than a child has for the parent who sends him on his way. But Dante the author has made sure that the attentive reader can see Virgil looming up to his full height just here, before we lose sight of him for good. Much of the tragic meaning of the *Inferno* and the *Purgatorio* is in Virgil, that "noble shadow," as we glimpse him near the summit of the Mountain.

The Plan of the *Paradiso Terrestre* (Cantos XXVIII–XXXIII)

The Terrestrial Paradise (the last six cantos of the *Purgatorio*) is outside the actual climb, like the *Antipurgatorio*, to which it corresponds in various ways. It is the scene of the climax and turning-point of the entire *Commedia* which was foreshadowed at the beginning: the moment when Virgil gives place to Beatrice. It marks the ambiguous earthly satisfaction of the "natural thirst" which awakened in Dante the traveler as the first day dawned on the beach at the foot of the Mountain; and here Dante the author reaches the end of his assignment for this *Cantica*. At the same time it shows the basis of the next *Cantica*, to which Beatrice will serve as guide: a wholly new movement of spirit into that final realm where all is clear in the Divine light. Thus it is evident that a great deal must go on in the *Paradiso Terrestre* if it is to fulfill its multiple functions in the grand design of the *Commedia*.

The garden of earthly felicity, Eden, was a difficult concept in Dante's thought, and in the thought of his time. When he wrote the *De Monarchia* he was content to say that it was a "figure" of earthly felicity to which natural reason can lead us, man's goal in this life corresponding to the celestial paradise beyond the grave. But in writing the *Commedia* he rather places man's one true and adequate goal beyond this life, where it is to be reached—or even apprehended—only by the grace of faith. What, then, becomes of "earthly felicity"? The nature of Eden and of man's relation to it was a many-sided problem for the theologians. Can man return to Eden now, after the fall? What was Adam's original state of innocence there? Was it natural in the classic sense? Does the Redemption wrought by Christ restore the innocence of Eden? Professor Singleton writes (*Dante Studies* II, page 274): "The question touched on nothing less than that most important problem (the biggest which the thirteenth century had been obliged to face) of the sharp distinction to be drawn between two orders, the order of nature and the order of grace. The revival of Aristotle's philosophy had indeed made that line the frontier of a whole range of urgent questions."

Anyone who wishes to explore the *Paradiso Terrestre* in the light of the best understanding available in our time must consult

Professor Singleton's *Dante Studies*, especially Number II, which is entirely concerned with these final cantos of the *Purgatorio*. Professor Singleton has searched out a uniquely useful collection of theological texts which relate to Dante's poem. And he has demonstrated just how the subtle Greek-Christian thought of the theologians was used in planning both the symbolism and the dramatic form of the poem. The more one mulls over these matters, the better one understands not only the conceptual but the poetic-dramatic structure of the whole, and the clearer the tiniest details become. In Dante's poem-making the art of the theologian, which traces out the intricate drama of human-divine relationships, is close to the art of the divinely love-inspired poet as he plots the climactic scene of his drama of enlightenment.

But on one's first few trips through this region, it is better to follow Dante the traveler, seeing and understanding what he does, than to try to catch Dante the author in his intricate plot-making. Dante the traveler first sees the garden in the tranquil natural light (Canto XXVIII); then the pageant of Revelation, with its elaborate iconography, in a supernatural light (Canto XXIX); then Beatrice (Canto XXX); then the "tree in the midst of the garden," and finally (Canto XXXII) the nightmare figures representing Dante's despairing vision of the Papacy, the Empire, and the House of France—the ugly history of human *treatment* of Revelation and its custodians. As always, the literal narrative "contains" all the meanings, but Dante the traveler does not—in fact cannot—open out the meaning as he goes. He has a series of experiences, delightful and painful, and of contrasting visions, brilliantly clear to the eye, but impermeable to his bewildered mind. They present the most indigestible paradoxes of the faith, as he encountered them in his own experience; and they will not be elucidated for him until Beatrice lifts him into the Divine light, beyond all earthly understanding. Meanwhile the literal narrative is extremely rich, and the very bewilderments of the traveler serve to show both the end of the journey of purgation, and the necessity of the supernatural journey to heaven, which is still to come.

We have seen that Virgil's final words, on the threshold of the garden, briefly indicate the freedom, inner harmony, and rectitude which his pupil has attained under his guidance. "Justice," the rule of reason, prevails in his psyche, and therefore he no longer needs external authority to restrain or guide him. They are about to enter the garden, earthly felicity itself (line 115):

> "Quel dolce pome, che per tanti rami
>   cercanda va la cura dei mortali,
>   oggi porrà in pace le tue fami,"

> ("That sweet apple, which the care of mortals
>   goes searching after through so many branches,
>   on this day will bring peace to all your hungers,")

as Virgil has said; and Dante's beloved Beatrice awaits him in that garden. Everything seems to show that the travelers have only to enjoy the felicity at the summit.

The garden (Canto XXVIII) certainly appears, at first, to answer every expectation. Its trees and flowering shrubs, its transparent waters and fragrant breeze, and Matelda singing beyond the stream, are given to us in verses that echo the more joyful love lyrics of Dante's youth. Matelda explains that its springlike freshness, though it resembles the nature we know, is immortal, being the direct utterance of God: the very scene of Adam's pristine innocence; and she adds, at the end, that it is what classic poets on Parnassus dreamed of as the Golden Age. The only trouble is that neither Dante nor Virgil can possess it: their classic moral virtues, harmonized by justice, qualify them to live in freedom on earth, but do not restore the state of man's innocence before the fall. That is why (as we have been told) Virgil "without hope lives in desire," and Dante's "thirst," though "natural," is not to be satisfied except by the grace that Christ brings. Dante with his insatiate thirst would at once embrace Matelda, were it not for the stream between them, which serves to hold his delight at that first moment of perception which is as close as man, after the fall, can come to innocence. Virgil is due back in his grave castle in hell, Dante in heaven; their vision of Eden, together, is only a moment between two incommensurable worlds.

According to the theology that Dante accepted, Eden is still real after the fall of man—perhaps even as a geographical place—but man cannot live there; at most he can pass through without stopping. This theological conception enables Dante to present Eden in the exact way in which he had experienced it. He would not deny all reality to the pastoral daydreams of his youth—or to the pretty legends of Genesis and the Golden Age. But he had found that he could not capture and hold innocent felicity, any more than he could that other version of the earthly summit, intellectual contemplation.

There is nothing to prepare Dante or Virgil for the pageant of Revelation, as it moves into view across the stream in a flash of lightning that miraculously stays (Canto XXIX, 16). Virgil's signal of bewilderment, when Dante looks toward him (as he had learned to do, for help), is the very last glimpse we have of him. For the pageant represents the historically cumulative Revelation of the Bible: the twenty-four elders signifying the books of the Old Testament; the traditional beasts of the four Gospels with the triumphal car of the Church, drawn by Christ the Griffon; and finally, elders representing the last books of the New Testament. The whole is lighted by the seven gifts of the spirit, and attended by the seven virtues as nymphs. The visible figures, venerable symbols as they are, "contain" the whole story of the relations of God and man through the last book of the New Testament, and so, of course, the truth about this garden where we are, but do not belong. As I have said, Dante the traveler was unprepared for the arrival of these strange, gorgeous apparitions just here; and he gazes at them as he might have, in childhood, at the mosaics high up in the church of San Miniato al Monte, absorbed in their literal splendor but with little attempt to open up their meanings. And Virgil, of course, can never penetrate to the meaning of the Christian Creed.

There was also nothing to prepare Dante for Beatrice's apparition in the car drawn by Christ (Canto XXX, 31), even though he had been expecting her ever since Virgil had told him, in the dark wood, that he would lead him back to her. Professor Singleton has explained that, in Dante's theological pattern, Beatrice is a "figure" of Christ. The analogies between the Beatrice of the *Commedia* and Christ are extremely intricate; suffice it to say, at this point, that Beatrice plays a role in Dante's individual history analogous to that of Christ in the history of the race and in the lives of all believers: she reveals the love which judges, convicts, and saves. Dante recognizes her (brought by Christ) at the same moment that he realizes Virgil is gone; and the terror of that loss is instantly mingled with remorse when the Beatrice whom he had abandoned begins to speak, calling him by name, "Dante"—the only time his name appears in the whole *Commedia*. There is nothing to hide him from his betrayed benefactress as she rehearses his infidelities, proving that the beauty and innocence of Eden is not for him, even though Virgil had brought him here. The comforts of philosophy are absent for this prolonged moment (Canto XXX, 31–91), as they were in hell, where "the good of the intellect" is lost forever: there is, indeed, nothing for Dante to see (turn as he will while Beatrice makes him remember) but his own inconstant psyche "crawling between heaven and earth" after Beatrice's death, by depriving him of her visible presence, had required of him a faith that was not forthcoming.

At this point neither reason nor faith is available; human life (in the person of Dante) is seen neither in the perspective of the *moralia, quid agas*, nor in that of the *allegoria, quid credas*. This is the climax of the *Commedia*, a peripety brought about by an act of recognition which destroys the whole rational motivation of the protagonist, opening his spirit, with great pain, to receive a wider and hitherto inadmissable vision. Just here the movement of spirit that brought us from Cocytus, the upward impulse of Eros, is ambiguously and ambivalently ended in Beatrice, so that Agape may take cover. But Beatrice makes sure that this first intolerable moment of recognition is held long enough—to a point like death, as Dante falls senseless—before she allows the complementary, life-giving aspects of her appearance to reach him.

The river Lethe, whose waters have the miraculous property of washing away all memory of evil, marks the boundary between Eden seen from the side of earth, and Eden in the order of grace. Dante has been on the earthly side while the infidelities of his life were rehearsed, but when he is overcome by remorse, Matelda pulls him across the stream, and there a new sequence begins. Having been led to the breast of the Griffon, where Beatrice is gazing, he sees its Divine and its human nature alternately reflected in her eyes. She then unveils, and for the first time since he saw her in life, her beauty is revealed to him: first her eyes, and then her smile. So we get two versions of Eden's delight after Redemption, as the bewildered traveler sees them.

When Dante tears his eyes away from Beatrice (Canto XXXII, 13) he sees the Divine procession wheel around and move past him toward the sun. He follows, with Matelda and Beatrice (who descends from the car), and they reach a very high tree—the tree of the knowledge of good and evil it must be, since the angelic presences murmur "Adam." Adam's disobedient sampling of its fruit had left it bare and leafless, but the Griffon now attaches his car to it, restoring what he owed (for the wood of the Cross was taken from this tree); and he says, "Thus is preserved the seed of all righteousness." The tree blossoms forth like the sudden coming of spring, and Dante mysteriously sleeps. These visions represent the ideal relations of church (Christ's car) and state (the tree) according to the doctrine of *De Monarchia*, which we glanced at before (page 75). The tree is one of those marvelous icons, rich with historic associations, which Dante used for his purposes. It represents here the obedience Adam lacked and that man must somehow acquire again; the Cross whereby (in Christ) man is enabled to obey again; and finally the Empire, secular discipline, the insufficient but necessary counterpart of the Divine sacrifice. All of these subtle matters, here presented in tightly packed visual symbols, will be elucidated in Cantos VI and VII of the *Paradiso*. At this point the traveler and the reader can only marvel rather blankly; but perhaps we are expected to notice that the whole sequence, with its music and its imagery of spring light (lines 52–84), pictures Redemption as it should have worked in human history, church and state harmoniously obedient to God's will, just as the beauty of Beatrice's eyes and smile picture Redemption as it should have been in Dante's small personal history.

As Dante has failed to be loyal to what Beatrice's beauty revealed to him, so the feckless human race has failed to cherish properly the Revelation of God's will in Christ, and, through Christ, in history past, present, and to come. The second part of Canto XXXII is devoted to a startling series of nightmare beasts, signs of the heresies, violence, stupidity, and corruption that have actually all but ruined both the Church and the Empire. Dante's vision of the relations of the Papacy and the House of France (lines 141–160) has already been quoted in connection with the tragic career of Henry VII (page 73). It is this wonderfully virulent bad dream, desecrating Eden and then leaving it empty, that ends Canto XXXII.

The last canto opens with allusions to the death of Christ (lines 1–12), and then Beatrice starts her little procession: the seven nymphs, Matelda, Statius, and Dante, slowly moving through the forest. A Christian reader such as Dante had in mind would, I think, be full of troubled questions arising from the end of the preceding canto. Beatrice hints at a few answers, to reassure the faithful that God's plan will not be defied much longer. But as she says herself, her words are dark: experts with a flair for secret codes are still trying, in vain, to interpret her prophecy that "a five hundred ten and five" will come to restore order. She is giving Dante a few instructions for his return to earth, rather than endeavoring to explain anything to him. But as all movement quiets down for the mysterious end of the canto and the *Cantica* (when Dante drinks of the stream Eunoe that restores all memories of good and so prepares him to "rise to the stars"), the action of Dante the traveler in the *Paradiso Terrestre,* and that of Dante the author in presenting it in poetry, are unobtrusively explained to us.

It is Matelda who enables us to understand Dante's movement of spirit in the exploration of Eden. She now (line 130) leads him to Eunoe, just as she has guided him throughout: drawing him, by his love for her, along the stream when he first enters the garden; telling him where to look when the Divine pageant appears; pulling him through Lethe when the time comes, and pointing him back to Beatrice after his strange slumber before the flowering tree. She is one of those female figures, inhabitants of various realms, who momentarily attract Dante, thus making objectively visible the particular mode of love that moves him there—like Francesca, who with her love moves his spirit down through the first circle of hell. Matelda is the very clue to life in Eden: innocence, or, as we are told here, perfect obedience (line 130):

> Com'anima gentil che non fa scusa,
> ma fa sua voglia della voglia altrui,
> tosto ch'ell'è per segno fuor dischiusa

> (As a gentle soul that does not make excuses,
> but makes her will of the will of another
> as soon as it is, by a sign, disclosed)

She is like Marco Lombardo's "simple soul" (Canto XVI), "who knows nothing, except that, being moved by a joyous Maker, she turns all willingly to what delights her"—but all that delights Matelda here in the garden is the direct sign of God's pristine will for man. Thus it is God's will for man on earth of which she "makes her will."

It is all very well for Matelda, who is apparently "native to that element," to live in that way, but it is not easy for Dante (or the reader) to "obey" the contrasting apparitions, clear to the eye but impermeable to the mind, which are the Word of God, the "outward signs" of his will, here in Eden. Beatrice lets Dante know that this brilliant but bewildering effect is intended (line 85):

> "Perchè conoschi," disse, "quella scuola
> ch'hai seguitata, e veggi sua dottrina
> come può seguitar la mia parola;
> e veggi vostra via dalla divina
> distar cotanto, quanto si discorda
> da terra il ciel che più alto festina."

> ("So that you may know," she said, "that school
> which you have followed, and see how its teaching
> can keep up with my word;
> and see that your way is from the divine
> as far removed as is removed
> from earth the heaven that hastens highest.")

Virgil's rational school, though it could lead Dante to Eden, cannot follow God's Word here, for Eden is *quid credas*: the "letter" of the *Allegoria*, the "sign" that points upward. That is why Dante's mind is "turned to stone," as Beatrice says (line 73), and all he can do is report what he has *seen*: "if not written, at least depicted" (line 76). That is just what he has done in writing this part of the poem: Beatrice's instructions are the clue to the style of the *Paradiso Terrestre*. The action of Dante the traveler is, as usual, closely analogous to that of Dante as poet: he is "signifying" in exactly that "mode" that Love "dictates" just here on the incomprehensible boundary between the human and the Divine.

This style or "mode" is similar to that which Dante uses at other frontiers between two realms of experience: the clear but undeciphered iconography of the Gate of Purgatory in the morning sunshine, for example; or the words on Hell Gate, which, simple as they literally are, prove too "hard" for the traveler and the reader. The whole of Cocytus, which serves as *terminus ad quem* and *terminus a quo* for the *Inferno*, as the *Paradiso Terrestre* does for the *Purgatorio*, is stylistically similar. The realistic intensity and unmitigated immediacy of the Ugolino episode corresponds to Dante's lacerating experience with Beatrice; the symbolic artifact of Lucifer, to the inexplicable symbolism of the Divine pageant and the tree in the midst of the garden. Immediate realism and uninterpreted iconography are two versions of the "letter that killeth." Both serve to show the traveler's mode of perception at that point of deathly paralysis when his old motive has succumbed, and the new motive, the "Spirit that giveth life," has not, as yet, quite taken over.

Beatrice

The mysterious figure of Beatrice is, of course, of central importance in any attempt to understand Dante and his works. In the *Commedia* Dante says his final word about her; he makes good on the famous promise of the *Vita Nuova*, "to write of her what hath never been written of any woman," concentrating in her role much of his final lore of love. In the following observations it is not my intention to dispel the mystery of her being, which Dante himself often stresses, but rather to meditate upon it, for it is a most suggestive mystery.

Professor Singleton has shown conclusively that Dante thinks of Beatrice as a "figure" of Christ. In the *Vita Nuova* this parallel is suggested in the dream of her death, and much more explicitly in her appearance (XXIV), preceded by Giovanna-Primavera, as "the true light" was preceded by John the Baptist. And we have just seen that she is staged in the *Paradiso Terrestre* as an analogue of Christ. But of course Christ means many things, and there are various "figures" of Christ in the *Commedia*. In what way, or ways, did Dante think of her as playing this role?

There used to be a great deal of controversy among *Dantisti* about whether the Beatrice of the *Commedia* is a real woman, Beatrice Portinari of Florence, or *only* a sign for something else, the Church or Divine Wisdom or Theology or the Holy Spirit. It is now generally recognized that the question in this form is wrongly conceived. Beatrice is as real as Virgil, and her significance, like his, is in the role which only a particular human being, in a particular time and place, could play. In this too she is analogous to Christ. Just as His Revelation is available only because He lived as a real man, so Beatrice could reach Dante only because she was a real woman—and just *that* woman. And so, in the upper reaches of the *Purgatorio,* she approaches as the woman Dante had known on earth: a name and a memory that tempts him as an apple does a child (Canto XXVII); as one to be found in the garden of youthful delights (Cantos XXVIII and XIX); then, finally, shaking his whole being as Aeneas shook Dido's, and burning him with Venus' ancient flame (Canto XXX). She is, of course, only a "shadow," but Dante forgets that, as Statius forgets Virgil's and his own "vanity" when they meet beyond the grave. Beatrice meets her erring lover, first of all, as the profoundly disturbing young woman of Florence.

According to Dante's Aristotelian psychology, the object to which the ever-loving psyche is attached forms it, well or ill; determines, therefore, the quality of its life—that is why love is the root of all evil and all good (*Purgatorio* XVII and XVIII). A woman (in Dante's experience at least) is the object most capable of attaching the spirit, and therefore the best indication of the quality of its life. Even at the time of the *Convivio,* when he was trying to renounce woman and attach himself solely to the life of reason, he had to use a female figure, "Lady Philosophy," to represent that intellectual object. A series of female figures in the *Inferno* and *Purgatorio* serve to make objectively perceptible the varying *foci* of his spirit: Francesca, the beginning of the fated descent; and the women in his dreams on the Mountain—Thetis, the Siren and the holy lady, Leah and Rachel. They represent only momentary modes of action, turnings of the path; Beatrice is the climax of this sequence, and the constant, if unseen, goal.

In the great scene across Lethe, Beatrice is as female as any of the others, even Francesca. Only an offended earthly woman could hold him so long at the brute fact of his infidelity, or find so many ways of humiliating him there. The effect is to paralyze the life of his spirit, like melting snow on the summit of the Apennines when it is turned to ice again in the winds from the north (XXX, 85). This metaphor restores, for the moment, the bottom of hell, Cocytus, where the treacherous find that even the tears that well up within them are frozen solid at the lids before they can be shed. Perhaps the ice would have claimed Dante permanently if Beatrice had not rescued him, when he could not rescue himself, by going to hell to make her appeal to Virgil.

All of this reaches Dante the traveler (and the reader) in the painful idiom of mortal love, but we know that Beatrice came to meet her lover here, not from hell or from earth, but from heaven, where she dwells as an immortal spirit. As early as the last part of the *Vita Nuova* we learn that the unique and far-reaching *meaning* of Beatrice depends upon her immortality, and indeed upon the faith in human immortality in general. When Beatrice died, Dante turned to the presently visible window lady, telling himself that she too revealed love to him; but then Beatrice, very much "alive" in heaven, though invisible, sent him dreams and visions to call him back to her. So she drew him again, away from this life to the unseen world in, or beyond, death. When he turned away from Beatrice a second time, to philosophy, he was turning to what is possible here on earth, and away from what is to be had only on the "evidence of things not seen." By the time of the *Commedia* most of his hopes for this life, both personal and political, had been disappointed: experience itself had told him that "the natural thirst" is not to be satisfied on this side of the grave. Instead of living then like Virgil, in desire but without hope, or trying to deny his "natural thirst," or changing his mind about what the human spirit really needs, he projected his deepest thirst, or need, or desire into the next world. He represents this final turn, from earthly life in reason's natural light to the postmortem life in Christian faith and hope, as a return to Beatrice. For it was her beauty that had first turned his spirit toward heavenly intuitions of clarity, order, and love.

The fidelity that Beatrice, as outraged woman, is demanding of Dante, is not that of marriage, for marriage has to do with this world, and death is thought to separate man and wife. It is more like what Francesca's romantically tyrannous love demands when it allows her, once loved, no excuse from loving in return, and seals her in death to Paolo's lost shadowy being. Of course Francesca's love imprisons her in its own darkness, while Beatrice's opens upward into the glory of God. But it is because Beatrice, like the absolute *donna* of *amor cortese* and the infatuated Paolo and Francesca, demands everything that she *can* be a figure of Christ. When Dante crosses Lethe he literally sees the Griffon reflected in her eyes, now as man, now as God. But he will not even begin to see into the meaning of all this until the *Paradiso*, when Beatrice talks to him about Redemption, alluding briefly to their passionate meeting in the garden (*Paradiso* VII, line 58):

> "Questo decreto, frate, sta sepulto
> agli occhi di ciascuno, il cui ingegno
> nella fiamma d'amor non è adulto."

> ("This decree [i.e., that man be redeemed by the Incarnation
> and sacrifice of Christ], my brother, is hidden
> from the eyes of everyone whose wit
> is not matured in the flame of love.")

That passage in the *Paradiso*—most of Canto VII—may be thought of as presenting the "spirit" behind the "letter" of the scene at the river Lethe.

As soon as Dante has crossed Lethe and so lost all memory of evil, and Beatrice has turned from him to gaze at the Griffon, she is less the young woman he knew in Florence than she is the immortal spirit whose real life is in the contemplation of God. But here in the *Paradiso Terrestre* Dante cannot see the glory of God, and so he lacks the clue to Beatrice's life and action. He can follow her slow pacing through the garden, note her attitude of grief or anger, record her words literally, as she tells him to do. But he does not really understand: he is like a preschool child watching a parent who is reading a book. The reader cannot see what moves Beatrice either, when she has finished scolding her lover and turns away to Christ the Griffon; and from this point through the *Paradiso* Beatrice lacks the kind of individual life or character which makes the other spirits in hell and purgatory so sharply visible to us. We divine the nature of an individual's action, i.e., his character, by noting the things to which he attaches himself, as Dante explained in the *Convivio*. That is the principle he uses in portraying the spirits in hell and in purgatory: he makes them visible by means of their physical settings and their dramatic interplay with those they remember from their earthly lives, and with Dante when he invades their realms. But when Beatrice turns from Dante toward the "evidence of things not seen," the movement of her spirit is not to be seen either.

It is probably this strange unindividualized quality of the Beatrice of the *Paradiso* that leads some *Dantisti* to conclude that she is not intended to be a woman at all, but only an abstraction like Wisdom. We cannot see her as *a* woman as we do Francesca, or Sapia (*Purgatorio* XIII), or La Pia (*Purgatorio* V). But we must see her as a *woman*, and one of great though undefined beauty, if we are to understand her role of guide for the rest of the journey.

In representing Beatrice beyond Lethe and in the *Paradiso*, Dante returns to the style of portraiture which he had used in his early love lyrics (*Vita Nuova* XXI):

Negli occhi porta la mia donna Amore;
Per che si fa gentil ciò ch'ella mira

(In her eyes my lady carries love,
and so makes gentle what she looks upon)

Her spirit is to be made visible, not through what it is attached to outwardly, but through the body, especially the eyes and mouth, of which it is the life and "form." The Aristotelian conception of the soul as the form of the body, and as making visible changes in the body as it changes the focus of its desire, underlies all Dante's moving-pictures of people, but it is of special importance in his representations of beloved women. As pointed out earlier (page 63), he explains this clearly in *Convivio* III, viii, where he discusses philosophy, the life of reason, as revealed in the analogy of a beautiful woman: "And inasmuch as the soul operates in the face chiefly in two places, because in these two places the three natures of the soul have some kind of jurisdiction, to wit in the eyes and in the mouth, it chiefly adorns these . . . Which two places by a beautiful simile may be called the balconies of the lady who dwelleth in the edifice of the body, to wit the soul, because here, albeit in a measure veiled, she doth many times reveal herself."

From the moment just beyond Lethe, when Beatrice unveils first her eyes and then her mouth (XXXII, 133), it is in those most responsive parts of the face that Dante will "see" her living spirit. In the sonnet quoted above, it is "love," hardly further defined, that appears in his lady's eyes; but in the *Paradiso* almost all of the successive heavenly visions come by way of Beatrice's guiding vision—her "eyes" in many senses. Dante never tells us what shape her mouth is, or what color her eyes: he assumes that his reader has "seen" a spirit in a beautiful and beloved face, and leaves it to him to fill in the specifications to suit his own taste. The effect of this style of portraiture is to make the Beatrice of the *Paradiso* strangely abstract yet at the same time most intimate. Thus, however mysterious, she is essentially a beautiful woman: she must be, to serve as guide to beatitude; just as she had to be a woman in order to play the more familiar role of jealous lover on the earthly bank of Lethe.

Beatrice is a "figure" of Christ: a particular woman who plays a role in Dante's individual history analogous to that which Christ played, plays, and will play in the history of mankind. I have mentioned the fact that Virgil too is a figure of Christ—another, different, analogue. Dante seems to have devised the roles of his two principal guides, in the drama of the *Purgatorio*, so as to suggest the many meanings which may be read in these complex analogical relationships. Virgil, like Moses, leads to the Revelation which is beyond him, but to which he will owe his own ultimate meaning. Beatrice also leads Dante to Christ, but since she came after, not before, Christ, she is brought by Him in the car of His Church. Thus her spirit—which Dante first knew incarnate in so beautiful a body—must be attributed to Agape, a gift descending from above, while Virgil is moved, rather, by Eros, love in the human clay, painfully toiling upward as far as it can in reason's sober light. But the mystery of Beatrice, in her manifold relationships within the great composition, is not to be dispelled. In composing the *Commedia* as the dramatic interplay between real, individual beings—Dante, Virgil, Beatrice, Christ, and the whole population beyond the grave—the poet was not so much trying to clear things up as he was meditating on the perennial and many-sided mysteries of the human situation.

«« IV »»

The *Paradiso*

The Action of the *Paradiso* (Canto I)

THE FIRST FOUR tercets of Canto I, like the inscription on Hell Gate and the beginning of the *Purgatorio*, briefly indicate the realm now to be explored:

La gloria di colui che tutto move
  per l'universo penetra, e risplende
  in una parte più, e meno altrove.
Nel ciel che più della sua luce prende
  fu'io; e vidi cose che ridire
  nè sa nè può qual di lassù discende;
perchè, appressando sè al suo disire,
  nostro intelletto si profonda tanto,
  che retro la memoria non può ire.
Veramente quant'io del regno santo
  nella mia mente potei far tesoro,
  sarà ora materia del mio canto.

(The glory of Him who moves all things
  penetrates the universe, and reglows
  in one part more and in another less.
In the heaven that most receives his light
  was I, and saw things which, to retell,
  he lacks both knowledge and strength who thence descends:
because, as it approaches its desire,
  our intellect becomes so deep
  that memory is unable to go back.

But in truth, as much of the holy realm
as I could treasure in my memory
will now be the matter of my song.)

Dante will try to sing of the ineffable glory of God, which he saw reflected in the nine spatial heavens as he rose from the top of the Mount of Purgatory to God, in the Empyrean, which is beyond space and time. Something will be said of the plan and the cosmic setting in the next chapter. But first let us consider the movement of spirit—contemplative, or mystical—which Canto I presents in several analogous ways as Dante the poet, and Dante the traveler, get started on their final and most marvelous voyage.

The action is abstractly defined in the third tercet:

because, as it approaches its desire,
our intellect becomes so deep
that memory is unable to go back.

As the human psyche approaches the one object that can satisfy that "natural thirst" which is not to be satisfied on earth, it gets out of its depth, and so (as Dante explains in his "letter to Can Grande") cannot remember what it perceived when it returns to the usual, groping, and unsatisfied human condition. The action of the *Paradiso* consists of many "approaches," first by way of the Divine reflections in the nine heavens, then by the closer visions of the Empyrean.

These four tercets constitute one movement—a short, very concentrated lyric. The structure of each tercet and the structure of the whole passage "imitate" the spirit's approach to its desire. The first line of each tercet indicates the goal:

1. The glory of Him who moves all things
2. In the heaven that most receives his light
3. as it approaches its desire
4. as much of the holy realm

The last line of each represents a sinking back to earth or to mere humanity:

1. in another less
2. descends
3. unable to go back
4. my song

The passage as a whole has a similar shape, for the first line, "The glory of Him who moves all things," is the highest, the closest to the goal, while the first line of the last tercet has us back on earth, where the poet aspires, almost in vain, to rise again, in memory and in his verse, to the Empyrean. Thus the four tercets are like many a fine love song, in which the line of the words and the melody is accompanied by a rising and falling in the strings, a ceaseless amorous suspiration or aspiration.

In the second movement of the canto (lines 13–36), Dante turns from his reader to invoke the aid of Apollo and all the Muses in his labors as poet. This also represents the spirit's longing approach to God, for Apollo, the father of the Muses, represents the sun, and so God himself. In writing the *Inferno* and the *Purgatorio*, the Muses sufficed; now Dante must come as close as he can to the very source of his inspiration, the Love which has inspired him in so many ways since the dark wood. This movement also ends with references to human weakness, and to Dante's own inadequacy.

After the invocation by Dante as poet, we are returned to Dante the traveler at the point where we last saw him in the *Paradiso Terrestre*, just after he had emerged from Eunoe, "cleansed and made ready to rise to the stars" (*Purgatorio* XXXIII, 145). We are reminded that it was noon there and evening here; and now we see Dante and Beatrice miraculously shoot upward into the sky. The rest of the canto is devoted to their flight.

First we get the incredible experience of Dante the traveler, as he is moved both spatially into the sky and spiritually toward God (lines 37–81). The hour of noon is indicated by the astronomical situation, and so we are reminded of the vast, visible, spatial cosmos. In that epic setting Beatrice has the look of a pagan goddess, perhaps reclining in the sky (line 46):

Quando Beatrice in sul sinistro fianco
vidi rivolta, e riguardar nel sole.
Aquila sì non gli s'affisse unquanco.

(When Beatrice, turned on her left side,
and gazing into the sun I saw.
Never did eagle so fix himself there.)

Then we are told with technical exactitude how Dante's spirit *is moved* with hers:

E sì come secondo raggio suole
uscir del primo, e risalire in suso,
pur come peregrin che tornar vuole;
così dell'atto suo, per gli occhi infuso
nell'imagine mia, il mio si fece,
e fissi gli occhi al sole oltre a nostr'uso.

(And just as the second ray always
comes from the first, and rises again
like a pilgrim wishing to return;
so from her action, poured through the eyes
into my imagination, mine [i.e., my action] was made,
and I fixed my eyes on the sun beyond our wont.)

As in the love lyrics of the *Vita Nuova,* and the *canzoni* addressed to Lady Philosophy, the visible beauty of the beloved woman reveals her action to Dante, and then he finds that his spirit is moved with hers: it perceives the Divine truths that she is perceiving. This is the beginning of Beatrice's guidance through the heavens—always her perception, then Dante's; then the amorous lift to a higher realm:

Quinci si può veder come si fonda
l'esser beato nell'atto che vede,
non in quel ch'ama, che poscia seconda.

(Hence may be seen how being-blessed is founded on
the action that sees, not that which loves,
which follows after.)

as she will tell him in the Primum Mobile (Canto XXVIII, line 109). He turns from the visible sun back to Beatrice; and then he wishes in vain to tell us how this first approach to the heart's desire feels, this movement of perception followed by delectation (line 67):

Nel suo aspetto tal dentro mi fei,
qual si fe' Glauco nel gustar dell'erba,
che il fe' consorto in mar degli altri dei.

(Gazing at her, such I became within
as Glaucus became, when he tasted the grass
that made him consort undersea with the other gods.)

The "example" of Glaucus comes, of course, from the visible world of nature and classic legend. Glaucus, the poor fisherman, having tasted the grass that immortalized him, dives into the sea to join the submarine gods, as Dante is now diving into the sky. Dante never loses this dimension of the paradisal voyage: even at the summit of heaven he can look back, past the planets, to the small earth, just as though he were riding in a sputnik. The *Paradiso* is thus, in one aspect, the tallest tale ever told by a returning traveler, and Dante can exploit the mode of childlike wonder whenever he wants to. But he knows that spatial movement, though analogous, is not equivalent to the movement of spirit; and having evoked Glaucus for us he adds (line 70):

> Trasumanar significar *per verba*
> non si poria; però l'esemplo basti
> a cui esperienza grazia serba.

> (To signify transcending humanity in words
> would not be possible; hence let the example suffice
> him for whom grace reserves the experience.)

As poet, the craftsman of words, he is beyond his depth here, and, moreover, as a man, he does not know how to conceive the experience (line 73):

> S'io era sol di me quel che creasti
> novellamente, Amor che il ciel governi,
> tu il sai, che col tuo lume mi levasti,

> (If I was only that of me which you created
> anew, O Love who rule heaven,
> you know, who with your light lifted me.)

What Love created anew was not the body, but Dante's rational psyche which, as Statius explained in *Purgatorio* XXV, is directly breathed into the fully developed fetus by God. The phrase "with your light lifted" is a reference to Saint Paul's account of his own experience of being "caught up into Paradise," (II Corinthians, 12): "whether in the body, I cannot tell; or whether out of the body, I cannot tell; God knoweth." Dante then tells us (lines 76–84) that, even as he shot upward into light and heard the harmony of the spheres, he was *commosso*, "disturbed," by not knowing what was happening to him; and with that return to the weak human mind this movement ends.

Beatrice's rescue of Dante in his bewilderment makes the fourth and final movement of the canto (lines 84–141). She gives him the appalling fact that he is actually leaving the earth faster than lightning, and then, to account for that as well as may be, briefly summarizes the theory of the cosmos and its moving principle. "All things have order among them, and this is the form that makes the universe resemble God" (lines 103–105). Moreover, each thing inclines to its principle, so fire moves upward, earth and all heavy things downward—to Cocytus, as we saw—and human souls by their nature incline toward God. So, she tells Dante (line 136):

> Non dei più ammirar, se bene estimo,
> lo tuo salir, se non come d'un rivo
> se d'alto monte scende giuso ad imo.

> (You should no more wonder, if I am right,
> at your rising, than at a river
> descending from a high mountain to the base.)

Beatrice's explanation gives us another way to see the action: the Love that is lifting Dante with its light is what moves "all things to diverse ports on the great sea of being" (line 112). Her words serve to restore Dante's shaken psyche to its proper focus, so that he may make another approach to God. The canto ends as Beatrice turns away from Dante, toward heaven once more.

Canto I is only the beginning, but, with Beatrice's explanations, it gives a foretaste of the mode of action of the whole *Paradiso*. Beatrice's references to the moving principle of the universe enable one to see that in one important respect the *Paradiso* corresponds to the *Inferno*: they represent the two timeless poles of human experience, while the *Purgatorio*, in the middle, represents trial and error, time and change. In both hell and heaven the human spirit, going as far as it can in a certain direction, meets the omnipotent will of God, while in purgatory, left rather more to its own devices, it only more or less vaguely *seeks* the divine. That is why the *Purgatorio* is a drama "of ethical motivation," whereas both the *Inferno* and the *Paradiso* are basically pathoses. But in hell God's will is suffered as the *gravezza* that pulls the lost spirits down to their allotted prisons, and the travelers all the way down to ultimate paralysis; while in heaven (as Canto I shows) God's will is felt as the spirit's own deepest desire, which miraculously lifts it beyond all earthly things. The clue to this heavenly paradox is in the *Purgatorio* (XVI, 79): "To a greater power and a better nature you lie subject, in your freedom." But in purgatory this is only a metaphysical concept, while in the *Paradiso* Dante wants to suggest, if he can, in his imagery of light and unimpeded movement, the *experience* of freedom and fulfillment.

Insofar as the spirit moves with the will of God, the *Paradiso* corresponds to the *Inferno*; but as a journey of enlightenment it is analogous to the *Purgatorio*. That is because Dante makes the heavenly trip as a man in this life: he does not see God directly until the ineffable end in Canto XXXIII; he depends on sensuous intermediaries for his perception, and on partial and successive intuitions. Hence the plan of this *Cantica*, the setting that serves to unroll the approaches to God, as the setting of the *Purgatorio* unrolls the journey to earthly felicity.

The Plan of the *Paradiso*

In his "Letter to Can Grande," Dante discusses the opening tercets of the *Paradiso* (which have just been described as a love song) from the point of view of their scientific and theological truth. The first three tercets (as he explains) contain implicitly the accepted theory of the cosmos, which is the setting of the last *Cantica*. He wants to defend his accuracy from those who might wish to discredit him, and he cites his authorities like an anxious Ph.D. candidate piling up footnotes: several works of Aristotle, *De Causis*, several books of the Old and New Testaments, and, for good measure, Plato and Lucan. He believed that the order of the heavens was confirmed by the naked eye gazing upward; by the mathematically worked out science of astronomy, and by the testimony of a long line of poets, philosophers, and mystics who since earliest times had been scanning the skies for signs of the order and meaning which the human spirit needs, and seldom finds on earth.

The astronomical scheme is the same in the *Paradiso* as in the *Convivio*; it is summarized in the diagram on page 179. The Primum Mobile is the largest sphere and the swiftest, whirling around the whole vast circumference and communicating its movement to the eight heavens below it, and ultimately to the earth. It is contained within the spaceless and timeless Empyrean, the heaven of God's light and love.

In the *Convivio* Dante tells us that the meanings which the visible heavens have for us here below were worked out in the course of thousands of years, as the inadequate surmises of the first stargazers were gradually developed and corrected. The ancients named the stars after their gods; then, later, Plato and Aristotle associated the intelligences that move the heavens with basic metaphysical concepts: Ideas, or Forms, or what the Scholastics call Universals. Not until Christ and His Church, he tells us, were the roles of the angels in moving the heavenly bodies—the Old Testament Seraphim and Cherubim and the rest—definitely understood. Beatrice tells Dante (*Paradiso* XXVIII) that even so great an authority as Pope Gregory (whom Dante had followed in the *Convivio*) could confuse two of the angelic orders. Except for that point, the diagram follows the *Convivio*.

In the columns to the right, in the diagram, the nine orders of angels and the three hierarchies of three orders each, in which they are grouped, are shown. Dante explains this arrangement as follows (*Convivio* II, vi):

> For inasmuch as the divine majesty is in three persons, which have one substance, they may be contemplated in three-fold manner. For the supreme power of the Father may be contemplated; and this it is that the first hierarchy, to wit first in nobility and last in our enumeration, gazes upon; and the supreme wisdom of the Son may be contemplated; and this it is that the second hierarchy gazes upon; and the supreme and most burning love of the Holy Spirit may be contemplated; and this it is that the third hierarchy gazes upon: the which being nearest unto us gives us of the gifts which it receiveth. And inasmuch as each person of the divine Trinity may be considered in three-fold manner, there are in each hierarchy three orders diversely contemplating. The Father may be considered without respect to aught save himself; and this contemplation the Seraphim do use, who see more of the first cause than any other angelic nature. The Father may be considered according as he hath relation to the Son, to wit how he is parted from him and how united with him, and this do the Cherubim contemplate. The Father may further be considered according as from him proceedeth the Holy Spirit, and how he is parted from him and

PLAN OF THE PARADISO

THE HEAVENS	SPIRITS THAT APPEAR IN EACH HEAVEN	SCIENCES ASSOCIATED WITH EACH HEAVEN	GOD AND THE ANGELS THAT MOVE THE HEAVENS	PERSON OF THE TRINITY CONTEMPLATED BY THE ANGELS: ORDERS	HIERARCHIES
10 EMPYRIAN (OUTSIDE SPACE AND TIME)	GOD AND ALL THE INHABITANTS OF HEAVEN	THEOLOGY	GOD		
9 PRIMUM MOBILE	ALL ANGELS	MORAL PHILOSOPHY	SERAPHIM	FATHER (POWER)	GOD THE FATHER
8 ○○○○○ FIXED STARS	ALL REDEEMED	METAPHYSICS PHYSICS	CHERUBIM	SON (WISDOM)	
7 ○ SATURN	TEMPERATE	ASTROLOGY	THRONES	HOLY SPIRIT (LOVE)	
6 ○ JUPITER	JUST	GEOMETRY	DOMINATIONS	FATHER (POWER)	GOD THE SON
5 ○ MARS	COURAGEOUS	MUSIC	VIRTUES	SON (WISDOM)	
4 ○ SUN	PRUDENT	ARITHMETIC	POWERS	HOLY SPIRIT (LOVE)	
3 ○ VENUS	AMOROUS	RHETORIC	PRINCIPALITIES	FATHER (POWER)	GOD THE HOLY SPIRIT
2 ○ MERCURY	HONOR SEEKING	LOGIC	ARCHANGELS	SON (WISDOM)	
1 ○ MOON	INCONSTANT	GRAMMAR	ANGELS	HOLY SPIRIT (LOVE)	

COMPARISON WITH THE PURGATORIO

PARTS OF PURGATORIO	PURG. CANTOS	PAR. CANTOS
EARTHLY PARADISE AFTER CROSSING LETHE	XXXIII	XXXIII
	XXX	XXX
EARTHLY PARADISE BEFORE CROSSING LETHE	XXVIII	XXVII
SECOND DAY IN PURGATORY; VIRGIL AND DANTE JOINED BY STATIUS	XXVII	
	XIX	XXI, XX
FIRST DAY IN PURGATORY; VIRGIL'S WISDOM	IX	X, IX
ANTI-PURGATORIO	I	I

EARTH

> how united with him; and this contemplation the Powers do use. And in like fashion may there be speculation of the Son and of the Holy Spirit. Wherefore it behooves that there be nine manners of contemplating spirits to gaze upon the light which alone seeth itself completely.

In other words, the order of the heavens, moved by angelic intelligences, reflects the Triune God. So does all creation, though more remotely and dimly, as mystics and theologians had been teaching since the first centuries of Christianity. Dante had been strongly influenced by the literature of the Trinity since youth, when he composed the *Vita Nuova* in three's. During the journey of the *Commedia* he sees the signature of the Trinity in every part of the universe, beginning with Hell Gate. The whole dramatic poem of the *Commedia* is composed in three's, from its three great *Cantiche* down to the *terza rima*. The Trinity would be the clue to all forms—of art, of life, of the world—if we could only see it; but "it alone seeth itself completely," as Dante tells us. The plan of the *Paradiso* is thus based upon the Trinity as all-pervasive but beyond our power of vision: we approach it through countless analogies, getting its light reflected back and forth among the things, spirits, and concepts we perceive as we rise through the nine spatial heavens, even though the ultimate light, light itself, is beyond our capacity.

The columns to the left in the diagram are intended to suggest relationships between the heavenly order and more accessible forms of order which we know here below. First come the sciences, which are symbolized by the ten heavens, as Dante explains in the *Convivio*. Next are the spirits that Dante meets in the various heavens. He is told that their appearance in the spatial heavens is only in deference to his human inability to see the spirit without sensory intermediaries, and that they all really have their beatific existence in the spaceless heaven of God's love. But the heavens in which they appear are appropriate; the nature of the angelic intelligences in each spatial heaven is analogous to the qualities the human spirits had shown in their earthly lives. Finally, in the diagram the parts of the *Purgatorio* that correspond to the parts of the *Paradiso* are indicated on the left.

Modern readers do not usually feel at home with angelic hierarchies, or even with the "august incomprehensibility" of the Trinity, as Joyce called it. But Dante himself tells Can Grande that his celestial setting is not there for its own sake ("by way of speculation"), but for a practical purpose. As always in the *Commedia* the setting is a framework for revealing the action, in this case the final supernatural journey of enlightenment corresponding to the more earthly journey to *human* wisdom in the *Purgatorio*. Even in the *Paradiso* Dante's subject is still the human spirit and its experience. That is why one way to learn to understand his ultimate religious vision is to compare and contrast the trip he takes in heaven with his trip through purgatory, where everything is closer to the life we know.

Thus (returning to the diagram) the first three heavens as we ascend, covered as they were supposed to be by the long shadow of the earth, and ruled by angels contemplating God as Holy Spirit, correspond to the *Antipurgatorio*, where Dante finds the spirits who, though saved by God's love, cannot yet see the upward path of moral wisdom. In heaven Dante meets spirits who on earth had been shadowed by inconstancy, ambition, or earthly love. It must be noted, however, that though this is only the threshold of heaven it serves to reveal the ultimate meaning of some of the visions which Dante found incomprehensible in the *Paradiso Terrestre*. In the Moon, Beatrice explains the limitations of human sense-bound perception. In Mercury, God's plans for human government—Empire in history—and for Redemption, are clearly explained by Justinian and Beatrice respectively. These expositions give the "spirit" behind the "letter" of the painful scenes and allegorical visions of Eden.

The heavens of the Sun, Mars, and Jupiter, ruled by angels that contemplate God as the Son, or Holy Wisdom, correspond to the first day of the purgatorial climb, when Virgil gradually makes available the light of his *human* wisdom. In these heavens Dante meets the spirits of theologians, righteous warriors, and just rulers: guides of the race who on earth had had the virtues of prudence, courage, or justice. These are Virgil's own classic virtues, but we are to understand that Virgil had acquired them by pedestrian thought and effort, while the virtues of the redeemed had been "infused," i.e., directly inspired by God. The purgatorial climb begins with the three steps which are an obscure sign of the Trinity, while the corresponding heavenly sequence opens with a direct reference to the Trinity itself: "Gazing upon his Son with the Love which the one and the other eternally breathes forth . . ." (X, 1). Both the purgatorial and the paradisal sequence are dominated by the Sun, which makes possible the sight of the eye, and symbolizes intellectual light, both human and Divine. If the reader will compare these parts of the *Purgatorio* and *Paradiso* (both of central importance), he will discover many illuminating analogies between them.

The angels that rule the three highest spatial heavens contemplate God as Divine Power. The diagram shows that this realm corresponds to the last part of the purgatorial journey, which ends as Dante reaches Beatrice in the *Paradiso Terrestre.* In both sequences Dante as the individual he is comes more and more into focus, the journey and the poem draw toward the end together, and traveler and poet begin to coincide. In both, Dante undergoes what may be called "tests," or "ordeals," and receives new signs of the special grace that sustains him. Thus his crossing of the wall of fire (*Purgatorio* XXVII), his loss of Virgil, and Beatrice's cruel reproaches (*Purgatorio* XXX) may be compared with his examination in Faith, Hope, and Charity, followed by a moment of deathlike but love-sustained total blindness (*Paradiso* XXIV, XXV, and XXVI). In *Purgatorio* Virgil bestows a kind of diploma in human virtue and knowledge when he declares Dante "King" and "Bishop" over himself, and in the *Paradiso* the celestial examiners certify his possession of the three supernatural virtues. In the *Purgatorio* this sequence ends at the river Lethe, which Dante must cross and drink from before he can continue (*Purgatorio* XXXI). In the *Paradiso* he has a vision of the river of light at the analogous point (*Paradiso* XXX) and must drink of it "with his eyes" before he can see the rose of eternity. Perhaps these two living streams, respectively liquid and visionary, should faintly remind the reader of the solid ice of Cocytus where all the rivers of hell come to their dead end.

In the *Purgatorio* the final cantos are devoted to the visually clear but impermeable signs which are Revelation; in the *Paradiso,* to the poetry of the Empyrean, and finally the ineffable vision.

As Dante climbs the Mount of Purgatory, moral and intellectual effort in the light of the sun alternates with darkness when he is moved or sustained by grace. In paradise he is lifted through various levels which are ruled by the Holy Spirit, then Divine Wisdom, then Divine Power. This sequence is one important clue to the rhythm of action in heaven: intellectual or mystical contemplation, as mentioned before. It suggests a continually varied interplay between God's Love (the Holy Spirit) which lifts Dante upward; his own perception of some truth, in the light of Divine Wisdom; and his own human love as it meets Divine Power. But this is offered only as a suggestion, and as a sample of the sort of notion that may occur to one when thinking over the marvelously elaborate and harmonious plan of the last *Cantica*.

On the Difficulty of Reading the *Paradiso*

Many of Dante's admirers agree that the *Paradiso* is the most difficult part of the *Commedia*. Eliot says that is partly because we have "a prejudice against beatitude as material for poetry." We may just hope to grow up to the *Paradiso*, he says, by the end of life. Dante himself often says it was the hardest for him to write, and in the second canto he warns his readers:

O voi, che siete in piccioletta barca,
desiderosi d'ascoltar, seguiti
retro al mio legno che cantando varca,
tornate a riveder li vostri liti:
non vi mettete in pelago; chè forse,
perdendo me, rimarreste smarriti.

(O you, who are there in your little boat,
longing to listen, following my way
behind my timbers singing as they go,
turn back to find your own shores again:
do not trust to the open sea; for perhaps,
once losing me, you would be left astray.)

He knew that it would not be easy, even for those who shared his belief, to read his poem with understanding.

The basic difficulty which the modern reader has is to recognize the movements of spirit the poem imitates, by analogy with experiences of one's own—to see, in other words, what Dante is talking about. He foresaw that; and he tries, by means of his legendary rivers—Lethe, which washes away all memory of evil; and Eunoe, which restores all memory of good—to show us where to look, and where not to look, in order to find the proper focus for the flight to heaven. But he knew that his paradise was "the substance of things hoped for, the evidence of things not seen," and that his faith—intense enough to produce vision, thought, and music—was very rare.

The mere place the *Paradiso* occupies, at the summit of the whole scheme of the *Commedia*, makes the technical problems it poses much harder than those of the other two *Cantiche*. In the *Inferno* his task was to present the lost directly and "literally," in the realm where none of the three "spiritual meanings" of human destiny was available. In the *Purgatorio* he was to show, first, the "moral meaning"; but it was natural to bring that out through the dramatic interplay of characters of different modes of moral sophistication, and through the concepts of Greek philosophy. When he came to the mysterious boundary between the human and Divine, in the *Paradiso Terrestre*, he had the rich and ancient vocabulary of Biblical narrative and ecclesiastical iconography to present the "allegorical meaning" as it appeared at that point. But the *Paradiso*, as the end of the journey, must convey the "anagogical meaning," the ultimate truth of human destiny, not in concepts, signs, or symbols adapted to the groping mind on earth, but as nearly as possible directly, in the Divine Light. That is the sense of Beatrice's promise (*Purgatorio* XXXIII, 100):

> Veramente oramai saranno nude
> le mie parole, quanto converrassi
> quelle scoprire alla tua vista rude.

> (But now my words shall be naked,
> as far as may be fitting
> to disclose them to your rude vision.)

The moment is just before Dante's immersion in Eunoe; Beatrice is apologizing for the dense symbolism of Eden, and foretelling the quite different style of the *Paradiso*.

Of course we cannot do without sensuously perceptible signs of some sort; language itself has to be sensuous and rational at once, as Dante explained in *De Vulgari Eloquentia*. And the plan of the *Paradiso*, based as it is on the visible heavens, recognizes that. Beatrice recognizes it when she explains Piccarda di Donati's visible and audible apparition in the moon (IV, 40):

> "Così parlar conviensi al vostro ingegno,
> però che solo da sensato apprende
> ciò che fa poscia d'intelletto degno."

("Thus must your powers be addressed,
for only through sense-perception do they get
what they then make fit for the intelligence.")

But Beatrice in the same passage explains that the real life of Piccarda and the other blessed spirits is not in the visible heavens where they appear to Dante, but in their contemplation (with the eye of the spirit) of God, outside space. Piccarda feels to us almost as real as her counterpart in the threshold of hell, Francesca. But when we leave the moon behind, in our ascent, the spirits we meet become less and less recognizable as individuals, just as Beatrice does in the *Paradiso Terrestre,* after Lethe, and for the same reason: we are closer to the invisible focus of their beings. Dante has to renounce the brilliant character-drawing and the absorbing dramatic narratives in which he actualized the *moto spiritale* in hell and purgatory if he is to be true to the spirit's life in heaven as he knew and felt it in himself. He will need, instead, the more "naked" words of theology, and the more abstract forms of music. That is why the *Paradiso* is often akin, in style, to the great *canzoni,* and Dante's studies of that form (in *De Vulgari Eloquentia* and the *Convivio*) are helpful here. But, coming to it from the other *Cantiche,* it takes a while to learn to do without the earthly- and infernal-human, and to rely, as we must, chiefly on thought and music, i.e., the beauties of *abstract* form and order.

From time to time the *Paradiso* becomes a song of devotion, for example, the first twelve lines of Canto I, and such passages are likely to reach a modern reader at once with their formal beauty. One of the most famous is the beginning of Canto XII, when Dante and Beatrice are encircled by two garlands of lights, which are blessed spirits:

Sì tosto come l'ultima parola
la benedetta fiamma per dir tolse,
a rotar cominciò la santa mola;
e nel suo giro tutta non si volse
prima ch'un altra di cerchio la chiuse,
e moto a moto, e canto a canto colse:
canto che tanto vince nostre muse,
nostre sirene, in quelle dolci tube,
quanto primo splendor quel ch'ei refuse.

Come si volgon per tenera nube
due archi paralleli e concolori,
quando Giunone a sua ancella iube,
nascendo di quel d'entro quel di fuori,
a guisa del parlar di quella vaga,
ch'amor consunse come sol vapori;
e fanno qui la gente esser presaga,
per lo patto che Dio con Noè pose,
del mondo che giammai più non si allaga:
così di quelle sempiterne rose
volgeansi circa noi le due ghirlande,
e sì l'estrema all intima rispose.

(As soon as the final word
was spoken by the blessed flame,
the sacred millstone began to turn;
and in its rolling had not all revolved
before another closed it in its circle,
and motion chimed with motion, song with song;
song which is as far beyond our muses,
our sirens, in those sweet instruments,
as the first splendor from that which it reflects.
As bend across thin clouds
two bows, in parallel and the same in color,
when Juno so directs her serving-maiden,
from the inner coming to birth the outer
like the speech of that fond girl
whom love consumed as the sun does vapor,
and make the people here divine,
through the compact that God made with Noah,
that the world shall never drown again:
so of those sempiternal roses
revolved around us the two garlands,
and so the farther answered to the nearer.)

The dancelike rhythm and the rich patterns of assonance and inner rhyme, in the Italian, call attention to the musical form; and a modern reader, accustomed to abstract arts like chamber music or ballet choreography, can enjoy the passage almost without reference to its meaning. But this "dance and high festival," as Dante calls it in the next line, emerges from the intricate interplay of love and perception when Thomas Aquinas, the Dominican theologian, pays tribute to Saint Francis; and Bonaventura, the

Franciscan, pays tribute to Saint Dominic. It is part of the recurrent celebration of the Trinity in the heaven of the Sun; and if one were reading the *Paradiso* as it was intended to be read, one would be led from the form of this passage to the form and order of the whole sequence of the solar heaven.

This sequence begins with a reference to the Trinity as Creator of all order, both physical and spiritual (X, 1):

> Guardando nel suo figlio con l'amore
> che l'uno e l'altro eternalmente spira,
> lo primo ed ineffabile valore
> quanto per mente o per loco si gira
> con tanto ordine fe', ch'esser non puote
> senza gustar di lui chi ciò rimira.

> (Looking upon his Son with the Love
> that the one and the other breathe eternally,
> the primal and ineffable value
> made all that revolves through mind or space
> with such order, that it is not possible,
> without some taste of Him, to contemplate it.)

It is an invitation to consider the Triune order, physical and spiritual, of the heavens, which Dante built into the plan of his poem; and, of course, behind that, the mystery of the Trinity itself. And how is one supposed to do that?—"Now, reader, stay on your bench, thinking over this foretaste, if you wish to be happy rather than weary," says Dante (X, 22). He knew that in the poem itself he could not provide the reader with all the mathematics, astronomy, and theology he would need; he could only allude to the necessary knowledge. If the reader wants to fathom the full meaning, he will have to stay on his schoolboy's bench and do a little background reading—Saint Augustine's *On the Trinity*, for instance, where it is explained (IX) "That a kind of Trinity exists in Man, who is the image of God, viz., the mind, and the knowledge wherewith the mind knows itself, and the love wherewith it loves both itself and its own knowledge . . ." Augustine uses such analogies in order to lead the reader upward, toward some conception of the Triune God. But one may also remember that Dante's account of the action of philosophic contemplation in the *Convivio*, (which he dramatizes in the middle of the *Purgatorio*, where we still have our feet on the ground), is in agreement with this Augustinian analogue of the Trinity: "the philosophising soul not only contemplates the truth, but also contemplates its own contemplation and the beauty thereof, turning upon itself and enamoring itself of itself by reason of the beauty of its direct contemplation."

In reading the *Paradiso* there is no end to this process of weaving back and forth between the pregnant formulas of the verse, the structure of the canto and *Cantica*, lower stages of enlightenment in the *Purgatorio*, and the theological and devotional literature of Dante's tradition: "you pass from point to point, led by its formal lines; you apprehend it as balanced part against part within its limits; you feel the rhythm of its structure," as Stephen Dedalus said of the process of apprehending the inner harmony of a work of art. Dante's cosmos is, in fact, bound to strike us as a work of art. Dante thought of it that way, too; but as God's art, not man's: the thing itself, not a fabric of human thought and dream. In reading the *Paradiso* it is never enough to enjoy its formal beauties if one is to understand it as Dante meant us to. For him the heavenliness of the heavenly vision lay not only in its form and order, but in his triumphant conviction of its *reality*.

That is why (for instance) he can turn from subtlest reflections of the Trinity, in the solar heaven, to the straightforward narrative of Saint Francis' life in the mountains around Assisi, where he himself probably lingered as an exile. In the heaven of Mars, cosmic signs of Christ's triumph give place to Cacciaguida, Dante's own ancestor, who recounts epic deeds of warriors of God and describes Florence in the good old days. The inconceivable Trinity, the lives of the saints on earth, the course of human history, Florence, and Dante's career there, are all real, and all parts of God's plan. He sees his heart's desire, the object of his faith and hope—most of it lost to sight on earth—actually there before him in heaven.

He tells us that it was hard, at first, even for him, to accept heaven as real. As he enters the milky substance of the moon, the first blessed spirits who appear out of the whiteness strike him as illusory (III, 16):

> tali vid'io più facce a parlar pronte,
> perch'io dentro all'error contrario corsi
> a quel ch'accese amor tra l'uomo e il fonte.

(so did I behold many a countenance, eager to speak;
wherefore I fell into the opposite error of that
which kindled love between the man and the fountain.)

The man who loved the fountain is of course Narcissus, doting on his own reflection. Dante's first impulse, as he comes up from the earth, is to assume that what he sees in heaven is too good to be true. But Beatrice reassures him; and then the higher he rises, the more his marveling sense of the reality of all he sees and hears and understands grows within him.

The *Paradiso* must, I think, be taken in very small doses. It requires a great deal of energy to be alert to Dante's many hints to his reader about the way to read it, and then to respond to the different kinds of poetry it contains.

Action Defined by Faith, Hope, and Charity (Cantos XXIV, XXV, and XXVI)

As Dante the traveler underwent the infernal experience, and then toiled up the Mount of Purgatory, he acquired only gradually the freedom to understand his own motives, and then to feel what he most deeply craved. It was not until the middle of the *Purgatorio* (XVIII, 4) that, enlightened and encouraged by Virgil, he became aware of a "new thirst." That thirst drove him more sharply the next day (XX, 1), and Dante the poet described it then as "the natural thirst, which nothing ever sates except the water which the little woman of Samaria begged for." When the mortal heaviness was removed by the waters of Eunoe, it was that thirst, or craving, or love, basic to the human psyche, that lifted Dante and Beatrice into the heavens (*Paradiso* II, 19):

La concreata e perpetua sete
del deiforme regno cen portava
veloci, quasi come il ciel vedete.

(Our native and perpetual thirst
for the god-formed realm was bearing us
swift almost as you see the sky.)

In the eighth heaven (*Paradiso* XXIV, XXV, XXVI), the "starry sky" where the spirits of the redeemed are visible as countless lights, Dante is asked to say what Faith, Hope, and Charity mean to him. His answers amount to a description of the love that, though unformulated, had been moving him all along: a definition of his action, which here, so near its goal, is clearly understood at last.

This part of the *Paradiso* corresponds to the upper reaches of the *Purgatorio* (as is indicated in the diagram on page 179) where Dante himself moves to the center of the stage, undergoes his tests, and then sees his motive in the light of the goal he is about to reach. On the threshold of the *Paradiso Terrestre*, figure of earthly felicity (*Purgatorio* XXVII), Virgil tells Dante, "Free, upright and whole is your will, and it would be a fault not to do as it says." It is that freedom in accord with reason that the traveler had been aiming at during the whole arduous climb guided by the classical cardinal virtues; and it is that mode of action, attainable by moral and intellectual effort, that Virgil regards as man's fulfillment, the best he can ever do. But, as we have seen, it does not satisfy Dante's "natural thirst," and it leaves Virgil, also, "without hope," to live in desire. Here in the starry sky, on the threshold of the Empyrean, figure of eternal felicity, Dante is about to see what Virgil could never believe in: the Object of love which (having been certified by Revelation) is beyond man and his reason altogether. And now he can see the God-given theological virtues, so different from Virgil's sober four, which have brought him to this point.

The definition of faith that Dante offers to his examiner, Saint Peter, is taken from *Hebrews* XI, which Dante knew, of course, in the Vulgate (*Paradiso* XXIV, 64): "the substance of things hoped for, and argument of things unseen." Faith *underlies* our hope, and so may be called "substance." And since it is from faith that mortal man, on earth, "must syllogize without further sight," it is also "argument," a source of reasoning. Hope, the next virtue, is immediately generated by faith. Beatrice points out to Saint James (XXV, 52), who is about to conduct the examination on this point, that Dante must have an all-but-unique endowment of hope, since it is enabling him, even now, while he is still in the first life, to see the things of heaven. Dante defines hope as "a certain expectation of future glory," i.e., immortality in God's light. Hope in just that sense—certainty of life and justification beyond the grave—was indeed crucial in Dante's motivation on earth. It enabled him to reaffirm Beatrice's existence and power after her death, at the time of the *Vita Nuova*, and to reaffirm the truth of his political and religious doctrines, when all the causes he loved seemed dead in Italy.

Charity, or love, comes from faith and hope; and one may think of these three virtues as another suggestive, though inadequate, sign of the Trinity in the human spirit. Faith would then correspond to the Father, Hope to the Son He eternally begets, and Charity or Love to the Holy Spirit that the first and second Persons breathe forth. The three virtues are one and inseparable, for, taken together, they define the motivation of the human spirit that has accepted, in the darkness of mortal life, the truth of the Christian Creed. It is, of course, faith, pointing to man's true goal, that initially creates this mode of action, this supernatural, supra-rational form of love. But love itself, in Dante's view (as we have seen throughout this book) is neither good nor bad until it is defined by its object; and all creatures have love.

The very revealing sequence which Dante devotes to the crowning virtue of love begins in Canto XXV, 118, when, blinded by the light of John, he cannot see Beatrice when he turns toward her; and it continues to XXVI, 70, when his vision is restored. Does this blindness suggest death—perhaps Beatrice's? Or love separated from the direct perception of its object, as the Christian's love of God must be on earth? Or the operation of the Holy Spirit, often described in religious writings as the most invisible and mysterious of all? In any case, the Apostle John tells Dante that he has only to rely on Beatrice, invisible as she is, to restore his sight, and meanwhile he must discourse on love, i.e., explain "whereon your mind is focused" (XXVI, 7).

Dante's discourse follows the development of his own understanding of love through the three phases described in the first parts of this book—youth, the middle of the journey, and the fulfillment represented by the *Commedia*. As he faithfully waits for Beatrice to restore his sight, he refers to the experiences recorded in the *Vita Nuova*, when the sight of Beatrice's beauty gave him the love which is satisfied at last here in heaven (XXVI, 13):

> Io dissi: "Al suo piacere e tosto e tardo
> vegna rimedio agli occhi, che fur porte,
> quand' ella entrò col foco ond'io sempr' ardo."

(I said: "At her good pleasure, soon or late,
let the cure come to the eyes that were the gates
when she came in with the fire I burn with always.")

Urged by John to explain further, Dante sets forth the Aristotelian conception of love (*energeia*) as the motive power of every creature of the universe—the conception he first expounded in the *Convivio*, and which Virgil briefly rehearses in the center of the central canto of the central *Cantica* (*Purgatorio* XVII, 91), in the discourse beginning, "Neither Creator nor creature, my son, was ever without love." Dante then (line 40) completes the picture with brief references to the Old and New Testament, and to Christ's death and resurrection; and his sight returns with music, as that of the saved Christian soul is supposed to do after the dark moment of death.

Though Dante evidently wants us to know that this account of love is in a sense "autobiographical," it does not bring out the confusion and pain of either of the two crucial shifts in his service and understanding of love, which he had undergone on earth: that from his romantic love of Beatrice to secular philosophy, and that from secular philosophy to his final religious vision. He dramatized the latter in the *Commedia* by the painful and incomprehensible loss of Virgil at the moment when Beatrice appears. But here, close to the summit of heaven, the drastic changes in his love and his understanding of love—and also the abysmal differences between the loves of all the infinitely diverse creatures of the world—all appear only in the perspective of Charity; variety is not frustration and terror, but harmony. This theme first appeared in *Purgatorio* XV, when Virgil endeavored to explain to his pupil the love that quiets the anguish of envy. It came out much more explicitly, and much more fully orchestrated (*Paradiso* III), when Piccarda explained the harmony of the varied wills and capacities of the redeemed within the joyfully accepted will of God. Now Dante himself, even before death, can by faith and hope affirm that order in the universe, and (most heavenly of all) his own participation in it.

In order to understand the relation between this conception of love, those Dante had held successively in the course of his life, and those he gets in the lower reaches of the journey of the *Commedia*, one must consider his emphasis on blindness even here, near Beatrice, and "in the world of felicity," as he puts it (XXV, 139). During the purgatorial climb he lays the foundations for his understanding of love by means of Virgil's explanations, but it is at night, when Virgil is silent, that the stars of Faith, Hope, and Charity preside over his journey. It is then that the psyche is most detached from particular delectable things, or persons, or concepts, by darkness and sleep, and it is, therefore, then, that the deepest "thirst" takes over. That thirst is always there, congenital and insatiable; but perhaps we do not even feel it except in the attentive darkness of faith. Dante thought that what really moves man, the love that makes him what he is, his "heart's desire," could only be defined by the faith and hope which can be perceived neither by the eye of the body nor by the eye of the mind. Only after the darkness of death does the saved soul actually *see* the thirst that had been driving it—except by the very rare grace which enables Dante to approach the content of faith and hope while still in the body and in this life.

The End of the Spatial Journey (Cantos XXVII–XXX)

In the Primum Mobile (XXVII, 97—XXX, 37) the focus is turned upon the cosmic setting, for this is the crucial ninth heaven, the boundary between space and time, and the eternity of God's light and love, which contains it. As Cocytus is the bottom of the universe, so the Primum Mobile is the top; and as Dante, in the *Inferno*, uses the passage through the center of gravity to help us imagine the paradoxical end of evil, so here he uses the unimaginable end of space to suggest the different, the supernatural, mode of vision which will be required beyond it, in the Empyrean.

When Dante first finds himself in the Primum Mobile, Beatrice explains it as the swiftest and outermost heavenly sphere, the source of all spatial change and movement, and hence of all measurement of time. From this point of view it is the outer edge of the universe, and Cocytus, the center of gravity, is the cosmic center. But Dante then finds (XXVIII, 16) that he is looking at a point of intense light, surrounded by nine concentric spheres, and Beatrice explains that the point of light is the Unmoved Mover, God, true center of *all* movement; and the Primum Mobile, in this perspective, is the smallest—though still the swiftest—of the nine spheres. It now appears that the center of gravity, which is only the center of our earth, is at the outer edge. This effect of mutually exclusive perspectives is, I think, akin to the "complementarity" of modern theoretical physics. Neither perspective is false, and neither is adequate: the God that moves all things may be conceived as the all-inclusive container just as well (and as inadequately) as He may be conceived as the central point. We cannot do without spatial metaphors, and here, where they cease to be sufficient, the human mind is out of its depth.

As the end of the spatial journey, the Primum Mobile is an essential element in the scheme of the whole *Commedia*. Dante explained, long before he wrote his masterpiece (in *Convivio* II, xv), that the Primum Mobile "has very manifest comparisons with moral philosophy," which, according to Thomas Aquinas, "disposes us rightly for the other sciences." Human motivation, or action—which Dante says is the subject of the whole *Commedia*, including the *Paradiso*—underlies the intellectual work of all the sciences, as well as conduct of every other kind. Moral philosophy is the science of motivation, and in its light, therefore, the purposes and relative values of the sciences are to be understood, and their practice regulated. Only God is above the Primum Mobile; the other heavens, to be compared with the other sciences, are all below it. It is here that Beatrice explains how the intelligences that move the nine heavens revolve at speeds proportioned to their love of God, which in turn is proportioned to the depth of their perception; and the Seraphim, who move the Primum Mobile, see the most deeply and move the most swiftly. Beatrice adds (XXVIII, 109):

> Quinci si può veder come si fonda
> l'esser beato nell'atto che vede,
> non in quel ch'ama, che poscia seconda.

> (Hence may be seen how being-blessed is founded on
> the action that sees, not that which loves,
> which follows after.)

The dynamics of the universe is like that of the human psyche, whose love is stirred and then formed by what it perceives, as Virgil explained far below in the middle of the *Purgatorio*.

It was pointed out earlier that in the *cielo stellato*, the heaven of the redeemed, Dante defines action with reference to the virtues of Faith, Hope, and Charity, whereby the dim human psyche apprehends and loves God. One may say that in the Primum Mobile the corresponding action of the *cosmos* is presented. The modern reader cannot, of course, take this organic or vitalistic conception of the universe seriously as science. But when one begins to see how the heavenly setting and the heavenly machinery, angels and all, make action visible, many subtle insights into the life of the spirit slowly appear.

But the end of the journey and of the poem can only be in God—i.e., in the Empyrean, and so beyond space, whether we take space as reality or metaphor. As we rise into the Empyrean, therefore, the focus is turned, from the cosmic setting of the whole *Commedia*, back to Dante, who now appears rather as the poet who endeavors to remember and record his final experience than as the traveler among the stars that the bodily eye can see in the night sky.

Dante's Special Grace as Seer and Poet (Canto XXXIII)

Just before the ascent from the starry sky to the Primum Mobile, all heaven falls silent, and then blushes crimson with anger, while Saint Peter denounces Pope Boniface, who has usurped (XXVII, 22) "my place, my place, my place," and "made my grave a cloaca for blood and filth." He proceeds to denounce other modern Popes, especially Clement, whose betrayal of Emperor Henry VII he foresees; and he bids Dante, when his mortal weight shall have carried him back to earth, "open your mouth,/ and do not hide what I do not hide." Clement is bitterly mentioned again (XXX, 133) when Dante is shown the throne reserved for his beloved Henry VII, high up among the redeemed. This sequence is one of the striking signs of Dante's conviction that his vision of heaven was, by a unique grace, intended specifically for him, and that it laid upon him the seer's fearful duty to bear witness against the wicked who occupied the seats of the mighty in his time and country.

When he rises beyond space, to the Empyrean, it is by this special grace that he "sees" the things of heaven. It enables him to see the redeemed, not as they actually exist now, but as they will appear at the Last Judgment when they resume their bodies. Just as he enters the Empyrean (XXX, 61) he receives the vision of the river of light, with its flowery banks and the jewel-like sparks that hover over it. Since the whole spatial setting has now been transcended, there is no point in trying to locate this river, determine its geometric relation to the Primum Mobile, or explain to oneself how it can turn into the lake of light, center of the many-petaled white rose of the redeemed, where the angels, like bees, pass in and out. The river suggests the glory of God in time, and Dante must drink of it with his eyes before he can see it turn into the rose of eternity. But Beatrice says that the river, its sparks, and its flowers, are only "foreshadowing prefaces of their reality"; and when they become the sempiternal rose, Dante, as poet, emphasizes that the rose is *his* vision by repeating *io vidi*, "I saw," three times (line 94):

> così mi si cambiaro in maggior feste
> li fiori e le faville, sì ch'io vidi
> ambo le corti del ciel manifeste.
> O isplendor di Dio, per cu'io vidi
> l'alto trionfo del regno verace,
> dammi virtù a dir com'io lo vidi.

> (Thus changed for me to a greater festival
> those flowers and sparks, so that I saw
> both courts of heaven manifest.
> O splendor of God, whereby I saw
> the high triumph of the realm of truth,
> give me the strength to tell what there I saw.)

The elements in this sequence—river, rose, reflected light, overwhelmed poet—make a composition of thought and feeling that comes out of the movement of the whole poem up to this point. But they do not depend upon the spatial setting, and the style is more like that of a metaphysical lyric than a dramatic narrative.

Beatrice gives place to Bernard, the great contemplative who was supposed to have seen God in this life (XXXI, 58). Bernard guides Dante's vision over the ranks of the redeemed, indicating Beatrice (who has now resumed her timeless place), the Virgin Mary, Lucia, and many others; and he explains their ordering in the rose. He then prays to Mary that Dante may be given the strength to see God, and so complete his journey and his preparation for the task of poet and seer that awaits him on earth. So Dante is led back to the ultimate source of the grace which makes poem and journey possible; for Beatrice told Virgil, and Virgil told Dante in the dark wood (*Inferno* II) that grace had descended from Mary to Lucia, Lucia to Beatrice, Beatrice to Virgil, and so from Virgil to Dante. Now that Beatrice and Virgil have completed their tasks of upward guidance, Bernard plays the part of Lucia, to bring Dante to the Virgin herself.

Bernard's prayer, which opens the last canto, simple in diction and in motive, nevertheless manages to present the essentials of the mystical doctrine of the Mother of God, with its significant paradoxes. The prayer is one of the renowned poetic summits of the *Commedia*; but it can be considered here only for what it shows about Dante's role as seer and poet.

One must remember, once more, Dante's lifelong habit of taking a loved woman, at every significant juncture of his life, as the objectively visible pattern of his spirit's movement: Beatrice, "Lady Philosophy," Francesca, Matelda. Between the rise from the top of the Mount of Purgatory and the arrival at the Empyrean it is Beatrice who focuses, and thereby forms, his spirit's life of perception and love. The Virgin may be thought of as the end of this sequence, the constant, but more or less unseen pattern which now, at last, comes clear. She was represented, in seven different attitudes, at the entrances of the seven terraces of purgatory, silently revealing the forms of the passion that purifies. Bernard addresses her as the pattern for all mankind—*termine fisso d'etterno consiglio,* "fixed goal of the eternal counsel"—and as the "wings" for Dante's miraculous flight.

Bernard's prayer opens as follows (XXXIII, 1):

> "Vergine madre, figlia del tuo figlio,
> umile ed alta più che creatura,
> termine fisso d'eterno consiglio,

tu se' colei che l'umana natura
nobilitasti sì che il suo Fattore
non disdegnò di farsi sua fattura.
Nel ventre tuo si raccese l'amore
per lo cui caldo nell'eterna pace
così è germinato questo fiore."

("Virgin mother, daughter of your son,
more humble and more high than any creature,
fixed goal of the eternal counsel,
you are the one who human nature
ennobled so that its own Maker
did not disdain to make Himself its making.
Within your womb was lit once more the love
under whose warmth, in the eternal peace,
has germinated, thus, this flower.")

The second and third tercets show how the Virgin is Dante's "goal," or pattern. He too, according to his formula, must, as seer and poet, receive God's Love (or God as Love) within himself, and then remake it in the poem he utters:

"Io mi son un, che quando
Amor mi spira, noto, ed a quel modo
ch'e' ditta dentro, vo significando."

("I am one, who when
Love breathes in me, take note, and in that mode
which he dictates within, go signifying.")

The Love which the Virgin received within produced the vast "flower" of God's countless redeemed, while in Dante it produced only the *image* of the white rose of eternity which we read about in the last canto. But the analogy is there; it was always Dante's religious practice to follow exalted patterns, and to find divine analogies in the movements of his own inner being. As Love's secretary he was "more high than any creature," yet he must also have been "more humble" in order to quiet his own ego enough to hear what Love breathed within him.

Now the Virgin takes him the rest of the way. When she turns from Bernard to look upon God, Dante, gazing at her as he had at Beatrice in order to rise through the nine heavens, is empowered to look straight in the Divine Ray. He sees God in three ways: His first vision (lines 85–90) is of a book in which all the beings, and all the diverse modes of being, are bound, likes leaves, together; and this is nevertheless a "single light," image of the Aristotelian Unmoved Mover. The second vision (lines 115–117) of "three circles of three colors and one magnitude" refers, of course, to the Trinity; and the third (lines 130–132), when "our effigy" appears in the center, to the Incarnation of the Second Person.

What are we to make of these visions? I do not wish to raise the question often raised at this point, whether Dante had a "true mystical vision," for I have no way to deal with it. Dante himself seems to have believed that he was one of the few who saw God in this life. But he insists that what he saw was limited by his small capacity; that his memory cannot recover it; and that even so much as he retains is beyond the power of language to tell, just as he had said in Canto I. His *experience* was certainly real, however one may interpret it; and as he approaches it again, in memory, and then falls back helplessly, just as he had in the first twelve lines of Canto I, he brings his miraculous poem to its miraculous, and only possible, end.

The movement of Dante's spirit in its approaches to the vision of God is very close to that of the poet who now endeavors to recover and retell it (line 55):

> Da quinci innanzi il mio veder fu maggio
> che il parlar nostro ch'a tal vista cede,
> e cede la memoria a tanto oltraggio.
> Qual è colui che somniando vede,
> chè dopo il sogno la passione impressa
> rimane, e l'altro alla mente non riede;
> cotal son io, chè quasi tutta cessa
> mia visione, ed ancor mi distilla
> nel cor lo dolce che nacque da essa.

> (Thence forward my vision was greater
> than our discourse, which fails at such sight,
> and memory fails at so great outrage.
> As he who, dreaming, sees,
> and after the dream the passion stamped
> remains, and the rest returns not to the mind;
> such am I, for almost wholly ceases
> my vision, yet still there drops
> within my heart, the sweetness born of it.)

After the complementary visions of the Unmoved Mover as book and single light, we are again made aware of the remembering poet (line 91):

> La forma universal di questo nodo
> credo ch'io vidi, perche più di largo,
> dicendo questo, mi sento ch'io godo.
> Un punto solo m'è maggior letargo
> che venticinque secoli alla impresa
> che fe' Nettuno ammirar l'ombra d'Argo.

> (The universal form of this node
> I think I saw, for now more amply,
> as I say this, I feel that I rejoice.
> One single instant, for me, makes greater lethargy
> than five and twenty centuries for the enterprise
> that caused Neptune to marvel at Argo's shadow.)

I leave the reader to "marvel" at the dramaturgic agility and the metaphoric daring of this passage, which nevertheless produces an effect of hushed concentration, intellectual contemplation, or Joyce's "silent stasis" of aesthetic contemplation, or both.

At the very end, the rise and fall of Dante's spirit, endeavoring to accept, or recover, or express his vision, give place to the movement of love "within the Divine will, whereby our own wills are themselves made one," as Piccarda put it on the threshold of heaven (III, 80). She was defining the beatitude of the redeemed in the next life; Dante believed that, by the grace of God, he had tasted it in this life (line 142):

> All'alta fantasia qui mancò possa;
> ma già volgeva il mio disiro e il *velle*,
> sì come rota ch'egualmente è mossa,
> l'amor che move il sole e l'altre stelle.

> (The high imagining here lost its power;
> but now were being rolled my will and my desire,
> like a wheel that is moved evenly,
> by the love that moves the sun and all the stars.)

Bibliographical Notes

WORKS BY DANTE

1. The Temple Classics edition (London and New York) contains all of Dante's works in the following six volumes:
   The *Vita Nuova* and *Canzoniere* (Italian and English)
   The *Convivio* (English only)
   The *Latin Works* (English only):
      De Vulgari Eloquentia
      De Monarchia
      Epistles and Eclogues
      Quaestio de Aqua et Terra
   Inferno (Italian and English)
   Purgatorio (Italian and English)
   Paradiso (Italian and English)
   This edition is the best for readers with little or no Italian. The translations are in prose, and usually quite accurate. Each volume has excellent notes, maps, and tables.
2. *Le Opere di Dante.* Testo critico della Società Dantesca Italiana. Florence: 1921.
   The standard Italian edition of all the works, in Italian and Latin.
3. Dante Alighieri, *La Divina Commedia.* Riveduto, col commento Scartazziniano refatto da Giuseppe Vandelli. Milan: 1952.
   The latest Società Dantesca edition of the *Commedia.* The commentary is very full, with many useful quotations, and paraphrases of the passages where Dante's language is difficult.

4. Dante Alighieri, *Rime*. A cura di Gianfranco Contini. Turin: 1946.
This collection includes all of Dante's poems not collected by himself in the *Vita Nuova* or the *Convivio*. It incorporates the results of the latest scholarship, and includes Professor Contini's erudite and perceptive comments. His introduction is now available in English in *Dante*, ed. by John Freccero. Englewood Cliffs: 1965.

REFERENCE BOOKS

1. Cosmos, Umberto. *Handbook to Dante Studies*. Oxford: 1950.
This is a guide to the unmanageable Dante literature for young people who plan to become *Dantisti*. But other readers may find it useful for their more modest purposes.
2. Gardner, Edmund G. *Dante*. London: 1905.
Still a convenient short compendium of the main facts.
3. Toynbee, Paget. *A Dictionary of Proper Names and Notable Matters in the Works of Dante*. Oxford: 1898.
This is a most valuable mine of information and, because it contains many quotations, of primary sources.

SOME CRITICAL AND INTRODUCTORY STUDIES

1. Auerbach, Erich. *Dante, Poet of the Secular World*. Trans. by Ralph Manheim. Chicago: 1961.
2. Brandeis, Irma. *The Ladder of Vision. A Study of Dante's Comedy*. New York: 1961.
3. *De Sanctis on Dante*. Essays edited and translated by Joseph Rossi and Alfred Galpin. Madison: 1957.
4. Eliot, T. S. *Dante*. London: 1929. (Also in his *Selected Essays*.)
5. Pound, Ezra. *The Spirit of Romance*. London: 1910.
This very influential book includes an essay on Dante.
6. Sayers, Dorothy. *Introductory Papers on Dante*. New York: 1954.
7. Sayers, Dorothy. *Further Papers on Dante*. New York: 1957.

STUDIES USED FOR THE TEXT

"Dante in Florence":

1. Dinsmore, Charles Allen. *Aids to the Study of Dante.* Boston and New York: 1903.
   This useful book contains translations of the important earliest accounts of Dante's life: those of Giovanni Villani, Boccaccio, Filippo Villani, and Lionardo Bruni.
2. Villani, Giovanni, e Compagni, Dino. *Cronache.* Parti scelte, collegate e commentate per cura di Nicola Zingarelli. Florence: 1934.
3. Davidsohn, Robert. *Storia di Firenze.* Vols. III and IV. Florence, 1957.
   This is the Italian translation of the monumental *Geshichte von Florenz,* Berlin: 1896–1927. I have used it here and there, in Part One of this book, for reference.

"The New Life":

1. Auerbach, *op. cit.*
2. Contini, *op. cit.*
3. *I Rimatori del dolce stil novo.* A cura di G. R. Ceriello. Milan: 1950.
4. De Sanctis, Francesco. *Storio della Letteratura Italiana.* I. *Le origini.* Milan: 1950.
5. Pound, *op. cit.*

"A Short Reading of the *Vita Nuova*":

1. Singleton, Charles S. *An Essay on the* Vita Nuova. Cambridge: 1949.
   This is the most complete and illuminating study of the *Vita Nuova* that I know. I have used it in this chapter and the next.
2. De Rougemont, Denis. *Love in the Western World.* New York: 1956.

"*Vita Nuova*: The Symbolism of Number, Figure, and Form":

1. Auerbach, *op. cit.*
2. Singleton, *op. cit.*
3. Saint Bonaventura. *The Mind's Road to God,* Trans., with an Introduction by George Boas. New York: 1953.

"Politics in Florence":

1. Davidsohn, *op. cit.*
2. Del Lungo, Isidoro. *Da Bonifazio ad Arrigo VII.* Milan: 1921.
3. Villani e Compagni, *op. cit.*

"The Revolution of the Blacks and Dante's Banishment":

1. Davidsohn, *op. cit.*
2. Villani e Compagni, *op. cit.*
3. Villani, Giovanni. *Selections from the First Nine Books of the Florentine Chronicles.* Trans. by R. E. Selfe, ed. by P. H. Wicksteed. Westminster: 1896.
4. The Toynbee *Dictionary* (cited under Reference Books) is also very useful for the events and personalities of this period.

"The Works of Dante's Middle Phase":

1. Nardi, Bruno. *Nel mondo di Dante.* Rome: 1944.
2. Nardi, Bruno. *Dal "Convivio" alla "Commedia."* Rome: 1960. The reader will find, in Professor Nardi's works, extended discussions of some of the problems of Dante's middle phase, and, in general, of the whole matter of his Aristotelian philosophy and its sources.

"*Convivio*: Dante's Apology for Turning from Beatrice to Philosophy":

The Cavalcanti poem will be found in *Rimatori*, cited under "The New Life."

"*Convivio*: Rhetoric to Allegory to Poetry":

1. Singleton, Charles S. *Dante Studies I.* Cambridge: 1954. In two of the essays in this book, "Allegory" and "Appendix: Two Kinds of Allegory," the reader will find very important and illuminating discussions of Dante's conceptions of allegory in the *Convivio* and in the "Letter to Can Grande."
2. *Aristotle's Poetics.* Trans. by S. H. Butcher, introd. by F. Fergusson. New York: 1961.
   In my introductory essay I endeavor to bring out the essentials of Aristotle's theory of poetry as the imitation of action. I think the Aristotelian theory very important for the conception of poetry which takes shape in the *Convivio*, and still more for the full poetry of the *Commedia.*

"European Politics: Destruction of Dante's
Hopes for the Empire":

1. Davidsohn, *op. cit.*
2. Villani, *op. cit.*

"*De Monarchia*: The State, the Church, and
the Course of History":

1. Tillyard, E. M. W. *Shakespeare's History Plays.* London: 1956.
   The standard work on the subject.
2. Davis, Charles Till. *Dante and the Idea of Rome.* Oxford, 1957.
   This careful study is not concerned with *De Monarchia* but with the sources and aspects of "Rome" as Dante understood it.

"The Rebirth of Poetry in the Full Aristotelian Sense":

1. Auerbach, *op. cit.*
   Chapter III of this work is an account of the sources and genesis of Dante's mature style.
2. Auerbach, Erich. *Mimesis.* New York: 1953.
   Chapter VIII contains a more extended discussion of the style of the *Commedia,* especially the *sermo humilis.*
3. "Dante Alighieri, A Symposium by Modern Critics." In *Kenyon Review,* Vol. XIV, No. 2 (Spring, 1952).
   Essays on Dante's art by Erich Auerbach, R. P. Blackmur, T. S. Eliot, F. Fergusson, Robert Fitzgerald, Jacques Maritain, Charles S. Singleton, and Allen Tate.
4. Aristotle, *op. cit.*
5. Montanari, Fausto. *L'Esperienza poetica di Dante.* Florence: 1959.
   The development of Dante's poetic art, culminating in the *Commedia.*

"Allegory as a Function of Dramatic Narrative":

1. Singleton, *Dante Studies I* and *Dante Studies II,* Cambridge: 1958.
   Professor Singleton's indispensable studies are concerned with the allegorical and symbolic structure of the narrative. The first essay in the second series provides general orientation; the rest are on the *Purgatorio.*

"From the Midst of Life to the World of the Dead":

1. Singleton, *Dante Studies I.*
   In the first essay, "Allegory," the prologue (*Inferno* I and II) is analyzed in its poetic structure and its symbolism.

"The Inscription on the Gate of Hell":

1. Eliot, T. S. *Poems 1909–1925.* London: 1925.
   From Eliot's notes to *The Wasteland*:
   411. Cf. *Inferno,* XXXIII, 46:
   'ed io sentil chiavar l'uscio do sotto all'orribile torre.'
2. Bradley, F. H. *Appearance and Reality: A Metaphysical Essay.* Oxford: 1930, p. 346.
   "My external sensations are no less private to myself than are my thoughts and feelings. In either case my experience falls within my own circle, a circle closed on the outside; and, with all its elements alike, every sphere is opaque to the others which surround it. . . . In brief, regarded as an existence which appears in a soul, the whole whole world for each is peculiar and private to that soul."

"The Canto as the Imitation of One Action":

1. Aristotle, *op. cit.*

"Lucifer: The End of Hell in Two Senses":

1. Eliot, *op. cit.*
2. Freccero, John. "Infernal Inversion and Christian Conversion (*Inferno* XXXIV)." In *Italica,* Vol. XLII, No. 1 (March, 1965).
   A learned and illuminating study of the traditional figures and symbols of this canto.

"The *Purgatorio* as the Center of the *Commedia*":

1. Singleton, *Dante Studies II.*
   Professor Singleton's second volume, subtitled "Journey to Beatrice," is the essential study of the traditional figures, symbols, and theological concepts which underlie the dramatic structure of the *Purgatorio.*

"The Setting and the Time Scheme":

1. Fergusson, Francis. *Dante's Drama of the Mind, A Modern Reading of the* Purgatorio. Princeton: 1952.
   The table on pp. 138–139 is taken from this book by kind permission of the Princeton University Press.
2. De' Negri, Enrico. "Tema e iconografia del *Purgatorio.*" In *The Romanic Review,* Vol. XLIX, No. 2 (April, 1958).
   My explanation of the plastic setting is based on Professor De' Negri's important study, and the table on page 133 is adapted from his by his kind permission.
3. Saint Bonaventura, *op. cit.*
4. *Basic Writings of Saint Thomas Aquinas.* Trans. by Anton C. Pegis. Vol. II. New York: 1945.
   Contains "Grace" (QQ, 109–114, *Summa.*)

"The Traveler's Growing Awareness: The Poetry of Day and Night on the Mountain":

1. Fergusson, *op. cit.*
   Chapter 4 is an analysis of Canto IX, the first dream.
2. Stambler, Bernard. "Three Dreams." In *Books Abroad,* May, 1965.
   A study of the mythic, iconographic, and psychological significance of the traveler's three nocturnal dreams.

"Virgil":

1. Auerbach, Erich. *Scenes from the Drama of European Literature.* New York: 1959.
   The opening essay, "Figura," is a very important study of medieval analogical thinking about history, according to which (for example) Moses is an analogue, or type, or "figure" of Christ. Auerbach shows how Dante's treatment of Virgil, Cato, Beatrice and many others is in this tradition.

"The Plan of the *Paradiso Terrestre*":

1. Nygren, Anders. *Agape and Eros.* New York: 1937–1939.

"The Action of the *Paradiso*":

1. Gardner, Edmund G. *Dante and the Mystics.* London: 1913.

By means of liberal quotations from the mystics, and from the *Convivio, Purgatorio,* and *Paradiso,* this book shows that Dante's basic conception of the psyche's life agrees with that of the Christian mystics before and after his time.

2. Mazzeo, Joseph Anthony. *Structure and Thought in the Paradiso*. Ithaca: 1958.
   This study brings out the kinship between the *Paradiso* and the Platonic conceptions of Eros and its goal.

"The Plan of the *Paradiso*":

1. Dunbar, H. Flanders. *Symbolism in Medieval Thought, and its Culmination in the Divine Comedy*. New York: 1961.
   This book is perhaps best used as a reference work, especially for the *Paradiso,* where so much of Dante's symbolism centers.
2. Saint Bonaventura. *On the Reduction of the Arts of Theology.* Trans. by Charles Glenn Wallis. Annapolis: 1923.
   This short work demonstrates how the Middle Ages thought that all knowledge was rooted in God, and theology, therefore, was the basic science.

"On the Difficulty of Reading the *Paradiso*":

1. Eliot, *Dante.*
2. Leonardi, Anna M. Chiavacci. *Lettura del Paradiso Dantesco.* Florence: 1963.
   A sensitive account of the different varieties of poetic beauty in the *Paradiso.*
3. Saint Augustine. *On the Trinity,* Book Nine. In *Basic Writings of Saint Augustine,* Vol. II. Ed. by Whitney J. Oates. New York: 1948.

Index